Letting Go

SUNY Series in Human Communication Processes
Donald P. Cushman and *D. Lawrence Kincaid,* Editors

Letting Go

A Practical Theory of Relationship Disengagement and Reengagement

Dudley D. Cahn, Jr.

State University of New York Press

Published by
State University of New York Press, Albany

© 1987 State University of New York

For information, address State University of New York
Press, State University Plaza, Albany, N.Y., 12246

Library of Congress Cataloging-in-Publication Data

Cahn, Dudley D.
    Letting go.

    (SUNY series in human communication processes)
    Includes bibliographies and indexes.
    1. Interpersonal relations.   2. Interpersonal
communication.   I. Title.   II. Series.
HM132.C325   1986   302.3′4   86-14549
ISBN 0-88706-452-3
ISBN 0-88706-454-X (pbk.)

10 9 8 7 6 5 4 3 2 1

To Leanne and Cortlandt

Contents

Preface

This book focuses on relationship disengagement and reengagement with an eye toward relationship satisfaction and growth. It is assumed that a better understanding of disintegrating relationships improves one's satisfaction and commitment to subsequent interpersonal relationships.

The study of relationship disengagement and reengagement is important from both a practical and a theoretical perspective. On the practical level, studies show that the disintegration of relationships creates loneliness, family disorders, and depression. For example, they tell us that nearly one-half of our romantic relationships and marriages end within two to five years after they are established. Such terminations of close relationships are associated with feelings of loneliness, self-doubt, and, at times, serious psychological, social, and economic deprivation. Researchers also tell us that the attempt to initiate new relationships is stressful. They claim that over one-half of the individuals one approaches as friends and most of the individuals one approaches as mates decline offers to form such intimate relationships. Such rejections are associated with extreme feelings of anxiety, the questioning of one's personal worth, and high stress.

Since success in interpersonal relationships is so comforting and satisfying, and problems in interpersonal relationships so stressful and dissatisfying, the theoretical treatment of relationship disengagement and reengagement must be approached with care and understanding. To that end, this book proposes a theory of relationship disintegration and reengagement based on the following propositions.

First, at the heart of an individual's decision to disengage from a stressful and dissatisfying relationship and to reengage in more comforting and satisfying relationships is an individual's subjective evaluation of other people's overt behaviors. One can distinguish between overt behaviors and interpretations or meanings associated with those behaviors. An individual's interpretations may be affected by such factors as familiarity and knowledge, emotionality and motivation, and behavioral interdependence and ideological beliefs. Decisions about relationships depend on each partner's process for identifying what overt behaviors represent.

Second, at the heart of an individual's subjective evaluation of other people's behavior as appropriate and as contributing to a satisfying and comforting relationship is the accurate communication of one's own values, fears, and aspirations, and the accurate communication of one's expectations regarding appropriate behaviors and how to respond to them. This proposition also implies that the realization that communication has taken place by others results in the perception of being understood. This means that when one coordinates behavior with others, in order for that coordination to take place, he or she must have expectations regarding the other and an understanding of the other's attitudes, values, and beliefs. In a similar manner, the other must have an understanding of one's attitudes, values, and beliefs, and well as expectations regarding what is appropriate behavior in a specific situation. Only then, when perceived understanding occurs, can coordination take place in a persistent and fulfilling manner. Thus, the perception of being understood is key to understanding how individuals subjectively evaluate interpersonal behavior and relationships.

Third, it is proposed that at the heart of partners' accurate perception of being understood are certain communication behaviors that govern and guide relationship disengagement and reengagement processes. When partners share the perception of being understood, they find their relationship more meaningful, special, and positive. The more partners feel understood by one another, the more they want to be physically close and emotionally intimate with one another. When partners do not share the perception of being understood, they find their relationship less meaningful, more stressful, and negative, with the results that they want to be more distant and less emotionally intimate with one another. Therefore, the communication behaviors that result in an accurate perception of being understood play an important role in relationship development, and the absence of these behaviors is key to understanding relationship disintegration. These three propositions undergrid the theoretical contribution of this book.

To return to the practical usefulness of this book, I would like to raise the following question: Where do people gain insight into the nature of interpersonal relationships? One way to do this is hands-on *experience*, but many people wish they had known more before coming involved with others. Another possibility occurs *after* the dissolution of a primary relationship. The guilt, anger, or depression drives some people to seek help in the form of individual or group therapy which may help them learn from the past and cope with their present situation. Because the experience of divorce or being fired from a job may leave them in financial and social ruin, they wish they could have avoided the disintegration of their mate or boss-employee relationships in the first place.

The final possibility for gaining knowledge about relationships is integrated into the educational system at an appropriate level. For many people, their university experience is the best place to undertake the study of interpersonal relationships because the importance of relationships is made salient by a shift from home, direct parental guidance, and long-term friends to a university environment where one interacts with strangers, makes new friends, dates new members of the opposite sex, and fits into a new hierarchy of superordinate-subordinate relationships.

Where in the university might one find courses that best suit one's relationship needs? Advanced undergraduate and graduate courses which emphasize or include communication processes are one of the best places to study the growth and decay of interpersonal relationships. The right kind of communication is the web that binds people together, and the wrong type is a wall that keeps them apart. In the study of mass or cultural communication, one learns how communication may be employed to link individuals into a society and enable that society to transmit its culture from one generation to the next. In the study of organizational communication, one learns how members of an organization accomplish tasks through coordinated actions that require certain types of communication. In the study of interpersonal communication, one learns how meaningful interpersonal relationships may be formed and molded through communication. It is perhaps impossible to study humans relating to humans from one generation to another, from one place in an organization to another, or from one stage to the next in a meaningful interpersonal relationship, without studying the subject of communication. For these reasons, I believe that college courses in communication and communication-related subjects—found in speech, sociology, psychology, and anthropology—are the best places for people to learn about significant interpersonal relationships.

In an effort to contribute to the growing literature on interpersonal relationships available in communication and other social science courses taught at American universities, this book is designed to serve as a primary or as a secondary text. It is useful as a primary text in graduate seminars in psychology, speech, and communication, as well as in advanced undergraduate courses such as "Communication and Interpersonal Relationships" or "Interpersonal Communication and Human Relationships." While there are numerous fundamental textbooks available for basic courses in communication, there are only a few written by communication scholars for more advanced courses in interpersonal communication. This book is also useful as a secondary text in social science courses which deal with marriage, family interaction, and divorce. While there are many works available on the growth of inter-personal relationships, this one, which takes an explicit *communication* perspective, is unique in its focus on the *termination* and *renegotiation* of relationships in *general.*

While I have included examples and studies from psychology and therapy literature, I do not intend this book to be psychological or therapeutic text. First, I believe that therapy is a highly individualized process, while I am trying to state generalizations about human be-havior. Second, I am writing about the common occurrence of people undergoing relationship change, while therapy literature often focuses on individuals who suffer serious emotional and psychological problems.

In an attempt to be both theoretical and practical, the book draws from a broad review of therapy literature but focuses on key concepts. In Part I, a survey of the alternative approaches to the study of satisfaction and commitment in interpersonal relationships (namely, quality, in-vestments, system constraints, and available alternatives models) shows that a combined approach is superior to any one. In Part II, a survey of the literature on theories of relationship development shows why a quality communication environment—as measured subjectively and objectively by the feeling of being understood—is key to an understand-ing of relationship reengagement and growth or deterioration in a variety of social and communicative contexts.

The aim of this book is threefold. First, by combining major perspectives on research in the social sciences, it attempts to present a comprehensive perspective on the development and disintegration of relationships for use as a text in university courses in speech, sociology, psychology, communication, and anthropology. Second, it focuses on key concepts that are theoretically useful to scholars who are conduct-ing research on communication processes, and practically useful to students who are interested in the subject of forming and disengaging from interpersonal relationships. Finally, it takes an explicit communica-tion perspective to help fill a need for texts in graduate and advanced undergraduate courses that focus on communication and interper-sonal relationships.

At this point, I wish to thank several people who have made this book possible. First, there is Don Cushman, State University of New York at Albany, who is one of the communication series editors. To Don, who frequently made suggestions regarding the different drafts of the book, I am especially grateful. Second, I express my appreciation to Lois Patton, Editor-in-Chief at SUNY Press, for her encouragement and editorial assistance. Third, I would like to thank W. Barnett Pearce,

University of Massachusetts, and Donald G. Ellis, University of Hartford, for their insightful comments and helpful suggestions regarding earlier versions of the manuscript. Of course, the responsibility for the accuracy of the final copy rests with me. Fourth, I thank Shirley Hammond for her secretarial assistance, and the students who have taken my courses in interpersonal communication for providing insight and enthusiasm for this project. Finally, I wish to express my appreciation to my wife, Sharon Cahn, for her patience, support, and helpful suggestions, and to my daughter, Katherine Marie Cahn, for her typing assistance.

Acknowledgments

Acknowledgments are made to the following sources for quotations and figures used in this book with permission.

Page 23   Entire poem by W. Tubbs which appears on page 5, "Beyond Perls," *Journal of Humanistic Psychology* 12 (Fall 1972). Copyright 1972 by the Association for Humanistic Psychology. Reprinted by permission of the Association of Humanistic Psychology and Sage Publications, Inc.

Page 57   Figure adapted from D. Cushman and D. Cahn, *Communication in Interpersonal Relationships*, Albany, NY: SUNY Press, 1985, p. 29. Copyright 1985 by the State University of New York Press. Reprinted by permission of SUNY Press and D. Cushman.

Pages 188–94   Material from D. Cahn and J. Hanford, "Perspectives on Human Communication Research: Behaviorism, Phenomenology, and an Integrated View," *The Western Journal of Speech Communication*, 48 (Summer 1984), Pp. 277–282. Copyright by 1984 by the Western Speech Communication Association. Reprinted by permission of the Western Speech Communication Association and J. Hanford.

Page 195   Figure 1 from D. Cahn, "Interpersonal Communication and Transactional Relationships," *Communication Quarterly*, Vol. 24, No. 4, Fall 1976. Copyright 1976 by the Eastern Communication Association. Reprinted by permission of the Eastern Communication Association.

Part One

Overview of Part One

Why do some people remain attached and others leave relationships? Empirical studies on the nature of relationship experience, including the decision to disengage and reengage, have been fragmented into specific lines of research dealing with quality, available alternatives, investments, and system constraints. Until lately, little attention has been given to the interrelations among these approaches. The approach taken in this book attempts to combine these diverse lines of research into a more comprehensive model of relationship development. Figure One illustrates this model.

The approach advocated here includes the quality, available alternatives, investments, and systems constraint models of relationship development. The quality model attempts to explain the development of comforting and satisfying relationships by focusing on *personal growth* and *relationship satisfaction* (Montgomery, 1981; Olson, 1972), *perceived self-concept support* (Sprenkle and Olson, 1978; Gottman, 1979; Cushman and Craig, 1976; Cissna, 1975; Clark, 1973; Watlawick, Beavin, and Jackson, 1967; Larson, 1965), and *perceived understanding* (Cahn, 1983; Witkin and Rose, 1978; Miller, Corrales, and Wackman, 1975; Bienvenu, 1970; Laing, Phillipson, and Lee, 1966). The key idea is that self-concept support produces perceived understanding, which in turn leads to increased feelings of self-worth and relationship satisfaction.

The conditions under which one feels committed to a particular relationship depend on the extent to which one finds personal and relationship growth, perceived self-concept support, and mutual perceived understanding in light of available alternative relationships (Thibaut and Kelley, 1959; Kelley and Thibaut, 1978), investment size (LaGaipa, 1977; Blau, 1967; Homans, 1961), and system constraints (Green and Sporakowski, 1983; Lewis and Spanier, 1979). Following interdependence theory, it is argued that individuals should be more satisfied with their relationships to the extent that they continue to be rewarding, minimize costs, and exceed their generalized expectations. Moreover, greater satisfaction with an involvement should increase commitment, provided alternative relationships are not available. Alter-

3

Figure 1
A Comprehensive Model of Relationship Factors

Quality of Relationship	Availability of Alternatives	Size of Investments	System Constraints
Perceived Understanding	Personal Quality	Personal	Personal
Perceived Support	Personal Quantity	Financial	Friends
Personal Growth Relationship Growth	Reciprocity	Social	Family Culture

native relationships may be perceived to be few or many (*quantity*), perceived to be of higher or lower *quality*, and more or less *reciprocal* than one's present primary relationship. Lewis and Spanier (1979) propose that alternative attractions negatively influence the link between relationship quality and commitment.

In addition, individuals feel committed to the extent that they perceive an investment of numerous resources in that involvement. Investments may be *personal, finanacial*, and/or *social*. Rusbult (1983) found that investments increase commitment and help to "lock" the individual into the relationship by increasing the costs of ending it.

Finally, individuals feel committed to the extent that they perceive system constraints. System constraints are external pressures which may be classified as *personal, friends, family*, and *culture*. Lewis and Spanier (1979) argue that external pressures to remain together positively influence partners' commitment to the relationships.

In Part One of this book, it is proposed that persons become more committed when they perceive that they have only inferior alternatives to the present relationship, when they perceive that they have invested numerous resources in that involvement, and when they perceive pressures from significant others to remain in the relationship. Although researchers tend to follow one of the above models, recent studies show that relationship development and disintegration of long-term heterosexual involvements, supervisor and subordinate working relationships, and friendships are best predicted by a combination of the models (Green, 1983; Green and Sporakowski, 1983; Rusbult, 1983; Farrell and Rusbult, 1981; and Rusbult, 1980).

A discussion of the combination of the quality, available alternatives, investments, and system constraints models would be incomplete without pointing to the important role of feeling understood in self-concept support and in relationship development and disintegration (Cushman and Cahn, 1985; Cahn, 1984; Cahn, 1983; Cahn, 1976). The recognition of individual self-concepts is a prerequisite for significant cooperation from others. Positive self-concept support is believed to be an important factor, if not the most important factor, in the development of individual self-concepts and the initiation and maintenance of significant interpersonal relationships (Cushman and Cahn, 1985; Watzlawick, Bevin, and Jackson, 1967). Moreover, self-concept accuracy is essential to predicting the effect of our behavior on others (Christensen and Wallace, 1976), to achieving an empathic understanding of others (Bernstein and Davis, 1982) to achieving relationship adjustment (Frank and Kupfer, 1976), and to achieving personal relational happiness (Corsini, 1956). When we misjudge others or they misjudge us, both parties experience disappointment. Thus, at the center of our feelings of personal worth and relationship satisfaction is our capacity both to understand others and to pattern others' expectations for us in an accurate and realistic manner, so that neither party finds the other's behaviors disappointing by rejecting or disconfirming one another's actions. Rejection and disconfirmation produce feelings of being misunderstood, which leads to relationship dissatisfaction and disintegration; while positive and accurate self-concept support results in feelings of being understood, which leads to relationship satisfaction and growth. The techniques involved in producing the perception of being understood are communication skills.

Positive and accurate self-concept support that produces feelings of being understood is the criteria for assessing or reassessing the quality communication environment for interpersonal relationships. Without positive self-concept support, an individual's attempts to validate his or her self-concept and to initiate interpersonal relationships will likely fail. Without self-concept accuracy, an individual, and those who interact with him or her, will misjudge and disappoint others, leading to relationship termination. Without communication skills, every interactional error has the potential to harm either or both persons' self-concepts and their relationship. These then are the criteria by which we may reassess our interpersonal communications environment and the interpersonal relationships that exist in it, in order to determine whether such relationships warrant continuation, repair, renegotiation, or disengagement.

It should be apparent by now that a clear and precise analysis of the processes involved in accurate and positive self-concept support turns upon our ability to construct messages such that others understand us

and convey that understanding back to us. The lack of self-concept support that produces feelings of being misunderstood results in discom-
forting and dissatisfying relationships from which one looks for opportunities to disengage. Positive and accurate self-concept support that
produces feelings of being understood results in comforting and satisfying interpersonal relationships to which one is attracted. Thus, from the
communicator's point of view, perceived understanding is central to the
validation of his or her self-concept and relationship growth or disintegration.

Part One focuses on the role of feeling understood in quality communication environments that promote self-worth and relationship
satisfaction within the context of investment size, system constraints,
and the availability of more desirable alternative interpersonal relationships. By combining the four models of relationship development, and
incorporating feeling understood as a measure of quality communication environments, the approach taken here leads to a greater understanding and improved predictability in relationship development
and disengagement.

To better understand why some people stay in and others leave
relationships, Part One combines four relationship models and focuses
on perceived understanding as a measure of quality in relationship
development. Chapter One deals primarily with the role of perceived
understanding in human communication and relationship development.
In the application of social rules to the human action process, perceived
understanding may be viewed subjectively as feelings associated with
perceived normative force.

Chapter Two examines the role of perceived understanding within
self-concept theory and symbolic interaction. In American culture,
identity, evaluative, and behavioral self-object relationships are separately evaluated (Thompson, 1972). These distinctions are discussed in
detail in Chapter Two. The point here is that the self-concept may be
regarded as an organized set of information that defines the relationship
of objects to the individual and is capable of governing and directing
human action. To better understand the role of perceived understanding as a vital component in the self-concept, it is necessary to distinguish
among the types of information we have on ourselves—which may be
social, unique, or preferred. These distinctions are also introduced in
Chapter Two. The point here is that the notion of preferred self-concept
is key to understanding the role of perceived understanding as an essential component in the self-concept.

It is proposed that perceived understanding is a concept that sup-
plements rules—given participants' views of social interactions—and

which functions as a generative mechanism for determining the relationship between communication behaviors enacted and their consequences. The role of communication skill in relationship development is discussed in Chapter Three. Self-assertion, listening, and collaboration skills are employed in systematic ways when one seeks to continue, repair, renegotiate, or disengage from a relationship.

Chapter Four, which deals with various consequences of communication, focuses on the role of feeling understood in quality communication environments that promote self-worth and relationship satisfaction within the context of investment size, system constraints, and the availability of more desirable alternative interpersonal relationships. By combining the four models and incorporating feeling understood as a measure of quality communication environments, the approach taken in Chapter Four leads to a greater understanding and improved predictability in relationship development and disengagement.

ONE

Feeling Understood in Interpersonal Relationships

> [T]he intentions with which people do things are of two main sorts—
> observations are made with the intention of discovering the way things
> are in the world; actions are performed with the intention of changing
> the way things are in the world.
>
> G. Langford, *Human Action*

Introduction

Yolton (1973) argues that action theory provides a philosophic basis for
understanding and explaining human behavior. Action theorists write
about intention, motive, reason, purpose, and action. Taylor (1964) distinguishes human action from other types of behavior when he notes
that to ascribe action to a person implies that a certain state of affairs
came into existence, the person intended this state of affairs (or something very close to it), and the person's behaviors were, at least in part,
instrumental in bringing the state of affairs into existence. Social and
communicative behaviors exemplify members of this class.

When studying the nature of actions, action theorists argue that
often it is impossible to identify causes, effects, and causal relationships.
When actions occur, one may not observe a physical change that
functions as a stimulus or cause, and nothing may appear to function as a
response or effect. Actions are described as arbitrary, learned, and often
unpredictable. Because they are different from stimulus-response types
of behaviors and physical events, actions fail to conform to physical laws
(i.e., the covering law model). They require teleological explanations in
the form of intentional models and theories which include the concept
of choice.

One realizes the role of choice in actions when one observes an
instance of goal-seeking behavior in which choice is obviously absent.
For example, a fully automatic airplane, equipped with navigating gear,
can display goal-directed behavior, but no one would claim that the
machine chose to reach that goal. Langford (1971) adds to the illustra-

9

tion by noting that the airplane has behaved as though it were goal-seeking; but in fact it was unaware of the goal, because it did not choose to go in that direction. Choice requires that there be alternatives and criteria for selecting among them.

In this chapter, I take the position (1) that rules function as criteria for choice among goals, and that feeling understood may be viewed subjectively as feelings associated with the normative force of a rule; (2) that in the context of interpersonal relationship development and deterioration, mutual perceived understanding makes relationships more meaningful; (3) that a need for more meaningful interpersonal relationships exists; and (4) that a valid and reliable instrument exists to objectively measure perceived understanding in communicative contexts.

Feeling Understood as a Measure of the Normative Force of A Rule

If action theory presupposes choice among goals and alternatives to these goals, how can one understand, explain, and predict human behavior? The answer lies in the study of rules.

Rules as Criteria for Choice

As constraints on the availability of choices, rules are guides to action. They function as criteria for choice among alternatives. These constraints are normative in contrast to the causal force of laws. That normative force governs human actions forms a basis for Cushman's and Whiting's (1972) communication theory. They argue that intentional behavior requires the existence of consensually shared rules or "standardized usages" that function like guide posts, because they indicate what should be done. A rule exists when people perform the same actions under certain conditions because each expects the others to so behave and each is aware of the others' expectations. Thus, a pattern of behavior is said to be rule-governed when there exists mutual expectations regarding what is appropriate in a given situation. A rule or standardized usage, then, is prescriptive because it serves as a criterion for evaluating the appropriateness of intentional behavior. Although rules are social conventions which can be violated or changed by individuals or groups, it is argued that when people know the rules, they tend to conform to them.

A rules theory of human action takes the form of a practical syllogism. For example, X intends to bring about Z; X considers that in order to bring about Z, he or she must do Y; and, therefore, X sets out to do Y (von Wright, 1971). It is argued that there exists a class of human behaviors governed by a particular set of rules and that persons have some degree of choice among alterative behaviors and rule sets, monitor and critique their performance, and act in response to normative forces.

In summary, actions differ from other types of behaviors and physical events because they presuppose choice among goals which requires the existence of rules as criteria for choice. These criteria act as normative forces. Next, I will introduce the concept of feeling understood, or perceived understanding, and explain how it serves as a measure of normative force.

Feeling Understood as a Measure of Normative Force

What is feeling understood, or perceived understanding, and how does it differ from empathy? Perceived understanding is not to be confused with empathy, as illustrated by Laing's multilevel model of interpersonal perception (Laing, Phillipson, and Lee, 1966). At the first level of Laing's model, persons A and B both have a direct perspective of some object or concept. At the next level, persons A and B both have a perspective of the other's direct perspective, which Laing calls a metaperspective. A comparison of these two levels represents the traditional notion of predictive empathy, because concern here is with accuracy or the degrees of consistency between B's direct perspective and A's view of B's direct perspective. Therefore, empathy is the ability to "get inside" another person, the message receiver.

At the third level, A and B both have perspectives of the other's metaperspective, called a meta-metaperspective. The perception of being understood or misunderstood involves comparison of one's meta-metaperspective with his or her direct perspective. The concern at the third level is not so much with accuracy as with a comparison of one's own direct perspective and meta-metaperspective. Thus, the feeling of being understood is different from empathy because it shifts the frame of reference from the feelings of the intended receiver to the feelings of the message source.

What is the role of feeling understood or misunderstood in a rules theory based on human action? In the application of social rules to the human action process, perceived understanding may be viewed subjectively as feelings associated with perceived normative force. From the individual's point of view, these feelings serve as the primary reasons for initiating, continuing, or abandoning courses of action. To the extent that one feels understood, one tends to undertake or continue to interact based on the belief that he or she has tapped into the appropriate set of rules governing human action (or interaction) for that kind of situation. To the extent that one feels less understood or even misunderstood, one suppresses actions based on the realization that there is a need to abandon one set of rules and behaviors and search for another set that is more appropriate for a given type of situation. Feelings of being misunderstood are likely to lead to a higher level of analysis in which one thinks about or discusses with others the answers to such questions as: What happened? What went wrong? Where did I fail? What should I have done? What am I supposed to do now?

In addition, it is thought that there are two classes of actions—coordinated and noncoordinated. The former requires other actors to achieve a goal while the latter does not, but may be conducted in the presence of others. Although human action may be coordinated or not, Cushman and Whiting (1972) have focused their attention on structured, coordinated social activity as a basis for a rules theory of human communication. Limiting the domain of communication inquiry to human actions involving coordination for which standardized usages exist may appear restrictive. However, evidence exists to indicate that this domain includes many important social interactions (Cushman and Cahn, 1985). One of these important areas concerns the disintegration of interpersonal relationships.

The Lack of Feeling Understood in Relationship Disintegration

> Perhaps it is true that unless (one) derives from human interaction the special quality of feeling understood, he will suffer the despair of meaninglessness no matter what he achieves and how well he understands everything else. Feeling understood appears then to be a necessary though perhaps not a sufficient condition for man to come to terms with the world and with himself.
>
> J. Luft, *Of Human Interaction*

What is happiness? That is a question with which great thinkers have struggled for centuries. At least part of the answer lies in the above quotation, in which Luft connects the meaning of life to human interaction and identifies the special quality of feeling understood as a connecting link. Thus, from Luft's point of view, happiness may be found in the web of one's interpersonal relationships, which in turn are a function of feeling understood.

Much has been written on the subject of human communication, and a great deal on interpersonal relationships, but few authors have attempted to relate these two subject areas. Focusing on that connection, this book attemps to show how feeling understood is produced by a quality communication environment that makes some interpersonal relationships more meaningful than others.

Although many people care about their interpersonal relationships and devote considerable time to analyzing and worrying about them, they often do not know what to make of them. In this book, I hope to provide some insights into the development, maintenance, and disintegration of relationships such as friendship, husband-wife, lovers, boss-employee, and teacher-student. If I am successful, one may better understand how, when, and under what conditions he or she should end or renegotiate a relationship. Moreover, one may better understand how to improve relationships the next time around. Taken all together, this information may shed some light on one's own happiness by getting people to examine how their interaction with others can help them to come to terms with the world and themselves. As the first step in this direction, this section explains how the feeling of being understood functions as a link between communication and the development of meaningful interpersonal relationships, and describes trends in American society resulting in interpersonal relationships that lack mutual perceived understanding.

Some interpersonal relationships are more meaningful than others. By meaningful, I mean that such relationships are special, because they are positive, close, and intimate. When I think about my past and present friendships, one friend seems more worthy of my trust and is more dependable than others when I need help. If I reflect on my past dating relationships, one had greater appeal and excitement than the others. Similarly, mate relationships are not all equal; some are characterized by greater love and commitment that others. It seems to me that *these distinctive interpersonal relationships are characterized by what Luft calls the special quality of feeling understood.* Essentially, a meaningful relationship is based on *sharing.* Partners may share ideas, feelings, and needs; they may share experience; they may share trust and respect; but perhaps most importantly, they share the feeling that each understands the other. *This mutual feeling of being understood is what makes some interpersonal relationships more meaningful than others.*

In order to better appreciate the role of perceived understanding as the interface between communication and relational development, one must first understand how communication produces perceived understanding. While this subject will be explored in greater detail in Chapters Two and Three, for the moment, I would suggest that a communication environment has quality to the extent that the communicators feel understood. For example, to the extent that I indicate to another that I accept that person for what he or she represents, the more that person will feel understood. The more each feels understood by the other, the higher the quality of the communication environment.

Obviously, if someone really offends another at first meeting, one probably avoids interacting with him or her in the future. Usually, however, social situations are more ambiguous, and one may continue to interact with another for some time before one realizes that the relationship lacks mutual perceived understanding. This may be due to the fact that when people meet they usually consider other factors as being important, when in the long run, mutual perceived understanding is the key.

While the relationship of perceived understanding and relational development will be explored in greater detail in Chapter Four, I would at least observe that the more communicators feel understood by one another, the more they want to be physically close and emotionally intimate with one another. When a close interpersonal relationship ends, one feels the emptiness—the vacuum or void that needs to be filled. Perhaps this explains why widows and widowers frequently remarry or see much more of their children or siblings than when their spouses were living, while unmarried persons spend more time with friends and relatives than do married persons (Townsend, 1968). The problem is that there is a need for more meaningful interpersonal relationships.

The Need for More Meaningful Interpersonal Relationships

Relational partners everywhere and throughout history have probably encountered at least some inferior communication environments and less than satisfying interpersonal relationships. But the lack of mutual perceived understanding may be greater in contemporary American society owing to three trends that are making it increasingly more difficult to create and maintain meaningful interpersonal relationships.

Increasing Demand for Personal Growth

The first trend is toward increasing demand for personal growth. Olson (1972) argues that, increasingly, individuals seek relationships that provide opportunities for personal growth. The problem with a relationship that facilitates the satisfaction of one's own needs, interests, and goals is that frequently, when and where growth does occur, it happens for only *one* of the persons involved in a relationship. The greater the growth for the one, the more likely those involved in the relationship grow further apart. I am reminded of Mike and his marriage to Linda. Linda argued that if Mike really loved her, he would let her leave the kids with him and permit her to move to a larger city over 150 miles away. There, she would get a job, live on her own indefinitely, make new friends, and escape from the responsibilities of married and family life. The idea was that she would use this time "to find herself," and when that was done she would be ready to return and settle down with him. Mike, understandably, was in a quandary because he felt that if he really loved her, he would encourage her "to do her own thing," but he admitted that deep inside he felt that something was wrong with the idea. Something was wrong; she never came back, and they are now divorced.

Some argue that by creating supportive conditions at home (such as sharing roles, encouraging the employment of both spouses, and permitting both spouses to have more social relationships outside the marriage), it is possible for both partners to satisfy their own and each other's needs (O'Neill and O'Neill, 1972). This is true only to a limited extent, however. Even where both partners grow as individuals, they may only grow farther apart if they do not *share* at least some of the same experiential basis for growth, because at least some of the experiences are not designed and used to sustain or further develop the relationship itself. It is not personal growth alone that makes one happy, but rather one's feeling understood by special others as one seeks and attains one's goals.

Increasing Social Mobility

A second trend identifiable in America is an increase in social mobility. According to the National Center for Health Statistics, the number of marriages increased in 1981 and 1982 for the sixth and seventh consecutive years. With the exception of 1974 and 1975, the number of marriages has risen every year for the past twenty-five years. If single, one may not have given much thought to when and whom one might marry, but statistics indicate that he or she will someday marry. In addition to the fact that more Americans marry every year, more divorce one another as well. The Bureau of the Census reports that in 1960 there were 393,000 divorces; in 1970, 708,000; and in 1979, 1.2 million. While the number of divorces is increasing, the ratio of divorces compared to marriages is also increasing. So, when one marries (or if one is married), there is a much greater likelihood that one may imagine that he or she will someday be divorced. Finally, the National Center for Health Statistics also reports that during the 1970's, the percentage of weddings involving a remarriage increased from 31% to 44%. Among those who remarry, nearly one-half divorce again (Hacker, 1979). Thus, not only are more Americans marrying and divorcing, more are remarrying and divorcing again.

In addition to an increasing number of marriages, divorces, and remarriages, social mobility in America is reflected in an increasing number of changes in jobs and geographical relocations. The Bureau of the Census reports that 45% of Americans moved during the period from 1975 to 1980, and that 77% of those twenty-five to twenty-nine years old moved during that period. It is a well-known fact that one-half of more high school graduates are going to college, frequently involving a move to a campus dormitory. Moreover, the Labor Department reports that for 1975–1980 almost 8% of all employed persons were employed in another occupation the previous year. These transfer rates vary with occupations ranging from zero for physicians, dentists, and farmers, to 20% for some blue collar workers. When the statistics on marriage, divorce, remarriage, geographic changes, and job changes are combined, it is clear that Americans live in a highly mobile society involving frequent changes in their interpersonal relationships.

Divorce, remarriage, geographic changes, and job changes may result in an improved social situation for some individuals, but emotional costs are high during the transition period when one terminates close interpersonal relationships and encounters loneliness and stress when attempting to form new ones. For those who move occasionally, and for those who live in areas with frequent turnover, relationships tend to be transitional, lacking in depth, closeness, and emotional intimacy. Furthermore, according to social research, over one-half of the individuals approached as potential friends and most of the individuals approached as potential mates or employers decline offers to form such close relationships, often resulting in extreme feelings of anxiety, the questioning of one's personal worth, and high stress (Cushman and Cahn, 1985). Therefore, the problem with increasing social mobility is twofold: more temporary and superficial interpersonal relationships, and more anxiety and stress.

Increasing Relational Options

The third trend in contemporary American society is toward increasing relational options. This century bears witness to rapid technological advances in transportation and communication that, when combined with an increase in geographic and job changes, result in more relationship choices, opportunities, and options than in earlier times. The fact that young people are considerably more mobile today than previous generations of youths, who tended to remain near home or on the family farm, enables many more young people to think beyond a social network limited to one's neighborhood or community and to make friends in college, distant camps, other countries, and other cities where they work.

I may serve as an example. Perhaps my case is a little unusual, but my parents, who have never been outside the United States, are amazed that I have visited or lived in seventeen different countries to date. They were surprised this year when I received as many Christmas cards from Japanese as Americans. Unlike some who marry their high school sweethearts, today's youths may date other students in college and one or more graduate schools. I imagine that our children will be more mobile yet, considering the fact that my fourteen-year-old daughter has already visited Hawaii and is talking about a high school trip to Mexico, which is more travel than her parents had accomplished by the time they graduated from high school. Perhaps not everyone is talking about foreign travel, but I am always amazed at how many of my students have either traveled to foreign countries or plan to do so in the next year or two. One of my students, who is from Long Island, is talking about a wedding in Hong Kong next summer!

The Need for Information on Relationship Growth and Disintegration

If today's individuals have more social options as a result of greater social mobility than earlier generations, what is the problem? In addition to providing people with more temporary and superficial interpersonal relationships, the three trends in contemporary American society also produce higher levels of uncertainty which, according to Berger to Calabrese (1975), lead to greater information seeking. I would also like to add that the prospect of relational change is often accompanied by physical and emotional stress, adding to one's need for information to reduce stress.

The need for information, then, is as follows. As more people demand increased personal growth, many find that society has not adequately prepared them to relate in a more meaningful way, one that also facilitates *mutual growth*, the kind that contributes in a more positive way to the relationship itself. They need information on how to better understand their partner's needs, interests, and goals, as well as their own; how to appreciate the unique qualities of others, and to support them while demanding support for themselves. Due to a greater social mobility, people need to know how to make new friends, find new lovers or potential mates, and to adapt to new spouses and bosses; in addition, they need information on how to better cope with the threats of loneliness and loss of self-esteem during transitional periods. Increasing relational options raises the question of how, when, and under what conditions is it wise to choose one relationship over another? People need information on how to make choices among such options. They need to know how to reassess current interpersonal relationships at home, at school, and at work, to assess available options, and to clarify a sound basis of judgment for exercising their options. Increasing relational options also raises the question of how one maintains current relationships when his or her partner is exposed to more alternative possibilities? Why should others want to preserve a relationship with you when they can choose among so many others? Thus, people need information on how to preserve the quality of their relationships as a hedge against losing their partners to others.

Relational Recidivism

The need for information on relationship growth and disintegration has resulted in a problem of *relational recidivism, which refers to the tendency for many people to either, at best, miss the opportunity to improve upon the relational quality of current social arrangements, or, at worse, repeat previous failures*—as, for example, in the case of remarriage, in which nearly one-half end in divorce (Hacker, 1979).

One reason for relational recidivism is that many individuals bring to their new interpersonal relationships behaviors, beliefs, and attitudes learned in a previous relationship. In many cases, this "baggage" creates a perspective and a set of expectations that doom from the start a subsequent relationship. For example, if an employee is told repeatedly by her insecure boss that she is unimportant, stupid, and incompetent at everything, she may develop negative attitudes toward herself that may continue to generate self-defeating behaviors in later relationships.

On the one hand, because of the pain and suffering experienced previously, one may overcompensate by trying hard to find someone who is very different from a previous friend, lover, mate, boss, or colleague. Unfortunately, a relationship with this new individual may produce a different set of problems for which one is unprepared, as illustrated in Dan's marriage. Dan disliked the fact that his wife, Joan, tried to discourage his desires to travel to foreign countries, eat at different and exotic restaurants, and meet new people. After their divorce, he became involved with a woman, Jackie, who enjoyed doing all the exciting things he liked to do. Dan was blind, however, to her suspicion and distrust of his friends, colleagues, and business contacts who were necessary for his occupational success. In time, Jackie's attempts to interfere with his connections undermined their relationship.

On the other hand, some people may get involved with another person who is too much like a previous partner. They may be attracted to a particular trait in members of the opposite sex that resulted in a previous breakup and will produce the same result in a subsequent relationship. For example, some people may be attracted to a weakness in others that makes them emotionally dependent but which also contributes to an overindulgence in alcohol that may lead to a subsequent relational failure.

Along with attitudes held over from previous relationship experiences, individuals bring numerous cultural myths to newly formed relationships. So pervasive are these myths that one hardly gives them a second thought; they appear to be truths. Some people express devotion to cultural myths that create such illusions as "marriage is everlasting" (as in "until death do us part," and where some think that "someday they will meet Mr. or Miss Right, fall deeply in love, and live happily ever after") or "a good friend is a friend forever." Meanwhile, researchers predict that 40% of our romantic relationships and 50% of our marriages will end within two to five years after they begin, and each year one or more of our close friends will lose interest in our friendship, move away, or die, leaving an empty space in our lives (Cushman and Cahn, 1985). Some believe that "opposites attract," although research favors equity and similarity of background (Berscheid and Walster, 1978; Coombs, 1966; Levenger and Breedlove, 1966). Others may associate love with "dependency" even though the dependent type of love may interfere with personal and relational satisfaction and growth (Hatfield and Walster, 1978). Some agree with the statement that "a girl who consistently plays hard-to-get inspires more passion than one who throws herself at a man"; yet the data suggest that in longer term relationships hard-to-get men and women do not elicit more intense liking in their partners (Walster, Walster and Berscheid, 1971; Walster, Berscheid and Walster, 1973). Parents may think that they can influence their children's romantic relationships, but research shows that such influence is usually viewed as "interference" and intensifies feelings of romantic love between members of a couple (Driscoll, Davis and Lipitz, 1972).

Owing to increasing relational options, people suffer from relational recidivism. To avoid getting involved in a syndrome in which subsequent relationships replicate failures of the past, it is important to see beyond one's previous experiences and cultural myths. One needs to better understand who one is, who the other person is, the nature of the interaction between the two, the factors that contribute to success or failure in creating and maintaining a positive, close, intimate interpersonal relationship, and how to work toward relational growth and satisfaction. These insights help to improve one's relationships in the future.

One key insight is that the mutual feeling of being understood is what makes some interpersonal relationships more meaningful than others. While intuitively it seems that the feeling of being understood is important in the development of meaningful interpersonal relationships, it is only recently that communication researchers have been able to measure and study it.

The Measurement of Perceived Understanding

A valid and reliable instrument exists for measuring the feeling of being understood or misunderstood, which is called perceived understanding (Cahn and Shulman, 1984). Essentially, the feeling of being understood, or perceived understanding, is inferred from cues in social interaction and refers to the communicators' feelings following their perceived successes and failures when attempting to communicate with one another (Cahn, 1981). In 1959, Van Kaam applied phenomenological techniques to investigate "really feeling understood." While Van Kaam studied "really feeling understood" as an unusual, peak emotional experience, the present approach includes the more common experience of varying degrees of feeling understood or misunderstood in human communication.

In order to develop an instrument for measuring perceived understanding, 224 university undergraduates were asked to describe their feelings when understood and misunderstood, and sixty descriptive adjectives were extracted from these descriptions of interactions. Another 182 students were asked to place these sixty terms in nine categories ranging from "most like feeling understood" to "most like feeling misunderstood." The many terms that clustered in the middle piles were eliminated from further analysis because they were considered the most ambiguous by the individual sorters. Sixteen terms were retained; eight were most descriptive of the perception of being understood and eight were most descriptive of the perception of being misunderstood. These terms were as follows:

To better understand the nature of perceived understanding, the reader is encouraged to recall a recent encounter with someone. By following these steps, the reader can measure the extent to which he or

Table 1
Feeling Understood-Misunderstood (FUM)

Feeling Understood (FU)		Feeling Misunderstood (FM)	
Satisfaction	_____	Annoyance	_____
Relaxation	_____	Discomfort	_____
Pleasure	_____	Insecurity	_____
Goodness	_____	Dissatisfaction	_____
Acceptance	_____	Sadness	_____
Comfort	_____	Failure	_____
Happiness	_____	Incompleteness	_____
Importance	_____	Uninteresting	_____
Total Checks (FU)	_____	Total Checks (FM)	_____

(FUM = FU − FM)

she felt understood in that encounter. First, place a check mark next to each of the above feelings experienced when interacting with the other person. Next, add up these checks in the two separate columns. Then, subtract the number of FM checks from the FU checks for an overall FUM score. The more positive the score, the more one felt understood in interaction with another person. Conversely, the more negative the score, the more one felt misunderstood.

I encourage others to measure perceived understanding in a variety of contexts; therefore, more refined versions of the instrument are included in the appendices, with instructions for scoring. Using the improved versions of the instrument, at least one study demonstrated significant relationships between feeling understood and interpersonal trust and attraction (Cahn and Frey, 1982). In addition, as indicated earlier, another study found that college students' feelings of being understood by their teachers are very important in the students' evaluation of their teachers (Cahn, 1984). Others ae encouraged to collect their own data to better understand how one's feelings of being understood and misunderstood in different situations are inferred from cues in social interaction, and how these feelings affect the development of specific types of interpersonal relationships, such as roommates, friends, steady dates, or brothers/sisters.

Summary

Action theorists view man as an organism able to do things. Distinguishing movements which are habitual, unreflective, and conditioned behaviors from actions which are intentional, conscious, planned, and purposive, rules theorists argue that the inner aspect of action consists of intention, while the outer aspect consists of social and communicative behavior, as well as event and its consequences. By focusing on the role of feeling understood in a rules approach derived from action theory, this chapter integrates subjective experience and overt behavior by studying communication behavior from the point of view of the communicators' own experiences.

Some interpersonal relationships are more meaningful than others. Superior interpersonal relationships are characterized by the special quality of feeling understood. The more communicators feel understood by one another, the more they want to be physically close and emotionally intimate with one another. The problem is that there is a need for more meaningful interpersonal relationships.

In a discussion of the three trends in contemporary American society, I argued that there is a need for information on relational development owing to the uncertainty produced by these trends. Moreover, these trends are producing problems in relational development resulting in relational recidivism. To help overcome relational recidivism and to fill the need for information on relationship development and deterioration, a valid and reliable measuring instrument for measuring perceived understanding is presented. By measuring the feeling of being understood in interaction, a better understanding of meaningful interpersonal relationships may be obtained.

Unfortunately, at a time of relationship change many previous experiences and cultural myths contribute to a problem of understanding of how to form, maintain, renegotiate, or disengage from interpersonal relationships. Thus, the need for information on the resolution of relational development problems is at least partially a response to three trends in American society that are creating uncertainty as to how to develop more meaningful interpersonal relationships.

I intend that this book help satisfy this need for information on how inferior relationships are identified and renegotiated, and how meaningful relationships are created and maintained. Therefore, the following chapters deal with the issues raised in this first chapter.

_____

TWO

On Maintaining One's Integrity in Developing Relationships

If I just do my thing and you do yours,
We stand in danger of losing each other
And ourselves.

I am not in this world to live up to your expectations,
But I am in this world to confirm you
As a unique human being,
And to be confirmed by you.

We are fully ourselves only in relation to each other;
The I detached from a Thou
Disintegrates.

I do not find you by chance;
I find you by an active life of reaching out.

Rather than passively letting things happen to me
I can act intentionally to make them happen.

I must begin with myself, true;
But I must not end with myself;
The truth begins with two.

W. Tubbs, *Beyond Perls*

Introduction

As suggested in Chapter One, a communication environment has *quality* to the extent that communicators feel understood. *Integrity,* which refers to the positive impressions one wants to sustain in interaction with others, is a link between the communication environment and perceived understanding. Integrity is extremely important in the study of communication and relational development, because if one successfully sustains intended impressions, one feels understood, but if unsuccessful, one feels misunderstood. Thus, I view integrity and the need to maintain it in interaction in a way similar to Rogers's (1951) view of self-regard and a basic need that leads one to seek self-regard from others.

To maintain integrity, one must assert a positive impression and solicit its acceptance. The accomplishment of these tasks requires some vision of who we are and what we would like to become, and an understanding of how these conceptions of self are supported or denied in social interaction through role-taking. The recognition of one's identity by others provides the individual with a feeling of self-worth and relationship satisfaction or with a lack of it in the absence of such recognition. One's self-concept or interactive identity is therefore a communication rather than a psychological phenomenon, because it is interactively established and sustained. Knowledge of the principles, processes, and skills involved in the presentation, development, and validation of self-concepts allows the individuals involved to exert influence over their sense of personal identity and the nature of their relationship.

It is the purpose of this chapter to explain how one maintains one's integrity in interaction with others by introducing three key concepts, namely, self-concept, self-concept support, and role-taking. Specifically, I intend to (1) explore the nature and scope of individual self-conceptions, (2) define interpersonal communication and identify self-concept support as a key message variable that ties the study of self-concepts to perceived understanding, (3) indicate how different kinds of role-taking provide different types of self-concept support, and (4) explain how self-concept rules guide communication behavior and the development of interpersonal relationships.

The Nature and Scope of Self-Concepts

Who am I? Undoubtedly each of us has wondered that on numerous occasions. The answer lies in the unique way in which we conceive of ourselves and present this conception to others. This self-conception is vital because the act of asserting ourselves in social interaction as a means of influencing other's perceptions of us and our relationship requires some vision of who we are and what we would like to become.

Why analyze the self-concept? We need to study the nature and scope of self-concepts because not everyone is alike. As unique individuals, we feel understood to the extent that others manifest support for the unique vision we hold of ourselves. In spite of this great diversity in individual self-concepts, an analysis of self-concepts reveals that there are common underlying elements that can help us better understand how others view themselves; this makes it easier for us to manifest support for others and for them to indicate their support for us, resulting in a higher quality communication environment with greater mutual perceived understanding.

Self-Concept Defined

In the tradition of symbolic interactionists like Cooley (1902) and Mead (1934), self-concept is defined as *the information an individual has regarding his or her relationship to objects, people, and places* (Cushman and Florence, 1974; Cahn, 1976; Cushman and Cahn, 1985). One better understands this definition by filling out a TST, which stands for Twenty Question Statement Test (Kuhn and McPartland, 1954; Spitzer, Couch, and Stratton, 1969), a test designed as a simple way to ascertain one's self-concept by eliciting the information one has on his or her relationship to other objects (Craig, 1981).

The reader may wish to take the test at this time. First, complete with short phrases the statements "I am (am not) . . . ," "I like (dislike) . . . ," "I have done . . . ," "I intend to . . . ." The goal is to produce at least twenty such statements, although there may be no limit as to the actual number. For an example, see Table Two. Next, ask others to do TSTs *on you.* In other words, if your name is Louis, ask a friend to complete phrases such as "Louis is (is not) . . . ," "Louis likes (dislikes) . . . ," "Louis has done . . . ." Hopefully, your respondents are able to produce about twenty such statements, too. To illustrate, we have included a second respondent, Bill's friend, Mike, in Table Two.

Real, Ideal, and Preferred Aspects of a Self-Concept

The information we have on ourselves may be real, ideal, and preferred. *Real self-concepts* refer to those self-object relationships which have been tested and supported in interaction. We know what aspects of our self-concepts are real because they appear on *both* our version of the TST and that of at least one other person's. While it is important that at least one other person agrees with us, the more people who share this perception with us, the better job we are doing in conveying to others the impression we intend. As illustrated in Table Two, Bill's real self-concept characteristics are identified by "R." They are being intelligent, talkative, assertive, thoughtful, easily angered, and a teacher; likes teaching, traveling, arguing, and good food; dislikes eating vegetables; has written a book, plays golf, and won a golfing trophy. These are discriptions that appear on both Bill's and Mike's TST.

Table 2
Who is Bill?
(Twenty Question Statement Test on Bill)

Bill on Bill			Mike on Bill
1. I am talkative	I	R	Bill is . . . talkative
2. I am assertive	I	R	Bill is . . . assertive
3. I am intelligent	I	R	Bill is . . . intelligent
4. I am easily angered	B	R	Bill is . . . easily angered
5. I am thoughtful	B	R	Bill is . . . thoughtful
6. I am helpful	B	Id	Bill is . . . hardworking
7. I am a teacher	I	R	Bill is . . . a teacher
8. I like teaching	E	R	Bill likes . . . teaching
9. I like traveling	E	R	Bill likes . . . traveling
10. I like good food	E	R	Bill likes . . . good food
11. I like to argue	E	R	Bill likes . . . to argue
12. I dislike vegetables	E	R	Bill dislikes . . . vegetables
13. I dislike Jazz music	E	Id	Bill likes . . . to eat desserts
14. I have written a book	B	R	Bill has . . . written a book
15. I play golf	B	R	Bill plays . . . golf and tennis
16. I won a golf trophy	B	R	Bill has . . . won a golf trophy

I = Identity Dimension
E = Evaluative Dimension
B = Behavioral Dimension
R = Real Self-Concept
I = Ideal Self-Concept

Ideal self-concepts refer to those self-object relationships that one thinks exist but that have not been tested in interaction or are not sustainable in interaction. Bill's ideal-self (identified by "Id" in Table Two) includes being helpful and disliking jazz music, because these are descriptions that appear *only* on Bill's TST.

Since not all aspects of real and ideal self-concepts as defined here are admirable, I need to introduce the notion of *preferred self-concepts*, which refers to those real and ideal self-object relationships that one thinks are assets. Defined earlier as one's desire to sustain an intended impression of oneself in social interaction, the term *integrity* consists of preferred real and ideal self-object relationships. As discussed in the next section, the confirmation of one's integrity results in feeling understood, while its rejection or failure to sustain one's identity in interaction results in feeling misunderstood. If we ask Bill to reflect on the matter, he might tell us that being intelligent, assertive, thoughtful, talkative, a teacher, liking his work and good food, traveling, having written a book, and winning a golf trophy are real self-concept characteristics that are also part of his preferred self-concept. He might add that being helpful is part of his ideal self-concept and also part of his preferred self-concept. Bill might prefer that his self-concept were limited to only these characteristics and did not include being easy to anger, liking to argue, and disliking vegetables. It should be noted that it takes some reflection on one's TST to determine one's preferred self-concept or what one's integrity means.

Identity, Evaluative, and Behavioral Self-Object Relationships

Following Thompson (1972), *identity, evaluative, and behavioral* self-object relationships are separately evaluated in American culture. This fragmented presentation of self and perception of others makes Americans more flexible and adaptable when dealing with one another when compared to other cultures, for example, the Japanese (Yoshikawa, 1982).

Identity Self-Concept. People may relate to one another on the basis of interdependent sociocultural roles. One cannot be a father or mother without children, nor can one be a teacher or boss without students and employees. There are many interdependent sociocultural roles, such as leader and follower, boyfriend and girlfriend, lovers, and best friends.

Specifically, an identity consists of one's formal role relationships and includes the attributes normally identified with those formal roles (Cushman & Cahn, 1985). To the extent that one engages in role relationships, he or she has some degree of an identity. This means that the longer one's list of interdependent sociocultural roles, the more identity one has available to reveal to others. For example, I am a father, husband, son, teacher, researcher, author, ex-military officer, onetime boy scout, former student, and the sum total of social attributes we normally associate with the roles that I am presently engaged in. An academic vita or a job resume frequently reveals a great deal of one's identity, because it lists one's past and present role relationships, implying that one has the social attributes associated with these roles. In Table Two, Bill is identified as a teacher and his being intelligent, talkative, and assertive are associated with this identity. Also, as far as we know, these statements are not evaluative, because they are not identified by Bill in the TST as being good or bad. They complete the statement, "I am (am not) . . . " "Bill is (is not) . . . ." The concept of an identity dimension is important because it enables one to engage in basic role-taking, which is discussed in the section on role-taking.

Evaluative Self-Concept. People may also relate to others by sharing values, feelings, likes, and dislikes. I can like or dislike something on my own, but the fact that you and I like or dislike the same things means that we can share these feelings with one another, thus forming a basis for a relationship.

The evaluative dimension of one's self-concept is derived from what one feels about those aspects of one's identity and behavioral self-concept. To the extent that one has such feelings, she or he has some degree of an evaluative self-concept. I enjoy jogging and writing, but I only read when I have to or when I need to kill time. I am really looking forward to visiting certain countries, but I'm not looking forward to visiting other countries that may be on the way. In Table Two, Bill's liking for teaching, traveling, good food, and arguing, as well as his dislikes for vegetables and jazz music, are reflective of his evaluative self-concept. They complete the statement "I like (dislike) . . . " or "Bill likes (dislikes) . . . ." The evaluative self-concept is important because it enables one to engage in reflective role-taking, which is discussed in the section on role-taking.

Behavioral Self-Concept. Finally, people may also relate to one another on the basis of activities and interests. While some behaviors necessarily involve others (e.g., being thoughtful, helpful, friendly, or considerate), some behaviors might not involve others and yet still be useful for forming a relationship. For example, I can perform a physical activity alone, such as exercise, but the fact that you also enjoy working out means that we can do it together, thus forming a basis for a relationship.

The behavioral dimension of one's self-concept is derived from what one does, is interested in doing, intends to do, or has done. To the extent that one has done and plans to do things, she or he has some degree of a behavioral self-concept. This means that the more one does, is interested in doing, intends to do, and has done, the more extensive is his or her behavioral self-concept. I swim, jog, talk and listen a lot, read and write, attend cultural events, go to movies, dance, and plan to travel to Yugoslavia this summer. In Table Two, Bill's playing golf, having written a book, and winning a golf trophy are behavioral self-concept characteristics. They complete the statements "I have done . . . ," "I am interested in doing . . . ," "I intend to do . . . ," or "Bill has done . . . ," "Bill is interested in doing . . . ," "Bill intends to do . . . ." The behavioral self-concept enables one to engage in appropriative and synesic role-taking, which is discussed in the section on role-taking.

Behavioral characteristics may be other- or self-oriented. Other-oriented statements on the TST reveal that one can separate other people from one's role and treat others as unique individuals. Bill's being thoughtful and helpful describe this type of behavior toward others. Self-oriented statements indicate that one treats others the same. Bill's being easily angered describes this kind of interpersonal behavior.

Implications of Self-Concept Analysis for Communication

The analysis of self-concept provides at least two implications for the study of communication and relationship development. First, one may discover through cross-person comparisons that some aspects of one's self-concept are ideal rather than real. To expand the bases for relationship development, one must convert these ideal characteristics into real ones and encourage others to do the same for themselves.

Second, one may discover that one's own or another's self-concept consists of primarily behavioral, evaluative, or identity characteristics. A primarily behavioral person may be a doer who probably acts without sufficient forethought. Others who wish to relate to him/her find that sharing activities is the sole basis for the relationship. If we define a companion as someone who shares one's activities and interests, then a behavioral person has only companions for friends. An evaluative person may be a complainer who does very little about anything. Others wishing to relate to him/her find that sharing values, attitudes, and feelings is the only way to develop a relationship. If we define a confidant as someone who shares one's feelings and values, an evaluative person has only confidants for friends. An identity person may be always in a role which discloses very little about his or her unique individual self, consisting of behavioral or evaluative characteristics. To relate to such a person, others must assume interdependent roles and find that the relationships are formal and superficial. To broaden the range of potential others who can relate to one in more meaningful ways, it is advantageous to develop all three dimensions of one's self-concept and to expand each dimension over time.

To see who one is to oneself and others, a personal may complete the TST and ask a friend or two to do the same. A comparison of TSTs reveals what ideal self-concept characteristics need to be converted into real ones, which real and ideal self-concept characteristics are part of one's preferred self-concept, and the bases on which others might relate to him or her. The comparison will also reveal if one has a more developed identity self-concept than either a behavioral or evaluative self-concept. After realizing the nature of one's own self-concept, one needs to know how it is supported or denied through interpersonal communication.

Interpersonal Communication and The Role of Self-Concept Support

As an integral part of messages each of us receives from others, our self-concepts are to some extent confirmed or denied in interpersonal communication. It is important to understand how self-concepts are supported and denied, because meaningful interpersonal relationships are based on mutual perceived understanding that results from reciprocal self-concept support.

Interpersonal Communication Defined

Although the research literature abounds with definitions of interpersonal communication (Dance and Larson, 1976), Cissna has synthesized them as "The confirmation of self-concepts and self-esteem through genuine, spontaneous dialogue between two persons based on psychological information about one another." (1980:58). This unified definition contains these essentials for defining interpersonal communication: a person-to-person relationship, genuine and spontaneous dialogue, psychological information, and the confirmation or validation of self-concepts. If one or more of these elements is missing, interpersonal communication is not fully realized. While the definition describes the ideal state of interpersonal communication, the elements of the definition take time to develop (Miller and Steinberg, 1975).

In keeping with this definition of interpersonal communication as an ideal, I am taking the view that an interpersonal relationship goes through stages of development in an interpersonal communication system that functions as a communication environment. Since communication systems have structure, purpose, and process (Cushman & Cahn, 1985), to describe a relationship in terms of an interpersonal communication system asserts that individuals are organized in some way (structure) for a reason (purpose) and that the relationship undergoes change over time (process).

Viewed as a system, the basic *function* of interpersonal communication is to regulate consensus with respect to individual self-concepts and to adjust consensus to the need for coordination and mutual understanding, particularly in the resolution of interpersonal conflicts and problems that occur when striving for such a consensus (Cissna, 1980; Cahn, 1976; Cushman and Florence, 1974). A coordination process emerges, according to Gauthier (1963), if and only if two or more individuals act in a manner determined by their mutual understanding. Coordination so defined depends not upon common goals but on a mutual understanding necessary for coordinated action.

In addition to function, an interpersonal communication system has structure and process. The *structure* is the set of rules that constitute the consensus of the system at a given moment (Cushman and Whiting, 1972). To describe the structure of communication that constitutes an interpersonal relationship is to describe the rules that guarantee coordination in defined situations. The basic *process* of interpersonal communication refers to the changes in communication patterns that the system undergoes over time as the relationship moves from one stage of development or deterioration to another. A relationship as a reflection of an interpersonal communication system is a stage of a temporal continuum or a sequence of changes in communication that evolves by responding to situations; the system's accommodation or failure to accommodate to novel developments is seen as growth or decay.

Self-Concept Support: A Key Message Variable

There are three types of interpersonal communication one can provide to any individual's presentation of self and/or attempt to initiate a relationship (Watzlawick, Bevin, and Jackson, 1967; Cahn and Tubbs, 1983; Cushman and Cahn, 1985). *Confirmation* feeds back to another that one accepts the other's presentation of self. Such a response is an overt indication of positive support for one's definition of self and is subjectively experienced as feeling understood. *Rejection* indicates to another than one understands the other's presentation of self but disagrees with it. *Disconfirmation* is an indication of neither acceptance nor rejection of one's definition of self. Frequently an ambiguous response, disconfirmation tells another that one is ignoring the reality of the other's presentation of self. While rejection is subjectively experienced as feeling misunderstood, disconfirmation is subjectively experienced as neither perceived understanding nor misunderstanding. According to Watzlawick and his colleagues, another's confirmation communicates to me that "I am right," another's rejection, that "I am wrong," and another's disconfirmation, that "I do not exist." It should also be noted that some researches argue that acceptance or rejection is the same as confirmation or disconfirmation (Cissna and Keating, 1979).

A communication environment is high in quality if one feels understood owing to a high degree of confirmation or accurate self-concept support perceived in the messages from others. Conversely, one's communication environment is inferior in quality to the extent that one lacks perceived understanding or is made to feel misunderstood owing to a denial of accurate self-concept support in the form of disconfirmation or rejection. Thus, perceived self-concept support contributes to the quality of a communication environment by making one feel satisfaction, pleasure, goodness, acceptance, and importance, as well as other possible feelings that make up perceived understanding (see Chapter One). When the feelings are perceived as mutual, perceived understanding becomes an intersubjective experience.

In general, *I receive self-concept support when I perceive that another person experiences what things mean to me, accepts me for what I represent, and makes me feel a sense of togetherness and relief from loneliness.* Specifically, I get that message when one confirms the identity, behavioral, and/or evaluative dimensions of my self-concept.

Identity, Behavioral, and Evaluative Dimensions of Self-Concept Support

The *identity* part of my self-concept is accurately confirmed by the existence (past and present) of those with whom I am socially or occupationally interdependent. My boss, students, friends, spouse, children, and parents support my identity simply because they exist and play the supporting roles. If it were not for them, I would lose a great deal of my identity. To the extent that they refuse to play the appropriate supporting roles, I feel misunderstood. For example, if a student were to tell Bill that she does not want to take his class because he does not know how to teach and is not intelligent, assertive, or talkative, he would feel misunderstood because she rejects his conception of himself. On the contrary, as illustrated in Table Two, Bill's identity is supported by others in regard to being intelligent, talkative, assertive, and a teacher. Because these characteristics are supported by others, they are part of his real self-concept.

The *behavioral* part of my self-concept is confirmed positively and accurately by my companions, that is, the people who often accompany me when I do the things I do. Barry can play golf alone, but you often play along with him. You choose to play with a partner because a sense of togetherness adds to your enjoyment of the game. While my behavior may not always need to be accompanied by others, it is reinforced by the support I receive when others accompany me as I do things. On the other hand, when others criticize the things I do, I feel misunderstood because part of my behavioral self-concept is being rejected. If no one ever did any of these things with me, I would feel misunderstood because part of my behavioral self-concept is being disconfirmed when

I am left out or feel that I am being ignored. Returning again to Table Two, Bill's behavioral self-concept receives confirmation in being easy to anger and thoughtful, writing books, playing golf, and winning a golf trophy. Because they are supported by other people, these attributes are part of his real self-concept.

The *evaluative* part of my self-concept is supported positively and accurately by my confidants, those with whom I share my deep feelings. Perhaps, I can talk to you, reveal to you my innermost concerns, share with you deep feelings, engage with you in the mutual resolution of interpersonal conflict, and elicit your help in the solution of my personal problems. Our relationship, which is evaluative in nature, is different from those based on interdependent roles (identities) or shared activities and interests (behavioral self-concepts), because I can talk to you about practically anything. You may not be related to me in any formal way, nor do we jog, play golf, or fish together, but I can share with you what I feel. While my evaluative self-concept is not totally dependent on my confidants, imperviousness is known to result in confused or suppressed feelings (Sieburg, 1976). This means that if others ignore or disagree with my attitudes, feelings, likes, and dislikes, I perceive these are overt indications of disconfirmation or rejection and subjectively experience lack of perceived understanding or the feeling of being misunderstood. In Table Two, Bill's evaluative self-concept is supported on these characteristics: He likes traveling, good food, and arguing, and he dislikes vegetables. These then are also part of Bill's real self-concept.

Table Two reveals that part of Bill's self-concept is not supported by others. As part of his identity, others do not confirm his being helpful and dislike for Jazz. Bill needs to communicate these parts of his self-concept to others to convert these attributes from ideal to real, unless of course he has tried previously and had these characteristics rejected or disconfirmed.

Implications of Self-Concept Support for Communication

The study of self-concept support or denial has the following implications for the role of communication in interpersonal relationships. First, if some of one's self-concept characteristics are more important to that person than other attributes, it is vital to the individual's growth and relational satisfaction that one receive support from others for those key characteristics. Thus, one must let them know what self-concept characteristics are most central to one's vision of self, learn what their vision is, and resolve the differences. Moreover, it is important for a person and the others in his or her social network to determine how long others can sustain support for one's self-concept. For example,

I may not continue for long to play the role you attribute to me, to experience the feelings that we have to share, or to enact the behaviors that we must perform together in order for you to receive sufficient self-concept support.

Second, an analysis of the specific types of self-concept support individuals need indicates how well they may get along in a relationship. If one is overly sensitive, uptight, and easily intimidated, and her male partner is insensitive, overconfident, and a bully, he will not supply her with a supportive environment. Either they both must change to create a communication environment in which she can develop interests and grow as a person, or they should consider changing partners. Therefore, it is useful to know and analyze the specific characteristics that dominate each person's self-concepts.

Third, the development of the self-concept, that is, the scope, depth, and configuration of one's self-object relationships as reflected on the TST, determines his or her ability to provide self-concept support to others and constrains the number and types of others who can and will provide self-concept support or denial in return. This constraint in turn limits the degree of mutual perceived understanding possible at different stages in a relationship, thus limiting the kinds and number of people who can or will want to be one's friends, lovers, and mates.

Fourth, the rate of change in self-concept development is an important predictor of how long relationships with others may last, because the type of self-concept support that one provides another person at one stage of relational development may not be enough to satisfy that person at a later stage of development. For example, if one changes faster than another, a strain is placed on the relationship. Moreover, if both change in different directions, the relationship is likely to terminate. Only if both change together in similar or supportable directions will the relationship grow.

Fifth, the distinction between preferred self-concept support and that which is not preferred is a unique way to view integrity; furthermore, it provides insight into how one maintains integrity in social interaction and helps others to do the same. One must determine which real and ideal self-concept characteristics one prefers, and then sustain them in interaction. Specific techniques are included in the next chapter.

Sixth, to the extent that one receives self-concept support on preferred characteristics, one develops a strong self-concept. For example, Lynn prefers being assertive, fearless, and outgoing, and discovers that others see her that way. On the other hand, if one receives self-concept support on characteristics one manifests but does not prefer, one develops a weak self-concept. For example, Mary does not prefer being viewed as meek and insecure, but she acts that way and is treated by others as though she is meek and insecure. Thus, the strength of the self-concept depends upon the consistency and frequency that the specific preferred characteristics are confirmed by others.

Self-Concept Support and Types of Role-Taking

If the identity, behavioral, and evaluative dimensions of one's real self-concept are derived from information regarding one's relationship to objects, people, and places, then it becomes apparent that the ways in which an individual can become aware of these relationships are the ways in which one is made to feel understood or misunderstood in social interaction. Mead (1934) argued that role-taking is the central mechanism by which one comes to understand one's own self-concept and the characteristics in others; if successful (real), one is able to indicate self-concept support for similar characteristics in others.

Types of Role-Taking

Thanks to the work of several researchers (Turner, 1956; Lauer and Boardman, 1971; Cushman and Craig, 1976; Craig, 1981), four kinds of role-taking may be differentiated in terms of the type of self-concept support each provides to others. The four types of role-taking are basic, reflective, appropriative, and synesic.

Basic role-taking is the process whereby one imaginatively constructs the attitudes and expectations of cultural and social organizational positions and is consequently able to anticipate and respond to the formal social roles of others. Examples of basic role-taking in our culture are acting like a son or daughter in front of one's parents and acting like a student in the presence of one's teachers. If a person's role-taking ability is limited to this level, he or she always performs in that role regardless of the situation. Take the case of my friend, Keith, for example. Keith is an ex-naval captain who always acts like a commander wherever he is. Even after retiring from the service to become a graduate student, he continues to act as though he is captain of the ship. I often feel the compulsion to ask him to be more "himself."

Self-concept support generated by basic role-taking includes indications that one understands what it means to be a father, a mother, a policeman, an American, a gas station attendant, and other standardized cultural and social roles. Effective self-concept support of the basic role-taking type requires that the other actually occupies these positions and that these positions are perceived and supported by messages from others.

As illustrated in Table Three, evidence of Bill's role-taking ability of the basic type are his *identity* statements on his TST, namely, being intelligent, talkative, assertive, and a teacher. If Bill's TST revealed only statements of this sort, his role-taking ability would be limited to the basic type. He would also be able to manifest to others only self-concept support of this type and in regard to only these characteristics.

Reflective role-taking is an evaluation of various basic role requirements and one's wishes, likes, and dislikes. As a teacher, I like giving lectures and dislike grading students; as a father, I like rewarding my daughter but dislike punishing her; as an American, I like freedom but dislike paying taxes. Self-concept support based on reflective role-taking involves indications that one understands what I like or dislike, what I see as good or bad, and what I think is beautiful or ugly. Effective self-concept support of the reflective role-taking type requires that the

Table 3
Real Self-Concepts for Bill and Mike
By Role-Taking Types
(Twenty Statements Question Test on Bill and Mike)

Bill's Real Self-Concept		Mike's Real Self-Concept	
1. I am talkative	B	I am nonassertive	A
2. I am assertive	B	I am meek	A
3. I am intelligent	B	I am intelligent	B
4. I am easily angered	A	I am insecure	A
5. I am thoughtful	S	I am status conscious	A
6. I am a teacher	B	I am a professor	B
7. I like teaching	R	I am a researcher	B
8. I like traveling	R	I am friendly	S
9. I like good food	R	I am concerned	S
10. I like to argue	R	I dislike criticism	R
11. I dislike vegetables	R	I dislike conflict	R
12. I have written a book	B	I have written a book	B
13. I play golf	B	I run in local marathons	B
14. I won a golf trophy	B	I won college track awards	B

     B = Basic
     R = Reflective
     A = Appropriate
     S = Synesic

other actually has these qualities and that they are perceived and supported by messages from others.

One's ability to role-take reflectively is identified from one's statements on the TST, just as one may use the TST to identify the evaluative dimension of one's self-concept. As illustrated in Table Three, evidence of Bill's role-taking ability of the reflective type are his *evaluative* self-concept statements, such as liking teaching, traveling, good food, and arguing. If Bill's TST consisted of only these statements, his role-taking ability would be very limited, and his ability to indicate self-concept support to others would also be limited to evaluations regarding these characteristics.

Appropriative role-taking is an individual's positive evaluation of an aspect of a role *and* the reduction of that self-object relationship to a permanent part of the self-concept. This results in what we commonly call a personality trait. For example, a male athlete in school may find that he likes one aspect of the role, namely, pitting his physical strength against other individuals. Thus, when he graduates from school, he may seize every opportunity to exercise that attribute, even though he is no longer a college athlete. Through a series of appropriative role-taking experiences, one acquires numerous self-object relationships that become person-dependent rather than role-dependent, meaning that one manifests the same self-object relationship across roles. For example, one must appropriate such self-object relationships as forceful, pushy, or arrogant. I once saw a cartoon in which a psychotherapist with pen and pad in hand was lying on his own couch while his client, who was formally dressed and wore a serious condescending facial expression, sat in the therapist's chair and held tightly on to its arms. The psychiatrist said, "One thing I have observed about you is that you tend to be dominant and overbearing . . . ." While this illustration may be an understatement, it reveals how one's personality may override situational differences.

Self-concept support based on appropriative role-taking includes indications that one understands that another is active, demanding, emotional, moody, and so forth. Effective self-concept support of the appropriative role-taking type requires that the other actually has these personality traits and that they are perceived and supported by others.

One's ability to role-take appropriatively is identified as personality traits on one's TST. Again, consider Table Three; evidence of Bill's role-taking ability of the appropriative type are his *behavioral self-statements that are self-oriented and not adaptive to individual differences in others*, like being easily angered. If Bill's TST revealed only statements of this sort, his role-taking ability would be limited to the appropriative type. He would also be able to manifest self-concept support only to others of this type and in regard to only these characteristics.

It should be noted that effort is required and care must be taken to properly distinguish some appropriative attributes from basic and synesic types of role-taking. This is due to the fact that a single attribute has many meanings. Therefore, the proper identification is made in the context of other statements on the TST. For example, assertive and talkative may refer to expectations associated with the role of teacher; if one is a teacher, then these attributes would be classified as basic, because they are associated with that identity. However, assertive and talkative may refer to personality traits, in which one has appropriated attributes he or she enjoyed in earlier roles. It is possible, then, for a particular attribute to be labeled appropriative or synesic on one person's TST and labeled basic on another's.

Synesic role-taking is the imaginative construction of the other's self-concept such that one can perceive the other's social orientation. Common synesic role-taking characteristics in American culture are cooperative, understanding, sympathetic, adaptive, kind, friendly, helpful, loving, sensitive, and tolerant. The client-centered approach to therapy of Carl Rogers (1951) illustrates synesic role-taking.

Self-concept support based on synesic role-taking involves indications that one sees that another is thoughtful, caring, and empathic. Effective self-concept support of the synesic role-taking type requires that the other actually has these qualities and that they are perceived and supported by others.

One's ability to role-take synesically is identified by *behavioral self-concept statements on one's TST that are other-oriented and show consideration of individual differences in others.* As illustrated by Table Three, evidence of Bill's role-taking ability of the synesic type is his being thoughtful. If Bill's TST revealed only statements of this sort, his role-taking ability would be limited to the synesic type. He would also be able to manifest self-concept support to others of this type and in regard to only this characteristic.

Implications of Role-Taking for Communication

The identification of four kinds of role-taking has important implications for the role of communication in relational development. First, if one type of role-taking dominates a relationship, the meaningfulness of the relationship is severely limited. Watzlawick, Beavin, and Jackson (1967) distinguish *complementary* relationships, in which two people are very different from one another (e.g., "opposites attract"), from *symmetrical* relationships, in which two people are quite similar (e.g., "birds of a feather flock together"). This distinction may be applied to the four types of role-taking.

In some relationships, people may relate to one another at the *same level,* forming a symmetrical relationship. If one's self-concept consists primarily of basic roles, then there is only a cultural, social, organizational self present. There is no unique individual self-concept with whom others can form interpersonal relationships. This occurs when one's boss is very formal and does not socialize with his or her employees. Workers say they do not know their boss very well. To be a more effective manager, this boss should be able to counsel employees on occasion, an event that requires one to temporarily vacate a formal role and perform reflective, appropriative, and synesic role-taking. So, if primarily basic, people may not get to know each other very well and feel that their relationships are empty, distant, and superficial.

If one's self-concept consists primarily of reflective characteristics, then there is only an evaluative self present. This happens when one is highly critical of others and things in general. Neighbors report that whenever they get together with this person, the discussion turns into a complaint session. Consequently, if primarily reflective, their interaction may always turn into "bitch sessions."

If one's self-concept consists primarily of appropriative characteristics, then one always acts as one wants irrespective of what others want; one lacks an appreciation of who others are as unique individuals. Such a person who observes an instance of aggressive behavior in another would assume and treat the other as though the other would react aggressively in all situations, when in fact this may not be the case. Therefore, if primarily appropriative, two people may be a powerful team, if they are alike on specific self-concept characteristics (e.g., both want to work for the same goals), but may experience a great deal of friction, if one's specific self-concept characteristics are incompatible with those of the other.

If one's self-concept consists primarily of synesic qualities, then one always acts as others want irrespective of what he or she wants; one lacks an appreciation of who one is as a unique individual. This person is whomever others want him or her to be. Thus, if both role-take at the synesic level most of the time, they may not get much done, because each is waiting for the other to make the decision (e.g., "What do you want to do? I don't know, what do you want to do?").

Second, while the fact that two individuals are limited in their role-taking ability to one type may not be a problem now, it may become a serious problem later on: Because they do not know each other very well in initial interaction, individuals tend to relate to each other primarily on the basis of roles, rather than as unique individuals (Miller and Steinberg, 1975). Thus, for a relationship to get underway, only basic role-taking is necessary at the early stages of relational development. However, as contact and interaction continue, the relationship has the possibility of making a qualitative change, potentially becoming increasingly more meaningful. In later stages of relational development, individuals need to relate to each other on the basis of unique characteristics, which requires the ability to manifest self-concept support through reflective, appropriative, and synesic role-taking. Miller and Steinberg (1975: 27) state it this way:

> In many cases, people interact for years without getting to "know" one another; they base their mutual predictions on sociological and cultural data. Typical examples are the husband and wife who have been married for twenty years and have never achieved the psychological prerequisite for interpersonal communication, or the father and teenage son who cannot talk to each other . . . or we may know of cases . . . where children have finished school and left home, and the parents and children suddenly realize that they know little about each other as individuals . . . They have never come to know each other as psychological beings, but only as cultural and sociological beings.

Third, if two people in a relationship engage in different role-taking types, forming complementary relationships, one may find the relationship less meaningful than does the other. If one person is primarily synesic and the other appropriative, the first may let the latter dominate the relationship. If one is primarily reflective, and the other appropriative, the first may want to "waste time" thinking things over, while the latter wants to "hurry and get the job over and done with."

Fourth, the specific self-concept characteristics relevant to each type also influence the nature of the relationship one may develop with others. If we return to Table Three to compare Bill's and Mike's real self-concepts as a means of analyzing the type of relationship possible between them, we discover that while they both are capable of all four types of role-taking, there are some important similarities and differences in the nature of each type. They can provide each other with some self-concept support in that they share being intelligent, teachers, having written books, being physically active, and winning athletic awards. In addition, Bill's thoughtfulness and Mike's concern and friendliness are potential assets in the development of their relationship; but Bill's aggressive and talkative tendencies may threaten Mike—who is meek, insecure, and status-conscious—and their competitiveness may further undermine their efforts to relate to one another. Thus, it is important in analyzing interpersonal relationships to study the specific characteristics for similarities and differences that might contribute to or undermine relationships.

Fifth, the development of one's self-concept and role-taking ability constrain the number and type of others who can or want to provide the person with self-concept support or denial. If one is receiving self-concept support on preferred characteristics, he or she feels understood; if not, one does not feel understood. If individuals' ability to role-take is limited to one kind, and if a different type of self-concept support occurs with each kind of role-taking, then one may be able to provide the appropriate type of self-concept support that produces feelings of being understood at one stage but probably not at other stages of relationship development. Therefore, it may be best for the positive growth of one's interpersonal relationships, and for one's own mental and emotional health, if he or she is able to manifest self-concept support using all four types of role-taking.

Sixth, the different types of role-taking represent greater orders of interpersonal awareness. The basic type is the first level, because it is based on sociocultural data; namely, role expectations and attitudes, which are acquired early in interaction (Miller and Steinberg, 1975). The reflective and appropriative types occur at the next level and are based on psychological data, specifically feelings and personality traits. The synesic type occurs at the highest level and is based on unique, individualized data regarding the other. Smith (1977) provides some research support for a developmental view of role-taking within small groups. In discussions lasting only an hour, Smith found that participants began with basic role-taking, moved to reflective and appropriative levels, and ended with synesic.

One may compare his or her role-taking abilities with those of others by examining real self-concept characteristics on one's TST (those that appear on one's own TST and on TSTs of others). Key questions are as follows: Does one reveal all four types of role-taking ability? Do other individuals in one's social network indicate role-taking at only one level? What specific self-concept characteristics might contribute most to one's relational satisfaction?

Through role-taking, one is made aware of another's confirmation, rejection, or disconfirmation. The question arises as to how the self-concept guides the development or disintegration of interpersonal relationships?

Self-Concept Rules: Guides to Communication and Relationship Development

According to Mead (1934), individuals, moving in their environment, are confronted by other persons, places, things, and messages.

When confronted by such material or social "objects," individuals must, if they are to commit themselves to an action, perform two tasks. First, they must determine what the objects in their experience are by associating them with and differentiating them from other objects of their experience. Second, they must determine the relationship of the objects to themselves in terms of appropriate actions in appropriate circumstances. An individual's knowledge of what objects are and how one should act towards them is a product of information based on past experience and vicarious learning from others. This does not mean an individual has in his experiential field only object relationships that include a relationship to one's self. For example, in the course of a day, I am apt to pass by many objects, people, and places that have little or no significance for me. When they have no particular meaning to me, I may not notice or remember them. On the other hand, how I relate to time ("I am always early"), height ("I am tall"), and politics ("I am a Democrat or a Republican") do provide information about myself and would therefore be a part of my self-concept.

The relationships that constitute the self-concept are important in at least three ways. First, the information an individual garners as a result of an encounter with one object applies to all other objects one places in the same class. Thus, an individual can make inferences about his or her relationship to an object without encountering the object. One need only to have encountered another object that has been placed in the same category as the first. Second, the self-concept provides us with expectations about the nature of objects placed in the same category, and therefore directs one's perception of his or her environment. It encourages people to take note of certain characteristics and to react to an object on the basis of those characteristics. Third, as the self-concept develops, it provides us with preconceived plans of action. A self-object relationship and initiating action. With such a system, a person is prepared to make sense out of his or her experience and to cope with the future. Thus, in the words of Blumer (1966:535), "The possession of a self provides the human being with a mechanism of self-interaction with which to meet the world . . . a mechanism that is used in forming and guiding his conduct."

As described above, in American culture, identity, evaluative, and behavioral self-object relationships are separately evaluated; but taken as a whole, they constitute a self-concept that is an organized set of information that defines the relationship of objects to the individual, which in turn governs and directs human action. Furthermore, the self-concept, as an organized set of structures, provides the rationale for choice in the form of a balanced repertory of alternative meanings, evaluations, and plans of action. Consequently, identity, evaluative, and behavioral self-object relations function as rules or imperatives for defining the self, evaluating objects, and acting in specific situations where those objects are present. The composite of all the rules one has regarding the relationship of objects to one's self is one's self-concept (Cushman and Cahn, 1985). It is the stability of this set of rules that makes an individual's identity, evaluations, and behaviors predictable by others. The self-concept or rules that govern and guide an individual's relationship to objects by directing human perception, evaluations, and actions contain, first, a definition of an object in terms of its relationship to the individual, and, second, an indication of the circumstances in which the rule is applicable.

What is the role of perceived understanding as a vital component in the self-concept? To better understand the answer to this question, it is necessary to distinguish among the types of information we have on ourselves, which may be real (those self-object relationships that have been tested and supported in interaction), ideal (those self-object relationships that one thinks exist but have not been tested in interaction or are not sustainable in interaction), and preferred (those social and unique self-object relationships that one thinks are assets).

The notion of preferred self-concept is key to understanding the role of perceived understanding as an essential component in the self-concept. Through the application of its identity, behavioral, and evaluative rules, the self-concept seeks the confirmation of one's preferred real and ideal self-object relationships, resulting in the feeling of being understood, while its rejection or disconfirmation results in feeling misunderstood. Although the notion of confirmation and disconfirmation seems rather simple, the actual way in which the self-concept employs perceived understanding is complicated by the fact that between initiation and termination the individual may construct, organize, and reorganize a plan of action based on the perception that his or her preferred self-concept is being understood or misunderstood by others.

The self-concept monitors and uses perceived understanding in two distinctly different ways (Cushman and Cahn 1985). First, perceived understanding alerts the self-concept to correct an individual's behavior when that behavior strays from the preferred self-concept conceived as a goal. Such a perception is used to adjust the individual's performance. Perceived understanding provides the individual with information about goals like the preferred self-concept, and the social self-concept provides the individual with rules for adjusting his or her performance so as to obtain the goals. Thus, when the individual has a fixed goal (i.e., a preferred self-concept) and is in the process of pursuing a standardized pattern of behavior in order to reach that goal (i.e., impression formation process), the self-concept provides the pattern of information needed for monitoring feelings of being understood or misunderstood in accordance with previously established rules for goal attainment.

Second, perceived understanding is dependent upon an individual's obtaining information about new ways of organizing action. It allows for some encouragement in an improbable direction to be recognized as beneficial and then to alter the individual's old course of action to a new course that maximizes those benefits. The judgment that a new course of action is beneficial and worth pursuing requires a previous organizational pattern for comparison purposes. The self-concept provides the previous pattern of organization and the information needed to recognize the implications of the new pattern, based on perceived understanding. Therefore, the new organization and pattern being pursued may also be represented in the self-concept as a new rule or pattern for action in specified situations.

When action is initiated, the individual engages in a process of evaluation to determine the "goodness-of-fit" between his or her belief about the appropriate choice and his or her progress toward attainment of his or her purpose (Cushman and Whiting, 1969). Although this evaluation may be biased by the subjectivity of one's perceptions and interpretations, it still typically allows for changes in subsequent actions and, more significantly, modification of the current, ongoing strategy. As such, the self-concept is more than a simple device for blindly tracking environmental variations or changes in internal reference signals. It incorporates one type of perceived understanding to assure goal attainment, but it also includes another type of perceived understanding to alter the goals themselves.

To summarize, the self-concept is a coordinator and initiator of actions in service of goal-seeking and systematic change. Between initiation and termination, the individual may be in the process of constructing, organizing, and reorganizing his or her plans of action regarding a preferred self-concept on the basis of perceived understanding.

Specific Recommendations

By now the reader may feel somewhat overwhelmed with the theoretical concepts of self, self-support, and role taking, as well as an endless number of specific self-concept characteristics that may be supported or denied in interaction. Given all that I have said about these topics, one may wonder how to assess the quality of the communication environment surrounding an interpersonal relationship.

The question is what should one know about one's self and another person that is most crucial to forming and maintaining a meaningful relationship as opposed to one that may be doomed from the start? First, it is important to know each person's *real self-concepts*, because they consist of the specific characteristics that form the basic building blocks for forming interpersonal relationships. This information is obtained by cross-person comparisons of real self-concepts, using a solicitation technique such as the TST. Second, it is important to know each person's *role-taking ability*, because this determines the nature, scope, and configuration of *self-concept support* each is capable of providing the other. This information is also obtained by cross-person comparisons of real self-concepts, using the TST. Finally, it is important to know each person's *preferred self-concepts*, because only confirmation of preferred self-concepts produces feelings of being understood. This information is obtained by reflecting on the self-concepts and mutually disclosing to one another those real and ideal self-concept characteristics each prefers.

Summary

Central to a conception of self as the information one has regarding one's relationship to objects are the identity, behavioral, and evaluative dimensions. Aspects of each dimension may be considered ideal, real, and preferred. The real self-concept characteristics are the building blocks of interpersonal relationships, because each one represents a way in which people may form a meaningful relationship. The more dimensions one develops, and the more extensive each dimension, the more basis a person has for forming a meaningful relationship with another person.

Individuals need to maintain their integrity, to convert ideal self-concept characteristics into real ones, and to manifest to others (and to support in others) only preferred characteristics. The more support one receives from others for his or her preferred self-concept, the higher the quality of the communication environment, the more one feels understood and the more one experiences personal growth and relational satisfaction.

The self-concept is established and sustained in social interaction by sharing symbolic information and taking the role of others. To conceive of a self one must "get outside of one's self" by imaginatively constructing the attitudes and expectations others have for him or her. Through the role-taking process, one is made aware of another's confirmation, rejection, or disconfirmation of one's self-object relationships. Four kinds of role-taking may be differentiated in terms of the type of self-concept support each provides to others. The four types are basic, reflective, appropriative, and synesic.

The self-concept monitors and uses perceived understanding in two distinctly different ways. First, perceived understanding alerts the self-concept to correct an individual's behavior when that behavior strays from the preferred self-concept conceived as a goal. Second, perceived understanding allows for some encouragement in an improbable direction to be recognized as beneficial and then to alter the individual's old course of action to a new course that maximizes those benefits.

The long history of interpersonal relationships as social phenomena suggests that human beings harbor not only a need for social structure and cultural organization that may be satisfied by the basic type of role-taking, but also a need for the special quality of perceived understanding that is satisfied only by the intimacy, human contact, and emotional support that are achieved by reflective, appropriative, and synesic types of role-taking. Perhaps it is as Fromm (1956) once stated, "The deepest need of man then is the need to overcome his separateness, to leave the prison of his aloneness. The absolute failure to achieve this aim means insanity . . .".

THREE

Communication Skills

The information we have regarding who we are is ... determined ... in interaction with others and (is) based upon our own and other's communication skills.

D. Cushman and D. Cahn,
Communication in Interpersonal Relationships

Introduction

The *quality communication model* has as its goal the achievement and maintenance of interpersonal understanding (Miller, Corrales, and Wackman, 1975; Laing, Phillipson, and Lee, 1966) and examines the communication environment or communication behaviors that encourage both individual and relationship growth (Cushman and Cahn, 1985; Montgomery, 1981; Miller, Nunnally, and Wackman, 1975; Satir, 1964; Gibb, 1961). Individual and relationship growth are in turn associated with feelings of self-worth and relationship satisfaction that are the product of perceived accurate and positive self-concept support and communication skills. The role positive and accurate self-concept support plays in the development, maintenance, and disintegration of interpersonal relationships is explored in Chapter Two. Feeling understood, which results from positive and accurate self-concept support, is demonstrated to be an important factor, if not the most important factor, in self-concept and relationship development, as well as in individual's feelings of self-worth and relationship satisfaction.

Without positive and accurate self-concept support, an individual's attempts to validate his or her self-concept and to initiate an interpersonal relationship will fail or lead to relationship termination. Without communication skills, every interactional error has the potential to harm one or both of the self-concepts involved, or the relationship itself. These then are the constituents of a quality communication environment, one which promotes self-worth and relationship satisfaction.

In the preceding chapter, it was argued that to create a quality communication environment communicators must know their own and the other's preferred self-concepts and have a highly developed role-taking

47

ability. In this chapter, it is argued that such an environment also requires communication skills to convey the appropriate type of messages that support and elicit support for one another's self-concept. Specifically, I intend to (1) describe the key communication skills and the mental and emotional orientation that underlies them, (2) describe the behavioral orientation that characterizes skillful communicators, (3) describe the advantages and phases of the collaborative behavioral orientation, and (4) make specific recommendations regarding the use of the three communication skills.

Key Communication Skills and the Communicator's Mental and Emotional Outlook

Three types of communication skills enable one to provide accurate and positive self-concept support to others. *Self-assertion skills* refer to one's ability to convey one's self-object relationships to others. *Listening skills* reflect one's ability to identify different types of self-object relationships designated by others. *Collaboration skills,* which build on one's self-assertion and listening skills, refer to the ability to develop appropriate means for reconciling differences in one's own and others' perceptions and expectations. These communication skills involve some vision of who we are and what we would like to become, as well as an appreciation of who others are and what they would like to become. Self-assertion, listening, and collaboration skills are employed in systematic ways when one seeks to continue, repair, renegotiate, or disengage from a relationship.

There is more to skill development than behavioral change alone. Beneath a given set of behaviors that represent a particular skill, there is a predisposition or tendency to behave in a particular fashion. This predisposition consists of intentions, attitudes, feelings, and motivations. While I readily admit that people do not always act in a manner consistent with their predispositions (due to social and cultural pressures or due to an inconsistent personality), I believe that most people tend toward consistency if they are free to do so. Therefore, a description of the skills essential to a quality communication environment must include an examination of the mental and emotional orientation that underlies these skills. A mental and emotional outlook consists of a communicator's concern for his or her own interests and those of others, positive feelings toward oneself and toward others, and task energy.

It has been said that there are two kinds of people in the world, those who divide the world into two kinds of people and those who do not. While some may legitimately argue against the use of a two-valued approach most of the time, I would point out that there are times when such thinking may produce insights. When it comes to the orientations that underlie effective communication, the notion that people tend to fall into one of two opposing categories appears useful.

Concerns for Self or Others

Let us begin with the observation that people often view human interaction with either their own *or* the other's concerns in mind. This is especially true in interpersonal conflict when one assumes that the other's concerns are in some way incompatible with one's own. On the one hand, having only the other's concerns in mind may produce altruistic behavior in American society. As a result of pressures from other members of a society and personality inclinations to be cooperative, one may sacrifice for others many or even all of one's own personal and individual needs, interests, and goals. When superficial relationships are not enough for a person in need of more intimate social contact, or when one has been subjected to periods of loneliness, he or she may need to be emotionally intimate or deeply involved with someone. In this case, one may need to sacrifice one's personal needs and interests to satisfy those of another. On the other hand, having only one's own concerns in mind may produce selfish behavior. Again, as a result of pressures from other members of a society and personal inclinations to be self-oriented, one may prevent others from satisfying their own concerns. When previous involvements result in dependency, one may feel stifled and subsequently turn to more selfish and demanding behaviors. In some cases, such people are simply unconcerned about the welfare of others; in other cases, they are only interested in doing better than another, even if their interests are not maximized (Deutsch, 1973).

Positive Feelings Toward Others

While people may have only their own or the other's concerns at stake, they may also be mutually trusting or suspicious; these are not themselves feelings but rather products of internal, subjectively experienced states one associates with another person. According to Brown and Keller (1979), the feelings behind trust or suspicion are as follows. First, *credibility* refers to the extent that the other is believable. A key component in trust is the realization that one means what one says. If the boss tells Mary that he is pleased with her teaching efforts but then writes about his dissatisfaction on her annual evaluation, she may become quite upset and feel that she cannot take what he says to be a valid indicator of how he really feels. Second, *predictability* refers to the extent that the other is living up to one's expectations. Another important fact is that one is consistent. Because Mary's boss said to her face that he was satisfied with her teaching efforts, she expected that he would indicate the same on the written evaluation. The fact that he did not follow through on the annual evaluation makes him appear unreliable to her. Finally, *confidentiality* means that the other uses information entrusted to him or her for one rather than against one. The factor of confidentiality is also very important. Mary might like to think that she can share her ideas, wants, and needs with her boss without fear of ridicule or intimidation. When her colleagues begin to criticize her for ideas expressed to her boss in private, she may feel hurt both personally and professionally.

If the feelings behind trust or suspicion are positive, one trusts, cares for, and is loyal to the other; if they are negative, one distrusts or is suspicious of the other. The more trusting one is of others who deserve that trust, the more optimistic and hopeful one becomes, the deeper one's relationships are with others, and the more comfortable one feels around them. According to Rogers (1961), the expression of positive feelings toward others takes the following forms: trusting behaviors, openness or disclosure, genuine regard or respect of others (i.e., positive self-concept support), an expressed concern for others, and behaviors indicating acceptance of others as they are (i.e., accurate self-concept support). Conversely, the less trusting one becomes, the more one tries to dominate others or to withdraw from the interaction; the less faith one has in oneself and in humanity, and the greater is one's isolation and loneliness.

Task Energy

The level of task energy refers to the amount of time, money, and effort one is willing to invest in the creation or maintenance of a relationship. In other words, how hard is one willing to work at preserving a relationship? Here task energy is limited to what is expended to be physically present, to interact with the other, to provide self-concept support to the other, to listen to and cue the other to attain accurate self-concepts, and to negotiate differences as they arise. While the amount of rest, good health, and money are factors that influence the energy available to expand on a relationship, commitment is one of the most important influencing factors, because it directs one towards preserving a relationship and helps one overcome the barrier created by the physical distance between relational partners (as discussed in Chapter One).

Behavioral Orientations

While I have been arguing that predispositions are important, the actual behaviors themselves are a more obvious component of any skill. As presented in Table Four, five different behavioral orientations—which may be arranged along the underlying dimensions of communicator concern for self or others, trust or suspicion, and level of task energy—may be defined in terms of the strategy, objective, and communication style associated with each behavioral orientation. In this section, I will describe each of the five communication behavioral orientations, and report research that shows which are most popular.

Five Alternatives

The first behavioral orientation is to *avoid* interaction. A strategy of withdrawal, avoidance is low in attempts to satisfy personal and other's concerns; it is also marked by suspicion toward the other and low in task energy. Because its objective is "lose-lose," everyone fails to make any gains. An "avoider" is a person so unconcerned about oneself and the other's needs, and so unmotivated toward positive attitudes and task energy, that he or she chooses to be physically absent, to avoid issues, or

Table 4
The Role of Communication in Five
Common Behavioral Orientations

Behavioral Orientation	Communication Strategy	Communication Objective	Communicator Style
Avoidance	To withdraw	Lose-Lose	Physically absent or silent
Accommodation	to acquiesce	Lose-Win	Give-in; don't make waves
Aggression	To compete	Win-Lose	Selfish, Argumentative
Compromise	To trade-off	Win & Lose	Wheeler-Dealer
Collaboration	To assert self, but respects interests of others	Win-Win	Supportive of self and other's self-concepts.

to remain silent. There is little if anything in this person's relationship with others to deter the threat of loneliness and separation.

The second behavioral orientation is to *accommodate.* A strategy of acquiescence, accommodation is low in attempts to satisfy personal concerns and low in task energy; but it is high in attempts to satisfy other's concerns and high in trust of the other. The object here is "lose-win" in favor of the other, where one gives up personal gains for the benefit of one's partner. An "accommodator" is one so concerned about the relationship and the other person that he or she suppresses personal needs, interests, and goals, and thus does not "make waves." While the "accommodator's" partner may derive considerable personal growth and satisfaction, the two are actually pursuing divergent paths because the "accommodator" is not deriving personal satisfaction and growth.

The third type, which is the opposite of accommodator, is a *competition*-oriented strategy. It is high in personal concerns and task energy but low in attempts to satisfy other's concerns and low in trust (or high in suspicion) of the other. Since the objective is "win-lose" in favor of oneself, one gains at the other's expense (zero-sum game). As defined here, competitors are typically argumentative, selfish, and confrontational because they are more concerned about their own personal needs than about their relationship. They beg and borrow excessively from their friends, steal from and cheat their colleagues and neighbors, and use coercion as much as, if not more than, communication.

Fourth, *compromise,* frequently the outcome of interaction between two competitors, is a strategy of trading involving "give and take," and involves some but not all degrees of both sets of dimensions. Albeit, it is designed to be a realistic attempt to seek an acceptable (but not necessarily preferred) solution of gains and losses for everyone involved. This strategy is not ideal because, regardless of the initial objective, in the end neither party may win using it if they both lose at least some of what they had hoped to achieve. Expert compromisers exchange offers and make concessions.

Fifth, *collaboration* is a strategy of "win-win" in which one's attempts to satisfy personal concerns and the other's concerns, and one's motivation regarding trust of others and task energy are also maximized. Everyone involved attempts to find integrative outcomes that completely satisfy everyone. The collaborator is assertive but respects the other's interests, needs, and goals, and captures the essence and virtues of competency in interpersonal communication because he or she is supportive of one's own and others' preferred self-concepts. While it may involve confronting differences, collaboration requires a problem solving attitude and includes sharing information about everyone's needs, goals, and interests.

Lack of Communication Skill: Empirical Research

What does empirical research show about people's actual attempts to communicate interpersonally? As for a lack of self-concept support discussed in Chapter Two, the lack of communication skills, especially those involving collaboration, leads to relational disintegration and may motivate relational disengagement. This is particularly true for the resolution of interpersonal conflicts that are primarily emotional in nature.

In interpersonal communication, one presents one's vision of self to those intimate others from whom one seeks and needs self-concept support in order to sustain one's view of self. The problem is that when conflicts arise people who are overly concerned about relationship maintenance and have very positive feelings toward their partner frequently fail to assert characteristics of their self-concepts that are important to them, which in turn decreases their ability to discover mutually advantageous outcomes. In a study that compared the communication behavioral orientation of mixed-sex stranger dyads with that typical of dating couples, romantic involvement was found to detract from the partners' ability to find mutually advantageous outcomes (Fry, Firestone and Williams, 1983). In contrast, wives who were more assertive and adventurous tended to have more successful marriages (McClelland et al., 1972).

In a study of relational satisfaction, Argyle and Furnham (1983) demonstrated that many people tend to deal with interpersonal conflicts in a highly emotional and critical manner. Kressel et al. (1980: 102) state that

> in many respects therapists may be better equipped than lawyers to help produce equitable, lasting, and less costly divorce settlements. The idea rests on various arguments, the principle one being that many of the real issues in settlement negotiations are emotional in nature and that lawyers are ill equipped to handle such matters and may therefore exacerbate the conflict between the parties.

Although in the first half of this chapter five different behavioral orientations were described in theory, research shows that people tend to deal with conflict in only one behavioral orientation. In their study of long term relationships, Argyle and Furnham report that criticism that is indicative of the competitive approach is a characteristic way of dealing with such situations. At least one other line of research supports the claim that people frequently deal with conflict in relationships by criticizing the other's behavior, habits, and style of life, again characteristic of the competitive approach. A comparison of verbal communication patterns in high and low marital adjustment groups (Ting-Toomey, 1983) reveals that people typically resort to confronting, complaining, and defending, all of which contribute to the disintegration of relationships. *Confronting* directly attacks, criticizes, or negatively evaluates the other's feelings/ideas, and consists of negative evaluations, loaded questions, and direct rejection. *Complaining* discloses discontent and resentment through indirect strategies of blame aimed at the other, a third party, and/or the situation. *Defending* persists in clarifying one's own position in spite of other's feelings/ideas and involves justifying one's own actions, those of others, and/or the situation. Thus, people typically begin a conflict in a manner directly attacking one another with criticism and negatively loaded statements, followed by attempts to justify oneself and blame the other. By complaining, instead of asserting the characteristics of one's self-concept that one thinks are important, one typically criticizes others by employing strategies that focus on the characteristics of other persons, places, or things.

Along with blaming others for one's problems, people frequently defend themselves by offering accounts for their transgressions. Accounts are explanations offered for actions called into question because they are unexpected or untoward (Scott and Lyman, 1968). *Excuses* are accounts in which one denies responsibility for an action but admits that the act is reprehensible, while *justifications* are accounts in which one admits responsibility but interprets the act in a more socially acceptable manner. In many cases, neither actually solves a problem but may be used to defend one's behavior, as Ting-Toomey found in disintegrating relationships. In a study of how parents explain to their children their decision to seek a divorce, Cushman and Cahn (1986) found that 55% of the parents chose to provide their children with explanations involving an excuse. Thus, people frequently rely on excuses as accounts, even though excuses may only be a form of defensive communication and do little if anything to help solve real problems.

Moreover, when dealing with the stress created by interpersonal conflicts, people resort to coping styles other than collaboration. Menaghan (1982), who examined the effects of coping strategies on relational stress and resolution of interpersonal conflicts in long term opposite-sex relationships, identifies four different coping styles. First, some individuals deal with the problem by compromising. Second, some individuals appear to be "accommodators" who resort to optimistic comparisons (relative to one's past and peers). Third, some individuals resort to selective inattention (away from negative aspects and toward positive features of the situation). Finally, others act as "avoiders" who withdrew from the interaction.

Menaghan (1982: 223) elaborates as follows:

> The first of these coping factors is the only effort focused on direct modification of the problems. The second and third seem to be aimed at deflecting or buffering the stressful impact of problems by modifying perceptions of the problems; and the fourth focuses on managing or controlling the unpleasant feelings that may be aroused by the problem.

Menaghan adds that, owing to the concessions characteristic of the compromising behavioral orientation, compromising fails initially to reduce ongoing stress and strain on the relationship in spite of fact that it eventually helps to alleviate some problems.

Research indicates that the alternatives to collaboration, sometimes including that of compromising, tend to result in destructive communication. Deutsch's (1973) research employing the Prisoner's Dilemma Game demonstrates that mutual perceptions of a shared cooperative orientation help to establish a relationship of mutual trust; similarly, mutual perceptions of a competitive orientation help to establish a relationship of mutual suspicion. Situations where one communicator is cooperative while the other is competitive in orientation leads to the initial biasing of perceptions of the other's communication in the direction of one's own motivational state. However, as interaction continues, mutual suspicion eventually sets in. As argued in the previous chapter, the more suspicious one becomes, the less one trusts others. The less trusting one becomes, the more one tries to compete with others or to withdraw from the interaction; the less faith one has in oneself and in humanity, the greater is one's isolation and loneliness.

What can be said about the behavioral orientations typical of much interpersonal communication? In sum, at a time when people might prefer to present a vision of self to those intimate others from whom one seeks and needs self-concept support, others tend toward withdrawal, accommodation, or compromise rather than collaboration. In some cases, partners' concern for relationship maintenance and positive feelings toward the other may interfere with their ability to discover mutually advantageous outcomes. In other cases, people tend toward competition and frequently criticize characteristics of others. Such an attack on the other encourages withdrawal, selective inattention, optimistic comparisons, or the offering of accounts, especially excuses, for one's transgressions.

Advantages and Phases of
The Collaborative Behavioral Orientation

We know that it is difficult to establish and maintain intimate or close interpersonal relationships. Through collaboration one can create and maintain in interaction basic essentials that contribute toward personal growth and relational satisfaction. How does one assert a strong, positive conception of self into a relationship so that it is supported in return, and how does one encourage and respond to the assertion of others in a manner that produces mutual understanding? As a means of answering these questions, this section presents advantages of collaboration and describes its phases.

The Advantages of Collaboration

The most constructive behavioral orientation is collaboration, because it contributes most to a high quality communication environment. A comparison of the alternative behavioral orientations indicates that collaboration contributes less toward long-term personal and relational stress and most toward personal and relational growth and satisfaction.

LOW PERSONAL AND RELATIONAL STRESS. In general, stress is defined as "the tension generated from an event which is unmanaged at that point in time" (Cole and Ackerman, 1981: 135). Stress may be either personal or relational in nature or a combination of both. The five behavioral orientations may be arrayed along both types of stress, each ranging from high (10) to zero, as illustrated in Figure Two.

Personal stress occurs within a person and refers to emotional and physical wear and tear on the individual. While a little stress may be positive and pleasurable—as when one experiences an uplift associated with falling in love, seeing a great performance, or watching an exciting athletic event—other "stressors" (such as strong feelings of anxiety, frustration, and anger) that are associated with "life crises" such as the death of a family member, a divorce, a marriage, a new job, or a change

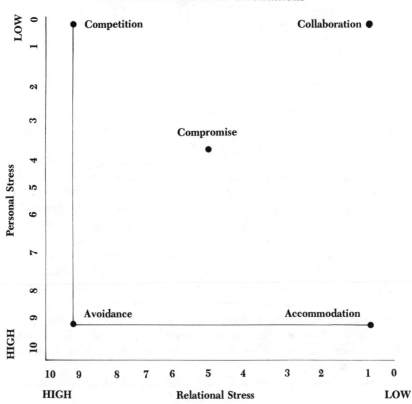

Figure 2
Two Dimensions of Stress Underlying
Alternative Behavioral Orientations

in one's location may contribute to ulcers, heart disease, hypertension, migraine headaches, and even suicide. Loneliness is also stress producing. Psychologists have long argued that stress improves performance, but only up a point at which efficiency drops off sharply. As reported by the Americans Academy of Family Physicians in *Time* (June 1983: 48), "two-thirds of office visits to family doctors are prompted by stress-related symptoms." Since many "life changes" contribute substantially to personal stress, Holmes and Rahe (1967) developed a stress scale for people to rate the amount of social readjustment required for various events. Some of the more common life events are awarded points on the Holmes-Rahe scale as follows:

Death of Spouse	100
Divorce	73
Marital Separation	65
Imprisonment	63
Death of a Close Family Member	63
Marriage	50
Pregnancy	40
Buying a New House	31
Christmas	12

Stress events such as these are thought to be cumulative, such that individuals totaling 300 or more units at any one time are very likely to suffer ulcers, burn out, or nervous breakdowns.

Relational stress occurs outside the individual and refers to wear and tear on a relationship. Whereas personal stress goes on within the individual, relational stress goes on *between* or *among* two or more persons. In opposite-sex long-term relationships, "new social roles of the sexes" is frequently mentioned as a relational stress producer. Because of the omnipresence of interpersonal conflict, a little relational stress is normal and unavoidable; but in the extreme, relational stress results in relational dissatisfaction and deterioration that eventually may result in social disengagement, such as breaking up, getting a divorce, or losing a job. Returning to the Holmes and Rahe Stress Scale, it is clear that extreme personal stress is associated with extreme relational stress, since the death of a spouse (100), divorce (73), and marital separation (65) score highest in personal stress and obviously involve relational breakdown as well.

As displayed in Table Five, the five alternative negotiation processes vary in the degree and/or nature of the type of stress underlying them. Again, collaboration bargaining is the most advantageous alterna-

Table 5
Dimensions of Stress Underlying Five Behavioral Orientations

Behavioral Orientation	Types of Stress
Avoidance	*High* personal stress/*high* relational stress
Accommodation	*High* personal stress/*low* relational stress
Competition	*Low* personal stress/*high* relational stress
Compromise	Moderate levels of *both* types of stress
Collaboration	*Low* personal stress/*low* relational stress

tive, because it alone reduces one's emotional and physical stress, as well as the stress on the relationship.

HIGH PERSONAL AND RELATIONAL GROWTH AND SATISFACTION. As depicted in Table Six, a comparison of the strategies, objectives, and styles of the five behavioral orientations reveals that they differ in their contributions to personal and relational growth and satisfaction. By failing to assert one's self, both avoidance and accommodation create conditions characterized by low feelings of self-worth and relational satisfaction, and no opportunities for personal or relational growth. By asserting one's self (but at the expense of others), competition creates conditions one may describe as high in feelings of self-worth, relational satisfaction, and personal growth for the competitor, but little or no growth in others. Thus, it is not uncommon for "accommodators" and competitors to be attracted to each other initially, but then to find that the stress and strain on the relationship as they grow apart often leads to relational deterioration and eventual disengagement. By gaining some and losing some of one's interests, needs, and goals, compromise consists of a strategy, objective, and style that contributes to moderate feelings of self-worth and relational satisfaction, as well as moderate personal and relational growth. Finally, by allowing self-assertion, encouraging effective listening, and promoting an integrative approach to problem solving, collaboration is the behavioral orientation that produces the highest quality communication environment by creating conditions that contribute to high feelings of self-worth and relational satisfaction for both partners, as well as maximum personal and relational growth.

Derr (1978) offers support for the collaborative behavioral orientation when he argues that it promotes authentic interpersonal relations, is used as a creative force for innovation and improvement, enhances feedback and information flow, and increases feelings of integrity and trust. When successfully used as a mode for resolving interpersonal conflict aimed at developing an integrated consensus through argumentation and role-taking, collaboration not only ends conflict but modifies the perspective of the individuals involved to a consensus framework that respects individual differences.

Phases of Collaboration

Collaboration is a behavioral orientation that may contribute to a quality communication environment by stimulating personal and interpersonal growth and satisfaction. In the following discussion, four phases involved in collaboration and adapted from Eiseman (1977) are described and illustrated with an extended example.

Table 6
Five Behavioral Orientations and
a Quality Communication Environment

Behavioral Orientation	Personal/Relationship Growth
Avoidance	Low feelings of self-worth and relational satisfaction; no personal/relational growth
Accommodation	Low feelings of self-worth and relational satisfaction; no personal growth; partners grow apart (high growth only for partner)
Competition	High feelings of self-worth and relational satisfaction; high personal growth for self; partners grow apart (no growth for partner)
Compromise	Moderate feelings of self-worth and relational satisfaction; moderate personal/relational growth
Collaboration	High feelings of self-worth and relational satisfaction; maximum personal/relational growth

CLARIFICATION OF PERSPECTIVES. First, communicators need to clarify their points of view for the understanding of others. Essential to collaboration, interpersonal communication calls for understanding the other as well as one's own position, and respecting one another's preferred self-concept. It also calls upon one to be aware of his or her own needs for self-concept support and to be alert to the other's use of unfair tactics against one.

To illustrate the first and the following phases of collaboration, the following extended example is offered. Suppose Linda and Jim were married soon after graduation four years ago and each has been employed since. Suppose further that Linda and Jim do not resort to unfair communication techniques to cloud differences of opinion that exist between them. In the first phase of collaboration, interpersonal communication between Linda and Jim reveals that Linda wants to take a year off from work and use a $10,000 inheritance (left to both of them) for a year of schooling, while Jim is against her taking a year off from work and favors banking the inheritance. Both indicate that these differences of opinion must be resolved because they are creating a strain on their marriage.

RIGID GOALS BUT FLEXIBLE MEANS. Collaborators are rigid in terms of goals but are flexible with respect to the means for achieving them. They are committed to a particular outcome but are able to entertain alternative ways to resolve their differences. Therefore, they accept only high personal gains for themselves and their partners and tend to pursue many alternative paths in an effort to achieve a mutual understanding.

In the extended example introduced above, Linda states that she wants to take a year off from work to attend a local university to acquire a Master's Degree in Business, which she says will advance her career in the long run. Jim, who is very satisified with his job, is adamantly opposed to her leave of absence because, after four years of their paying off debts for an automobile and furniture for the apartment, he would like to put the money in the bank to earn interest. Jim and Linda say that a completely satisfactory understanding must neither break up their marriage nor result in one or the other having to give up his or her ambitions, needs, and goals. Moreover, it must enable Linda to advance her career while providing greater financial security for Jim. Thus, while Jim and Linda appear to be rigid with respect to goals, they report that they are willing to entertain a wide variety of means for attaining them.

DEVELOPING MUTUAL UNDERSTANDING. To resolve differences in opinion or points of view in a manner that is mutually advantageous to everyone involved usually requires first that partners increase their range of perspectives, solutions, or alternatives. After identifying the differences in interests, goals, and needs of the partners, each person must try to think of their positions as end points on a continuum with many intermediate views. For example, Linda could earn her degree on a full-time basis, on a part-time basis, or not return to college at all and do something else instead. Jim, meanwhile, could bank all $10,000 or $5,000 or $1,000 or none at all. At this point, however, a premature understanding that consisted solely of Linda agreeing to return to school on a part-time basis and Jim banking $7,500 would result in a compromise with each person getting less than desired.

In addition to increasing the range of perspectives, the partners would benefit by trying to discover new perspectives, solutions, or alternatives that are *related* to the matter at hand, such as time, money, interests, security, status, or other factors that were not considered at first. Perhaps, in the case of Linda and Jim, a time dimension could be introduced in at least two ways. Linda could attempt to complete the degree in one year or spread it out over two or more years. Jim could invest the entire inheritance for an indefinite period or invest all of it now and some of it later. Moreover, since Linda expressed a desire to get away from it all, she could consider getting away from some aspect of her work that is especially bothersome to her. Perhaps a vacation or a change in her job situation—such as a different task, new co-workers, or a different department (or even a new job)—would satisify her need for a change.

Another technique for generating mutual understanding involves reordering the partners' views on the matter at hand. Such a shift creates an entirely new perspective. Realizing that there are other possible solutions to the problem, each person must take a new look at the matter. For example, in Linda's and Jim's case, each one's interest in preserving the relationship deserves mention. Presumably, Linda is interested in working most of the time, which contributes financially to the marriage. In fact, she states that obtaining a Master's Degree may make her more valuable to her employer and better guarantee her tenure and advancement in the long run. Jim's concern about savings reflects his interest also in the long-term financial security for the couple. They need to realize that neither Linda's desire for time off or Jim's desire for financial security may be achieved in the event of a marital breakdown, especially if it means divorce. The threat of severe financial loss at this time, which neither party wants, may motivate the couple to see the value of the newly discovered alternatives to the problem, to realize that there may be a way to reach mutual understanding, and to make an even greater effort to achieve it.

Using the acceptable elements of the possible alternative opinions, points of view, and solutions, the partners work together to find a choice that meets the needs of everyone involved. In the case of Linda and Jim, an example of an understanding that is mutually advantageous might be as follows. As soon as possible, they could take a three-week camping trip that they both want. Linda could return to her job after the vacation and enroll part-time at the university for one year, at the end of which she could request a leave of absence to attend to her studies full-time, following which any remaining credits could be obtained on a part-time basis. In the meantime, most of the inheritance could be banked to draw interest for one year, at the end of which one-half could be spent on Linda's education and the remainder could stay in the bank indefinitely. This solution has the potential of completely satisfying both Linda and Jim; while on a vacation with Jim, Linda is "getting away for a while," upon return she commences work on her degree and looks forward to a semester of full-time graduate student status next year; Jim gets to bank most of the money for one year and one-half of it after that. Although other agreements are possible, this is an example of an understanding that both parties may find mutually satisfying and that may enhance their interpersonal relationship.

IMPLEMENATION OF A MUTUAL UNDERSTANDING. While the discovery of a mutual understanding is often a challenging task, all the time and effort spent on its pursuit is wasted if appropriate measures are not taken to put the solution into effect. As a result of the preceding phases in the collaboration process, Linda and Jim have a greater understanding of each other's needs, desires, and beliefs. Each may feel that his or her position has a valuable contribution to make in the long run to their relationship and that each's ideas are to be taken into account in any decision the couple reaches. They may take pride in the fact that they asserted themselves and participated in the process of reaching a mutual understanding. The partners may need to reinforce these attitudes during the next few months to guarantee the successful implementation of the mutual understanding.

Specific Recommendations

Assuming that communicators know their own and the other's preferred self-concepts and have a highly developed role-taking ability, communication skills in the form of self-assertion, listening, and collaboration are necessary to convey the appropriate type of messages that support and elicit support for one another's self-concept.

Self-Assertion

First, try to be assertive where appropriate. What is "self-assertiveness?" How does it differ from passive accommodation or aggressive competition? One is a passive "accommodator" when he or she fails to effectively stand up for his or her interests, goals, and needs when they are ignored or violated by others. Such behavior is self-denying. An aggressive competitor stands up for his or her own interests while ignoring or violating those of others. This person's behavior is primarily self-enhancing at another's expense. An assertive person is one who stands up for his or her interests as well as those of others. Thus, the assertive person is self- and other-oriented.

While assertiveness is supposed to be beneficial for a relationship in the long run, it may not always be applicable. One should consider the importance of the situation and determine whether on occasion there are serious disadvantages that outweigh the advantages of being assertive. It helps to ask one's self, "How will I feel tomorrow if I am or am not assertive today?"

According to Miller, Nunnally, and Wackman (1975), there are six skills involved in self-assertiveness.

1. Speaking for self: Identifying one's self as being central in one's awareness.

2. Making sense statements: Describing what one sees, hears, touches, tastes, and smells.

3. Making interpretative statements: Describing what one is thinking, believing, and assuming.

4. Making feeling statements: Describing what one is feeling.

5. Making intention statements: Describing what one wants, wishes, and desires.

6. Making action statements: Describing what one does or how one behaves.

Rather than express themselves openly, many people prefer to succumb to unfair, unkind, and subjective forms of destructive communication. Bach and Wyden (1968) identify numerous unfair communication techniques. "Avoiders" may withdraw, evade, or walk out; "accommodators" may apologize prematurely, make promises they do not intend to keep, and store up hurts and anger ("Gunnysacking"); competitors may use intimate knowledge ("Beltlining"), bring in unrelated issues ("chain reaction"), employ humor that belittles, attack indirectly (i.e., through the children or one's friends), throw everything into the argument (except the "kitchen sink"), always demand more ("must win"), and set traps ("sandbagging"). These and other tactics discussed by Bach and Wyden are designed to convert differences of opinion or understanding into an ego and emotional conflict in which one contestant views "winning" or "losing" the conflict as support or injury to one's self-concept.

When being assertive, one should express concern for the interests of others, tell how one feels, and explain what one wants. This is called the assertive response. It is important to be emotionally honest and share all feelings, negative as well as positive, but in a way that does not use or abuse the other person. For example, after Mike was late for the second date in a row, Mary waited for the appropriate time and place to discuss the matter and told Mike that his being late made her feel slighted and unimportant. Then, she asked him to either be on time in the future or to call earlier and let her know how late he would be.

Listening

Second, try to listen to others in order to identify their interests, needs, and goals. One reason we fail to hear what others are saying is that our egos get in the way. Instead of digesting what the other person says, we sometimes think of how we can impress the other in a manner *we* think is positive. I am reminded of a couple who were on a dinner date. The fellow said he wanted to take the young woman to an expensive restaurant (which he thought would impress her). Although she said she knew the restaurant and suggested other less expensive places that she really preferred, he stuck to his original plan and took her to the restaurant *he* thought would impress her. Of course, she did not enjoy the evening as much as she might have. The problem was that he did not listen.

As a listener, you can encourage interpersonal communication by confirming the other as a person. Your verbal and nonverbal messages say to the other person, "I'm listening; I care about your interests, needs, and goals; I am interested in your point of view, and what you have to say." The lack of confirmation may suggest to the other person that he or she does not even exist. He or she may perceive that you are ignoring what was said and that you are not really interested in taking the time to pay attention to one's thoughts and feelings.

Verbal and nonverbal messages may be "heard" in a manner other than intended. Miller, Nunnally, and Wackman (1975) describe four skills that help clarify communicator intent.

1. Checking Out: Asking the other person to report on what he or she senses, thinks, feels, wants, or does.

2. Stating Intention and Asking for Acknowledgment: Stating clearly what the other wants and then asking him or her to report on what he or she heard.

3. Acknowledging the Sender's Message: Reporting back to the other what one saw and heard in his or her own words.

4. Confirming and clarifying: Acknowledging the accuracy of the other's attempts to paraphrase one's original message.

When perception checking, you say in your own words how you perceive what the other person is saying. Phrases such as "I hear you saying..." and "Are you saying that..." are especially useful. Such paraphrasing functions to give the other person a statement of your understanding of what was said and the opportunity to correct your understanding if inaccurate.

Collaboration

Although self-assertion and effective listening are important communication skills, collaboration is necessary for genuine and mutual understanding. To collaborate successfully, you and your partner must try to establish an atmosphere of support that encourages openness, trust, and cooperation. Two types of atmosphere or "communication climates" that appear threatening or defensive and unthreatening or supportive are described by Gibb (1961) in the following sets of paired characteristics:

Defensive Climate		*Supportive Climate*
1. Evaluation	vs.	1. Description
2. Control	vs.	2. Problem Orientation
3. Strategy	vs.	3. Spontaneity
4. Neutrality	vs.	4. Empathy
5. Superiority	vs.	5. Equality
6. Certainty	vs.	6. Provisionalism

An *Evaluation* consisting of praise and blame immediately arouses one's ego defenses, whereas a nonjudgmental *description* may be worded in a way that does not ask the other to change behaviors or attitudes. *Control* refers to attempts to dominate another's behavior, whereas a *problem orientation* implies a desire for collaboration. While *strategy* involves hidden motives and agendas, *spontaneity* is straightforward and free of deception. *Neutrality*, as defined by Gibb, refers to a lack of concern for the welfare of others, while *empathy* includes an expression of respect for the worth of others. *Superiority* tends to arouse feelings of inadequacy in others, while *equality* expresses a willingness to enter into participative planning with mutual trust and respect. Finally, *certainty* appears dogmatic, while *provisionalism* suggests tentativeness, a desire to withhold one's judgment until all the facts are in.

While the above listing of defensive and supportive characteristics of communication climates may appear in an "either-or" format, climates typically exist somewhere in between such extremes. The more supportive the communication climate, the more interpersonal the trust and openness, thus reducing the need to avoid, accommodate, or compete. As defenses are reduced, the more communicators can concentrate on one another's perceptions and achieve mutual understanding.

Mutual understanding requires that communicators participate in the decisions, agreements, solutions to problems, and resolution of conflicts that affect them. To the extent that they feel safe enough to assert their interests, needs, and goals, listen to the expression of others, and cooperate in the process of achieving an understanding, communicators perceive that they are understood. This perception, if mutual, contributes to personal and interpersonal growth and satisfaction.

The Paradigm Case

In one of my college classes a professor drew on the board what at first appeared to be a circle, and then he asked us what the figure was. After students guessed a circle, a zero, and the letter "O", we began to suggest some really wild answers. To give us a clue, he then asked us for the (technical) definition of a circle. Remembering some geometry, a student offered as a definition the statement that a circle is a curved connected line in which all points on the line are equidistant from the center. The teacher then proceeded to show us that no matter how precisely man or machine tried to draw a circle, a highly precise measuring instrument would show that not all the points on the curved line are exactly equidistant from the center. Thus, he concluded that a circle only exists in our heads as a definition. "In reality, what we have on the board," he said, "is man's imperfect attempt to draw a circle. So, too," said the professor, "no relationship between persons is perfect. We have only people's attempts at creating in reality what we perceive in our minds as being a perfect relationship." He used this technique to alert his students to the fact that, like a circle, no relationship can be perfect. Perfection is only a goal to which one strives. Moreover, one should expect problems in any and every interpersonal relationship. One should not enter into a relationship expecting perfection, but rather look for a relationship that permits the partners to manage the inevitable conflicts as they arise.

Some must wonder what one looks for in another person when dating, interviewing for a job, or trying to make new friends. The key idea here is to use a paradigm test to determine whether this prospective friend, worker, or mate is the type of person who can help you work out the problems that necessarily arise in a relationship. The paradigm case is one that involves self-assertiveness, effective listening, and collaboration. Differences of opinion, interpersonal conflicts, and problems needing resolution may serve as the content in paradigm cases.

First, instead of trying to find a relationship that will be perfect, or avoiding the problems and conflicts that arise, one should assert one's interests, feelings, and needs to see if the other is willing to create and maintain the kind of supportive climate described by Gibb. Then one should try to listen to the interests, feelings, and needs of the other, to see if one can support them in future interaction. This is contrary to the encouragement one may hear to marry a problematic person because "in time, he or she will change." On the basis of personal experience, many people now admit that this is simply not so. Finally, one should see whether the other is willing to invest the time and effort to develop understandings that are mutually advantageous or prefers to avoid, accommodate, or compete. While compromising may be preferable on some occasions, is the other willing to go the extra distance to collaborate? Why not learn about the other's communication skills while dating, initially interacting, or interviewing, rather than wait until after the person becomes a friend, mate, or employee and it will take more time, money, and effort to disengage from the relationship?

Summary

Differences in perspectives may damage some interpersonal relationships, but the skillfull application of communication designed to develop mutual understanding may actually contribute to personal and relational growth and satisfaction. Communication skills, particularly self-assertion, effective listening, and collaboration, encourage honesty and openness because they seek to satisfy everyone, require consensus before action is taken, and distribute power in a relationship more equally. Thus, collaboration reinforces positive feelings toward the other (respect, trust, support), requires an understanding of everyone's interests, goals, and needs, and fosters cooperation and interdependence.

The major disadvantages of collaboration are that it generates initial feelings of frustration and inadequacy and requires high task energy (time and effort) and other valuable resources in the short-run. On the other hand, the major advantages of collaboration are that it provides greater clarity about one's own desires and beliefs, a genuine sense that one's contribution is valued and will be routinely taken into account, increased appreciation and respect for the potential contribution of others, the combined functioning of talents that previously cancelled each other out, more creative and stable solutions to complex problems, and, in long run, greater productivity.

Although collaboration appears straightforward, it is not an easy or simple communication skill to learn. However, once collaboration and its underlying skills of self-assertion and effective listening are developed, it becomes a powerful tool for producing mutual feelings of perceived understanding, for achieving one's goal of maintaining one's integrity, and for maintaining a quality communication environment by cooperating with others in a manner that contributes to personal and relationship growth and satisfaction.

FOUR

Commitment Versus Letting Go

Commitment is the focus of energy, the stick-to-it-iveness that varies so
much from one person to another.

C. Brown and P. Keller, *Monologue to Dialogue:*
An Exploration of Interpersonal Communication.

Introduction

Researchers tend to follow one of four models of relationship
development, namely quality communication, availability of more desirable alternatives, system constraints, and size of investments. Persons
become more committed when they are satisfied with a relationship
(quality communication), when they perceive that they have only
inferior alternatives to the present relationship, when they perceive that
they have invested numerous resources in that involvement, and when
they perceive pressures from significant others to remain in the relationship (system constraints). Although researchers tend to follow one
of these models, recent studies show that relationship development and
disintegration of long-term heterosexual involvements, supervisor and
subordinate working relationships, and friendships are best predicted
by a combination of the models (Green, 1983; Green and Sporakowski,
1983; Rusbult, 1983; Farrell and Rusbult, 1981; and Rusbult, 1980).
Thus, each model has been useful, but a combination of all four leads to
greater understanding of relationship development and more accurate predictions.

It is the purpose of this chapter to explore the nature of commitment and relationship satisfaction. Specifically, it will explore quality
communication, availability of more desirable alternatives, system constraints, and the size of investments models; in addition, a more comprehensive approach to commitment and relationship satisfaction will
be offered, and specific recommendations will be set forth.

Quality Communication and the Nature
of Relationship Satisfaction

Examining the communication environment or communication behaviors that encourage both individual and relationship growth, the *quality communication model*, introduced in Chapter Three, has as its goal the achievement and maintenance of interpersonal understanding. Individual and relationship growth in turn are associated with feelings of self-worth and relationship satisfaction that are the product of perceived accurate and positive self-concept support and communication skills. The role that positive and accurate self-concept support plays in the development, maintenance, and disintegration of interpersonal relationships is explored in Chapter Two. Feeling understood, which resulted from positive and accurate self-concept support, is demonstrated to be an important factor, if not the most important factor, in self-concept and relationship development, as well as individual's feelings of self-worth and relationship satisfaction. The role of communication skill in relationship development is discussed in Chapter Three. Self-assertion, listening, and collaboration skills are employed in systematic ways when one seeks to continue, repair, renegotiate, or disengage from a relationship. Without positive and accurate self-concept support, an individual's attempts to validate his or her self-concept and initiate an interpersonal relationship will fail or lead to relationship termination. Without communication skills, every interactional error has the potential to harm either or both self-concepts involved or the relationship itself. These then are the constituents of a quality communication environment, one which promotes self-worth and relationship satisfaction.

For the individuals involved in a relationship, the question of whether to let go starts with the extent to which the partners *share the feeling that each understands the other*. Some may argue that this is not the case. They might claim that people work for certain bosses because they have no choice and need the money, students go to college because they need a degree, and people marry because they need to procreate and raise children. If such considerations were the only realities of social life (and they may be for *some* people), one would not mind being embedded in empty, distant and impersonal relationships. However, this is not the case for many people who are interested in improving the quality of their interpersonal relationships. Many working people do change jobs, and many employers want to avoid worker complaints, negative evaluations, and grievances against them, just as many people want to avoid being fired and having their futures adversely affected by a negative job performance appraisal. College students do try to avoid some teachers and take others. Some workers affect the careers of others through written evaluations and by filing written grievances. Some people divorce each other, and some children run away from home. If functional utility were the key factor in preserving interpersonal relationships, ones' social world would be very different from what it is for most of us living in the United States today. Instead, I argue that there are many ways in which one may satisfy one's needs for income, education, intellectual stimulation, sex, and children; but one reason that a person stays with a particular source of such need satisfaction is because that source also satisfies one's need to feel emotionally committed to others.

Availability of Alternatives and the Nature of Commitment

The conditions under which one *feels* committed to a particular relationship depend on the extent to which one finds meaning, satisfaction, and a sense of togetherness in light of available alternative relationships. Therefore, one may evaluate the worth of one's interpersonal relationships in terms of two kinds of comparisons (adapted from Thibaut and Kelley, 1959) involving perceived understanding—one against a neutral point and the other against available alternative relationships—and in terms of investments in the relationship and system constraints.

Comparison Levels

A *neutral point* exists where both the feelings of involvement are minimal. One would evaluate one's feelings of involvement with another that fall above the neutral point as positive and desirable; those falling below are negative and undesirable. As desires and expectations are fulfilled in a relationship, the neutral point increases, resulting in the anticipation of even greater emotional rewards in the future.

Although the neutral point is a useful comparison level for determining the emotional value of a particular interpersonal relationship, we also need to consider a second kind of comparison that is just as important, because it is the actual standard one uses to decide whether to disengage from a particular relationship. This comparison level is the lowest level one will accept in light of the *available alternative opportunities.* This level is a threshold or a point at which one or both partners perceive that another person outside their relationship understands them more than does one's partner. When this threshold is reached by either or both partners, it is then that dissolution of the relationship becomes a real possibility.

Available alternative relationships appear more desirable when one partner (or both) realizes that another relationship offers more emotional commitment than he or she thinks possible at present. An alternative partner, kinship affiliations, a different job or boss, and even educational opportunities (i.e., going away to school) may make relationship termination more attractive if the alternative appears to provide more gratification than offered by the current relationship. The perceived desirability of alternatives is established in much the same manner as is satisfaction with the current or primary relationship, except that in this case a relationship with an alternative person constitutes the object of comparison.

Conversely, one is more committed to a relationship when alternatives are not available. In studies of dating and romantically involved partners, Rusbult (1980a, 1980b, 1983) defined available alternatives as another person, several others, or spending time alone, and he asked subjects to rate the appeal of the alternatives. In another study of job commitment and employee turnover, Farrell and Rusbult (1981) asked workers to evaluate the appeal of unemployment and finding similar employment as alternatives to their present employment. In all of these studies, it was found that commitment to present relationships increased as the quality of the available alternatives declined.

Available Alternative Relationships: Fact or Fancy?

Since either real or anticipated alternatives can be a strong inducement to end a relationship (Thompson and Spanier, 1983), the question arises as to whether the so called available alternative really does in fact offer greater relational satisfaction, or is it merely an illusion? Consider the following statement written by Leo, a married man.

> I am having an affair with Rita, the most exciting woman I have ever known. My job takes me to another town most weekends, and that is how I met and got involved with Rita, who is nothing like June whom I've been married to for the past 10 years. Rita always spends considerable time getting ready to see me, something my wife seldom does. When I get to her apartment on Friday or Saturday nights Rita has a cold beer ready for me, and we sit and talk about things. I must admit that I do most of the talking, because she is such a good listener and is very interested in what I do all week. We usually have a quiet candle light supper, just the two of us, and then we frequently take a bottle of cold duck to bed. I

know that she has a 3 year old son named Joey, but he usually stays with Rita's mother on weekends. Rita has made it very clear to me that she is in love and wants me to leave June for her.

Compare this situation to the one at home where life is just the opposite of what I like. When I arrive at home on Sunday night, I am met by chaos. The kitchen is a mess, toys are all over the living room, our 6 month old baby is crying, and our other two older children are running through the house playing cowboys and Indians, because there is no place outside for them to play. June doesn't let me drink in front of the kids, and she usually says that she is too tired to have a little fun after the lights go out. It seems like all we can talk about is what mischief the kids got into today or our money problems. You see, there is no comparison between what Rita has to offer me over my life with June.

What does one make of Leo's situation? If one concentrated only on Leo for a moment, one might think that a Leo-Rita relationship will provide Leo with a more meaningful existence than a Leo-June relationship. Superficially, it may appear to Leo that the Leo-Rita relationship is more desirable and attractive than his marriage. The problem is that the alternative may be merely an illusion, for two reasons. First, the "love" Leo and Rita feel for each other may be passion and infatuation that may not last; second, the circumstances surrounding Leo's relationship with Rita may change if and when he spends more time with her. Let us consider each of these reasons in more detail.

Passion Versus Companionate Love

Hatfield and Walster (1978) distinguish between passionate love, defined as a wildly emotional state, and companionate love, which refers to friendly affection and deep attachment to another person. The cultural myth supports the notion that men and women should stay passionately in love forever. When Leo first met June, he probably felt passion and infatuation for her, but as the months and years passed by, his feelings changed. Leo, who subscribes to the cultural myth on the everlasting nature of love, is made overly susceptible to Rita's influence.

What Leo may not understand is that the passion he now feels for Rita may only be temporary. Researchers have found that romantic love with its passion and infatuation does not last (Mathes and Wise, 1983; Cimbalo, Faling, and Mousaw, 1976; Driscoll, Davis, and Lipetz, 1972). The longer a couple has been married, the less passionately they love one another. Thus, Leo needs to realize that the loss of his passion for

June is due to the "ravages of time," something that will also affect his feelings for Rita, and that the companionate love that he feels for June is the result of shared understandings, emotions, and habits.

Changing Circumstances

Not only will Leo's "love" for Rita become less passionate in time, just as it did for June, but if and when Leo moves in with Rita or marries her, he is in for a big surprise—one that is three years old and named Joey. When dating Leo, Rita took time and great care to properly orchestrate the conditions under which she and Leo spent time together. She left Joey with her mother for the weekend, hired a maid to clean house on Friday so that it would look nice all weekend, and performed more mundane tasks during the week so that Friday and Saturday nights would be free of (real world) intrusions. Perhaps Rita and Leo could perpetuate their fantasy world if they were to see more of each other, but I would bet that things would have to change eventually. Joey, who may turn out to be one very spoiled little boy, might be around more. During the week, Joey might turn the house into a mess until it gets cleaned by the maid on Friday. Therefore, some errands, people, and other commitments might begin to intrude on the relationship, as they did in his marriage to June. Of course, all this need not occur, but it might; if it does, then the dating period offers Leo only the illusion of a better life with Rita.

Loneliness as an Alternative

Research shows that loneliness is clearly not a desirable state of being (Weiss, 1973), and in fact it is worse than many people imagine. Loneliness has been shown to correlate with low self-esteem (Jones, Sansone, and Helm, 1983), feeling of alienation, the belief that the world is not a just place (Jones, Freemon, and Goswick, 1981), boredom, restlessness, and unhappiness (Perlman, Gerson, and Spinner, 1978). Thus, Peplau and Perlman (1979) defined loneliness as a response to a discrepancy between desired and actual relationships.

A number of factors may contribute to the development of loneliness. Researchers have reported findings that link the following interaction antecedents to loneliness: high communication apprehension and low communication competence (Zakahi and Duran, 1985), shyness and fear of rejection (Cutrona, 1982), and low self-disclosure (Chelune, Sultan, and Williams, 1980). I am sure that, in time, numerous interaction antecedents could be identified. I suggest that a more broadly based construct, psychological in nature and based on the communicators' views of social interaction, functions as a generative mechanism for determining the relationship between the antecedents of interaction and a consequence of such interaction, like loneliness. This intervening construct is perceived understanding or feeling understood. Cahn and Frey (1982) found that feeling understood functions as a link between the quality of one's interaction with others and a climate of support and trust between people.

What communication behaviors function as the antecedents of interaction that produce feelings of being understood or misunderstood, which in turn reduce or lead to feelings of loneliness? Jones, Hobbs, and Hockenbury (1982:685) have implicated a specific class of communication behaviors termed "partner attention," a lack of which leads to loneliness.

> By definition, partner attention included comments or questions referring to the partner in the conversation, to the partner's preceding statement, or to the partner's attitudes, activities, or experiences and thus constituted an index of the extent to which the subject reinforced his or her partner with personal attention.

Jones and his colleagues found that high-lonely subjects made fewer partner references, less often continued the topic introduced by the partner, asked fewer questions of the partner, and emitted fewer partner attention statements.

Except for the addition of topic continuation, the general category of partner attention used by Jones and his colleagues was identical to the one previously found by Kupke and his colleagues to be functionally related to interpersonal attraction. Kupke, Hobbs, and Cheney (1979) found that the extent to which partners attended to one another was significantly related to their attraction for one another. In a subsequent experiment, Kupke, Calhoun and Hobbs (1979) showed that experimentally induced increases in the frequency of personal attention were significantly related to increases in attraction ratings, and that the subjects who received training in personal attention received significantly more positive ratings of attraction as compared to subjects trained in different conversational behaviors, subjects in a minimal encouragement group, and subjects in a no-treatment control group.

In sum, research findings on perceived understanding, along with results reported by Jones and Kupke on partner attention, indicate that feeling understood functions as a link between certain communication behaviors, social skills, or quality of interaction, and specific outcomes such as support, trust, and interpersonal attraction on the positive side and loneliness on the negative side. In any case, loneliness is not a viable alternative to interpersonal relationships, but rather it is an indicator of an inferior set of relationships in need of repair or replacement. Before taking drastic steps, however, one must also consider one's social network and the size of one's investments in the relationship.

System Constraints

Consider the following examples.

Mary may not want to do the tasks the way her supervisor wants them done, but if the organization backs up the supervisor's demands, she may feel compelled to cooperate.

Jack may not enjoy the company of his parents friends, but may spend time with them anyway simply to please his parents.

Jerry and Julie may be unhappily married, but Jerry may be committed to a job that requires that he maintain the marriage.

Like the availability of more desirable alternatives, social contacts encourage Mary, Jack, and Jerry to maintain less than desirable relationships.

Comparison levels are complicated by the fact that interpersonal relationships do not exist apart from larger social systems. What does it mean to be identified as part of a larger social system? A system is a set of components that influence one another and that constitute a whole or unity with a purpose. To call a set of components a system implies that the components are related in some way and that the principle of organization or interdependence makes the whole work toward some end. A social system as a set of interrelated components is organized and guided by a socially agreed upon set of expectations in the form of rules, which in turn influence the formation, development, and deterioration of interpersonal relationships that are a part of that social system. Functioning as *system contraints,* the complex of rules that constitute a social system obligates, prohibits, or permits particular interpersonal relations and individual behavioral sequences. Albert (1968) clarifies the relationship between a social system and behaviors when she states that rules represent what is expected or hoped for, required or forbidden. They are not a report of actual conduct but a system of criteria by which conduct is judged and sanctions applied. Thus, a social system with its set of rules contrains an interpersonal relationship.

The results of several studies lend support to the claim that family and friends may influence one's commitment to a relationship. Studies of married persons demonstrated that social approval was associated with marital adjustment (Burr, 1973). Lewis (1973) showed that support from one's own family and friends was positively related to several relationship formation indices and negatively related to premarital disengagements. Krain (1977) found that support from family and friends was associated with courtship progression. Parks, Stan, and Eggert (1983) found that romantic involvement was positively associated with perceived support from one's own network of family and friends, perceived support from the partner's network, attraction to the partner's network, communication with the partner's network, and the number of people met in the partner's network. Therefore, it appears that partners are more likely to maintain a relationship if their social network is supportive of it. The existence of system constraints helps explain why some individuals choose to say in a dissatisfying relationship even if there is a more desirable alternative. Out of a sense of duty and feelings of obligation, one may feel constrained from putting one's self first.

While a more desirable alternative decreases one's commitment to the present relationship, the lack of system constraints may also be a factor. If there is little or no system constraints in effect, individuals are quite free to satisfy their own personal desires and seek more desirable alternatives to the present relationship.

Because one's commitment to a relationship depends on one's relational satisfaction or dissatisfaction and the system constraints, some partners maintain a less than desirable relationship because they are under the influence of external pressures, while others may choose a more desirable alternataive because of lack of such constraints. Moreover, given a particular level of dissatisfaction, a change in system constraints may provide an opportunity for disengagement. A friendship, love affair, or marriage could break up because the absence of certain people eliminated external pressures that helped to keep the relationship together physically. Thus, changes in the network of friends, relatives, and other important persons may have implications for the maintenance of an interpersonal relationship.

Investment Size

Although one might view a couple's relationship as inferior in quality, the partners remain emotionally committed to their relationship because each partner's sense of well-being is determined by the entire set of interpersonal networks in which their relationship is an integral part. In addition, *investment size* is also a key factor in commitment to an interpersonal relationship. Investment size refers to the number of resources one has expended to create and maintain an interpersonal relationship. Rusbult defined investment size as the extent to which the persons involved in a relationship had "put things into" their relationship and the extent to which there were objects, events, persons, and activities uniquely associated with their relationship. In studies of friendship, dating, and romantic involvement (Rusbult, 1980a, 1980b, 1983), investments were measured by ratings of emotional and monetary investments, self-disclosure, mutual friends, and shared memories, activities, and possessions. In a study of job commitment and employee turnover (Farrell and Rusbult, 1981; Rusbult and Farrell, in press), investments were measured by ratings of length of service, job tenure, retirement programs, nontransferable training, spouse's employment, homeownership, and community ties. While some investments are intrinsic to a relationship—such as time, effort, and self-disclosure— others are extrinsic—such as shared friends, memories, joint possessions, and mutual activities. Once expended, it may be difficult if not impossible to withdraw either type of investments from a relationship.

Regardless of the degree of dissatisfaction experienced in a relationship, people may be reluctant to disengage from it if they have made a sizable investment in it. This is apparent from the following examples.

> A less than favorable friendship may continue if friends have invested time and effort in joint experiences.

> Inspite of problems in the relationship, young lovers may continue to date or court one another for the same reasons.

> An unhappy marriage may survive because of many joint ventures, travels, projects and accomplishments, joint ownership, children, and difficulties overcome in finding a mate in the first place.

In addition, some women undergo a traditional socialization process that prepares and trains them for the stereotypic role of "housewife and mother," resulting in a key investment that makes some women work hard to keep a marriage together; meanwhile, many husbands traditionally spend all or a major portion of their income on the home, cars, and food that they share with their spouses, counting as a monetary investment. A supervisor-subordinate relationship may be dissatisfying, but one continues it because he or she experienced considerable difficulty getting the job in the first place, successfully completed comprehensive job training or years of education in a particular field, received hard-earned tenure, seniority, promotion, rank, or privilege. In all three of Rusbuilt's studies cited above, commitment to the relationship was found to increase as investment size increased. Therefore, it is important for those who want to maintain a relationship to build one that becomes increasingly interdependent.

While the size of investments accounts for why some people do not choose a more desirable alternative to a less than satisfying relationship, the lack of investments helps to explain why others break up a relationship. Since investments accumulate over time, the shorter the relationship, the less likely efforts on one or the other's behalf have had enough time to accumulate into a sizable investment. Thus, newly formed relationships are less stable than those that have already developed over a number of years. In addition, those who do not want commitment want to avoid building interdependency into a relationship.

Because one's commitment to maintain a relationship depends on one's relational satisfaction or dissatisfaction tempered by the size of investments, it is possible to be dissatisfied with a relationship but remain committed to it or to be motivated to shift to a more desirable alternative. Moreover, given a particular level of dissatisfaction, a change in the size of the investment may result in disengagement. A friendship, steady date, or marriage could break up simply because a change in circumstance makes it necessary to spend more time and energy than one wants in order to maintain the relationship. Therefore absence due to moving, job changes, and other transfers may not "make the heart grow fonder."

Relationship Reassessment: When to Stay and When to Let Go

In this section, I intend to describe a relationship that should continue, one that should be repaired, and one from which the partners should disengage. For purposes of illustration, let the self-concepts depicted in Table Seven serve as examples.

Relational Continuation

Combinations of the two comparison levels (neutral point and available alternatives) establish four different kinds of behavioral and emotional commitment, which in turn set the conditions for four different kinds of interpersonal relationships. In the first combination of circumstances, the emotional involvement is above the neutral point and

Table 7
Reassessment of Relationships

Person A	Person B	Person C	Person D
intelligent	honest	hard worker	critical
talkative	good listener	intense	manipulative
supportive	funny	persuasive	cutting
good listener	exciting	intelligent	aggressive
thoughtful	hardworking	talkative	self-centered
exciting	talkative	critical	persuasive
honest	intelligent	manipulative	mean
hardworking	supportive	forceful	intelligent
funny	thoughtful	supportive	quick
playful	playful	self-centered	likes to put down
confrontative	good-looking	goal-directed	confrontative
understanding	helpful	unsure of self	insecure
needs support	artistic	uptight	physically attractive
self-derogating	creative	nervous	forceful
organized	affectionate	unhappy	goal-directed
intense	atheletic	creative	sexually appealing
persuasive	quick	affectionate	honest
loyal	productive	good listener	exciting
good-looking	sexy	physical	hardworking

higher than the comparison level for alternatives. In this case, the partners are committed to the relationship with or without investments and system constraints.

Using Table Seven, suppose one considers a relationship involving persons A and B. Both perceive themselves and one another as being intelligent, talkative, supportive, good listeners, and thoughtful. In terms of self-concept support, these qualities contribute to the intensity of the relationship by providing a common set of real self-concept qualities to admire, while creating supportive, accurate, and intense interaction. In addition, they perceive themselves as hardworking, exciting, and honest, complementing specific aspects of one another's self-concept and encouraging its development and growth. Finally, they agree that they are funny and playful, adding more common positive self-concept qualities. Each has some additional characteristics that are positive but different from the other, thus allowing each a unique complement to one another's self-concept and a unique contribution to their relationship, because they bring to their relationship self-concepts that contribute to its success.

Relational Repair

In the second combination, the emotional involvement is above the neutral point but lower than the comparison level for alternatives. In this case, the partners are less committed to the relationship unless there are sizable investments and system constraints.

For such a relationship, consider one that involves persons A and C, as depicted in Table Seven. At first glance, it appears that there is a basis for some mutual self-concept support because they have several self-concept qualities in common; they are both intelligent, supportive, hardworking, intense, talkative, and persuasive. There are, however, several important differences between them. Person C is critical, manipulative, self-centered, and goal-directed. These qualities in C, along with being forceful and persuasive, make person A a likely target for C's criticism and manipulation. This is especially true for someone like person A who is loyal, caring, and nice. Person A's self-concept qualities of talkative, honest, and confrontative suggest that person A try to deal with these friction points by calling C's hand. The stability and configuration of this relationship then rest on A's and C's ability to understand the common basis for their relationship and their willingness to undertake interactional repair strategies (Cushman and Cahn, 1985). Therefore, persons A and C present conceptions of self that have the potential of either contributing to relational success or destroying it.

Relational Disengagements

SITUATION ONE. In a third combination of circumstances, the result of emotional involvement is below the neutral point but higher than the comparison level for alternatives. While this would be a relationship lacking in satisfaction, it might still be a stable one, at least for the time being, because no alternative appears at present to provide a higher degree of emotional commitment, or because there are sizable investments and system constraints. Keep in mind that when the opportunity arises, this relationship might quickly dissolve in favor of a new alternative.

SITUATION TWO. In a fourth combination, the emotional involvement is below the neutral point and lower than the comparison level for alternatives. Obviously, in the absence of substantial investments and strong system constraints, this would be an undesirable relationship that is probably about to end.

To illustrate the kind of relationships from which one should disengage, consider persons A and D in Table Seven. Here, it appears that both partners perceive themselves and one another to be intelligent, physically attractive, and sexually appealing, providing positive self-concept support on these qualities. Person D, however, is also critical, aggressive, manipulating, cutting, self-centered, mean, puts people down, and is confrontative, which erodes person A's self-confidence, especially since he or she is lacking in support, self-derogating, and thoughtful of others. In short, their relationship is a destructive interaction pattern, because person D harms the positive qualities of A's self-concept and upsets the foundation for a more satisfying interpersonal relationship. For both, disengagement from the relationship appears necessary. If a more desirable alternative is available, they may disengage now; otherwise, they may wait until such circumstances prevail.

Specific Recommendations

While the messages that characterize a particular relationship may contribute substantially to the satisfaction or dissatisfaction felt by the relational partners, either or both individuals may feel compelled to continue the relationship due to considerable investments, system constraints, or a lack of more desirable alternatives. In this next section, recommendations will be made regarding relationships that are satisfying with no better alternative being available, somewhat satisfying but with a better alternative available, dissatisfying but with no better alternative being presently available, and dissatisfying with a better alternative available.

First, if one feels at least some emotional commitment to a particular relationship, and no alternative offers you greater relational satisfaction, one will probably want to continue that relationship. If this is not the case, at least one may appreciate the fact that relationships characterized by high emotional commitment owing to considerable self-concept support represents a goal for those who want to improve the quality of their interpersonal relationships.

Second, if one feels at least some emotional commitment to a particular relationship and an alternative offers greater relational satisfaction, the nature of the first relationship will have to be repaired so that it offers one greater emotional attachment, or one may want to disengage from that relationship. One should, however, ask one's self the following critical questions:

1. Is the first relationship growing? Since a growing relationship offers the potential of developing into a closer and more intimate one, one may not want to pull out too soon. In a relationship marked by at least some emotional commitment, the relationship appears to offer growth potential.

2. Is the alternative merely an illusion? Since the growth potential offered by an alternative relationship may be only an illusion due to changing feelings over time and changing circumstances, in the long run, one may not be better off switching partners. In a relationship marked by at least some emotional commitment, the change may not be worth the risk.

3. Has one and/or one's partner made sizable investments in the relationship? One should consider the size and quality of the investments including time, effort, and self-disclosure, shared friends, memories, joint possessions, and mutual activities.

4. What are one's system constraints? One should consider his or her social network and see where his or her important social contacts stand regarding the relationship.

Third, if one feels no emotional commitment to a particular relationship but no alternative offers greater relational satisfaction, one may want to continue that relationship; however, he or she might be better off trying to develop new relationships that offer greater emotional involvement. One should consider where he or she lives, the nature of present relationships, and what one might have to do to create a situation in which he or she may have more opportunities to meet others.

Fourth, if one feels no emotional commitment to a particular relationship and an alternative offers greater relational satisfaction, the nature of the first relationship may have to be improved drastically to offer greater emotional attachment, or one may want to disengage from that relationship. A person should determine the answer to the following two critical questions:

1. What must be done to turn the first relationship into a growing one? If there is the potential of developing such a relationship into a closer and more intimate one, a person may not want to pull out just yet. However, in a relationship marked by no emotional commitment, there may not be much likelihood for growth potential, and the sooner one accepts that fact, the sooner he or she can take actions toward creating more positive alternative relationships.

2. Is the alternative merely an illusion? Since the growth potential offered by an alternative relationship may be only an illusion due to changing feelings over time and changing circumstances, in the long run, one may not be better off switching partners.

Since in the first combination of circumstances, the partners probably feel committed and act committed to the relationship, a high quality relationship is one in which both feel understood at least to some degree and no alternatiave offers greater emotional involvement. The more both feel understood, the better the relationship. Thus, a relationship marked by at least some emotional attachment would benefit by emotional enhancement. Where there is very great mutual emotional involvement, such a relationship should be maintained and represents a goal for those interested in improving the quality of their interpersonal relationships.

In the second and third combination of circumstances, however, efforts must be taken to repair the nature of the relationship by improving the quality of its communication environment in order to create conditions for the growth of emotional commitment. Finally, the fourth illustration requires emergency measures because it has been allowed to deteriorate to a considerable extent.

Before leaving the question of commitment verses letting go, a caveat is in order. One should realize that either comparison level (neutral point or availability of alternataives) could change over time, differ among contexts or situations, and vary from one person to another. Moreover, a satisfying relationship raises one's comparison levels, while an inferior relationship lowers them. Finally, as a personal inclination, some people may perceive greater understanding from people generally and have relatively higher comparison levels than others who may generally perceive less understanding or more misunderstanding in their relationships (Cahn, 1981). If one wonders about his or her own general inclination, he or she may take the perceived understanding test, trait-version (see Appendix B). Results will reveal the extent to which one tends to feel understood or misunderstood in everyday interactions with most others. Presumably, if a person who generally perceives that he or she is understood is involved with a person who generally does not, the former views the potential for emotional commitment quite differently from the latter.

Summary

Researchers tend to follow one of four models of relationship development, namely, quality communication, availability of more desirable alternatives, system constraints, and size of investments. Although researchers tend to follow only one of these models, recent studies show that relationship development and disintegration of long-term heterosexual involvements, supervisor and subordinate working relationships, and friendships are best predicted by a combination of all four models. Therefore, Chapter Four focuses on the role of feeling understood in quality communication environments that promote self-worth and relationship satisfaction within the context of investment size and system constraints, and the availability of more desirable alternative interpersonal relationships. By combining the four models and incorporating feeling understood as a measure of quality communication environments, the approach taken here leads to a greater understanding and improved predictability in relationship development and disengagement.

What is the role of perceived understanding in the reassessment of interpersonal relationships? By distinguishing emotional commitment from acting committed, we can see the important role played by feelings of being understood or misunderstood in the development and disintegration of interpersonal relationships. When perceived understanding is absent, one may act committed but his or her social web is empty, distant, and impersonal. To the extent that one lacks meaningful interpersonal relationships, the more one needs to reach out and develop new and more meaningful contacts in order to avoid suffering the meaningless of despair. When one's emotional commitment to a relationship is low, an alternative may more easily offer greater relational satisfaction; thereby, forming conditions for the disintegration and eventual dissolution of a relationship. To the extent that one finds meaning in his or her relationships, the closer and more intimate the relationship becomes and the more difficult it is for alternatives to appear more desirable.

Part Two

Overview of Part Two

At least one dictionary defines loneliness as being alone or solitude. This is the cultural myth about loneliness. The implication is that loneliness is tied to the number of one's social contacts, as though the fewer relationships one has the more lonely one feels. Rather, I suggest that loneliness has more to do with the quality of one's interpersonal relationships than quantity.

Loneliness may be experienced when intimate interpersonal relationships end, but it may also occur when one enters new social arrangements. The vacuum or void or emptiness that is initially experienced is known as loneliness. Most people can recall feeling lonely. Perhaps one lost a relative, partner, or friend due to death, divorce, loss of job, or move from a geographical location. A key point is that one may experience loneliness in the presence of other people if there are no close and intimate relationships (Jones, 1981). According to Peplau and Perlman (1979), loneliness is not identical with solitude. People tend to feel lonely when they temporarily find themselves embedded in a network of inferior, superficial, and impersonal relationships, because such relationships tend to appear unsupportive, rejecting, or impervious. Thus, loneliness has little to do with the quantity of available social contacts and more to do with the quality of the communication environment that supports an interpersonal relationship. Therefore, in fact, Peplau and Perlman (1979) defined loneliness as a response to a discrepancy between desired and actual relationships. In a comparison of the motivation to be intimate (the need to get deeply into topics and to share feelings, ideals, and wants with others) with the motivation to affiliate (the need to be with others), McAdams and Constantian (1983) found that being more intimately involved with others is qualitatively different from affiliating with them, provides greater satisfaction in one's relationships, and creates less need to pursue other relationships to fill a perceived lack. Thus, loneliness has little to do with the quantity of available social contacts and more to do with the quality of the communication environment that supports an interpersonal relationship.

Recent research supports the claims that, for those who have previously experienced a meaningful relationship, loneliness is a subjective state in which one feels that the quality rather than the quantity of his or her relationships is lacking. In an experimental study, Williams and Solano (1983) found that lonely subjects listed as many "friends" as non-lonely subjects and were equally likely to have their choice reciprocated by these "friends," but there was a difference in quality. The lonely subjects did perceive a significantly lower level of intimacy in these relationships than did nonlonely subjects, and they were also likely to have this perception validated by the "friends." Moreover, Wheeler, Reis, and Nezlek (1983) found that the strongest predictor of loneliness was interaction meaningfulness (emotional closeness, intimacy, and quality of interaction). The more meaningful one's interactions, the less lonely one was.

Part Two focuses on the following questions: How does one re-engage in more comforting, satisfying and intimate relationships? More important, perhaps assuming one enters such a relationship, how does he or she maintain it and make it grow even deeper? Empirical research on re-engagement and relationship growth clusters around several approaches. The approach taken here attempts to integrate these various research efforts into a more comprehensive model of relationship re-engagement and growth. Figure Three illustrates this model. The comprehensive model combines motivation, communication behavior, levels and characteristics, and intimacy.

Motivation

In an attempt to set up new and better relationships, one must better understand the needs of others in general. The motivation model is founded on the idea that attempts to develop comforting and satisfying

Figure 3
Model of Reengagement and Relationship Growth

Motivation	Communication Behavior	Levels/ Characteristics	Intimacy
ego support	positive regard	Isolative	Self-Concept Support
self-affirmation	discussion	stereotyped	compatibility
stimulation	self-disclosure	preintimate	similarity
security	empathy	intimate	reciprocity
			respect
			Perceived Under-standing

relationships must focus on a better understanding of the entity that he or she identifies as self. One's self is "a conception made up of the individual's sense of distinctiveness, unity, continuity, causal power, and uniqueness" (Wright, 1984: 117). The observation of models or social learning (Bandura, 1977), in addition to input from significant others or symbolic interactionism (Webster and Kobieszek, 1974) and self-perception (Bem, 1972), cue the other person to act in certain ways and to be a specific type of person. These various learning approaches may be viewed as complementary parts of a broader process of self-referent motivation (Wright, 1984, 1978, 1977).

Because of a concern for the well-being and worth of the entity one identifies as one's self, a person's behavior is guided by self-referent motives. Five self-referent motives are as follows: First, one tries to maintain and affirm or reaffirm his or her sense of individuality (Fromkin, 1972, 1970). Second, one tries to assert or reaffirm his or her more highly valued self-attributes (Jones, 1973; Swann and Hill, 1982; Swann and Read, 1981; Bailey, Finney, and Helm, 1975). Third, one tries to change his or her self-attributes in the direction of growth. Fourth, a person attempts to avoid or neutralize situations that threaten the worth of the self (Kelvin, 1977).

At its simplest, Wright's theory of relationship development proposes that relationships are maintained and grow because they are *rewarding*, and they are rewarding because they facilitate the fulfillment of self-referent motives. Therefore, a person's self-referent tendency to maintain his or her sense of individuality is facilitated by a partner who is seen as having *ego support value*, that is, one from whom the other receives support, encouragement, and an impression of one's self as a unique individual. The tendency to assert or reaffirm one's sense of self-worth is communicated by a partner who is seen as having *self-affirmation value*, that is, someone who facilitates the expression and recognition of one's more important and highly valued self-attributes. The other's tendency towards growth is facilitated by a partner who is seen as having *stimulation value*, that is, one whom the other regards as interesting and stimulating. One's tendency to avoid or neutralize situations that threaten the worth of the self is facilitated by a partner who is seen as having *security value*, that is, a partner who is regarded as safe and nonthreatening.

Communication Behavior

What types of communication behavior meet one's self-referent needs and therefore appear rewarding? Anderson, Russell, and Schumm (1983) found several communication behaviors that produce quality relationships, namely, positive regard, discussion, self-disclosure, and empathy. These behaviors may be viewed from the perspective of the message sender who wishes to communicate in a way that facilitates the development of superior interpersonal relationships, as well as from the perspective of the message receiver who desires messages that will enhance his or her self-regard and the relationship. From either perspective, these communication behaviors are indicative of positive feedback, love, or unconditional regard, and add up to self-concept support and the feeling of being understood.

Levels and Characteristics

In an attempt to identify empirically the stages of relationship development, Prager (1983) employed a multidimensional analysis. Every interpersonal relationship that goes from impersonal to intimate —be it friend, mate, neighbor, colleague, boss-employee, teacher-student—appears to go through these four stages: (1) *isolative,* in which one has few social relationships and is extremely private and reserved; (2) *stereotyped* relationships, in which one may have many friends, colleagues, neighbors, dates, and so forth, but the relationships lack depth and commitment; (3) the *preintimate* stage, in which one has close relationships but has not yet committed to any; and (4) the *intimate* stage, in which one has close friends and a deep, enduring, committed relationship.

At each stage of a developing relationship a different set of characteristics influences the growth of the relationship (Cushman and Cahn, 1985; Cushman, Valentinsen, and Dietrich, 1982). At the stereotyped stage of relationship development, the characteristics vary with the type of relationship desired. For example, if one intends to form a friendship, the key characteristics at this stage of the relationship are authenticity, trust, and helping behaviors (La Gaipa, 1977; Crawford, 1977; Gibbs, 1977). If, on the other hand, one intends to form a mate relationship, physical attractiveness, sex appeal, intelligence, affection, and ideal "mateness" are the key defining characteristics of the second stage (Hill, Rubin, and Peplau, 1976; Berscheid and Walster, 1973; Pam, Plutchik, and Conte, 1973; Cavior and Boblett, 1972; Murstein, 1972). These characteristics for both friendship and mateship are defining and are qualitative in nature, for their importance remains constant throughout the later stages of relationship development. Finally, at the last stage of development, intimacy (Wise and Lowenthal, 1975), self-concept support (Cushman, Valentinsen, and Dietrich, 1982), and feeling understood (Cahn, 1984, 1983) emerge as key characteristics. These characteristics are incremental, because their importance grows as the relationship develops.

Intimacy

The communication that fulfills the other's self-referent motives and encourages the relevant characteristics for a particular type of interpersonal relationship is not enough for the development of a superior relationship. One must also communicate in a manner that facilitates intimacy. The intimate relationship is personal, free of formality, and involves a high degree of closeness, spontaneity, emotional commitment, responsibility, and mutuality (McCall and Simmons, 1966).

Intimacy is facilitated by self-concept support in the form of similarity, reciprocity, compatability, and respect (Wise and Lowenthal, 1975). *Similarity* is limited to commonalities in behavior and interests, of which shared experiences and ease of communication are the most important. According to Homans (1961), similarity in sentiments does develop through increased interaction. Involving a high degree of involvement, commitment, and understanding in any type of relationship, *reciprocity* means giving and receiving. One offers and receives trust, receptiveness, and openness for a mutual sharing of the self. In friendship, for example, reciprocity refers to mutual helping and support. *Compatability* refers to comfort, ease of the relationship, and likability. In other words, the other person enjoys being with the partner. Finally, *respect* refers to the attributes the other respects in his or her partners. Individuals tend to choose "ideal-self" partners (Shapiro, 1953). In a study of friendship, Wise and Lowenthal (1975) found that the qualities of intimacy are similar throughout the life span.

The Role of Actual and Perceived Self-Concept Support and the Feeling of Being Understood

In the study of communication, actual self-concept support is a sender variable, while perceived self-concept support and the feeling of being understood are receiver variables. Thus, the study of feeling understood shifts the perspective of the communication researcher from the actual message behavior of the source to the perceptions of the message receiver. One may intend to support another's self-concept, but if the other erroneously perceives instead a lack of support, he or she feels misunderstood. The perceived lack of self-concept support and consequent feelings of being misunderstood function as reality for individuals and govern their subsequent social and communication behavior (Cahn, 1981). For example, if a woman fails to perceive that another person is providing her with self-concept support, she feels that mutual understanding has not occurred and generally acts accordingly by initiating actions and messages that reveal and communicate feelings of misunderstanding. While shared understanding is an important aspect of communication, the point being made is that a person's social and communication behavior depends more on one's frequent *perception* of being understood than on the actual fact that one's self-concept is supported.

As a relationship evolves, the type of self-concept support that produces feelings of being understood moves it from pre-intimacy to intimacy stages. Cahn (1983) found that at an early stage of relationship development perceived understanding that is produced by self-concept support accounted for only 1 to 1.5% of the total variance in initial interaction. In later development between people who knew each other over sixteen weeks, Cahn (1984) found that perceived understanding accounted for 44% of the total variance. Therefore, a comparison of the findings of these two studies suggests that the Perceived Understanding Instrument indexes relationship development, since perceived understanding appears to be more important later on in longer-term relationships.

A high quality, close, intimate interpersonal relationship is subjectively experienced by the participants involved as the feeling of being understood. In positive, growing, close interpersonal relationships, partners share the feelings of satisfaction, pleasure, goodness, acceptance, comfort, relaxation, happiness, and importance. Conversely, a low quality relationship is subjectively experienced as the feeling of being misunderstood. In negative, empty, and impersonal relationships, one feels uninteresting, and experiences annoyance, discomfort, insecurity, dissatisfaction, sadness, failure, and incompleteness. While the feelings of being understood or misunderstood may seem less important compared to other factors early in the development of an interpersonal relationship, as the relationship matures, perceive understanding may become the most important factor in the development of intimate relationships.

Chapter Five functions as a transition chapter between Parts One and Two. In Chapter Five, emphasis is placed on the key features that relationships have in common and the unique characteristics that distinguish one type from another. The integrated model that underlies Part Two manifests itself in a variety of ways in different relationships. In each relationship, the stereotypic level has different and unique characteristics, be it a friendship, mateship, boss-employee, or teacher-student relationship. However, the levels remain constant across the different types of relationships. Intimacy is achieved by self-concept support that produces feelings of being understood.

The way one talks to another person is unique to the characteristics and level of that type of relationship, and the characteristics that are unique to the relationship are qualities that one must manifest to cue the relationship intended. For example, because one kind of disclosure that is characteristic of a client-therapist relationship could be most revealing of intimate details but prevent a friendship or a boss-employee relationship from growing, the type of disclosure must be appropriate for the type of relationship. The same goes for positive regard. One can express positive regard, but if it is not expressed for the appropriate characteristics, an individual may fail to cement the relationship and further intimacy, because the characteristics refer to the aspects of one's self-concept that should be supported—different qualities for different types of relationships. Thus, levels and characteristics determine the type of communication that must take place in each type of relationship to move from the stereotypic to the intimacy level.

Following Chapter Five, the next four chapters of Part Two apply the ideas from Chapters One through Four to developmental problems in specific types of interpersonal relationships: friends (Chapter Six), mates and lovers (Chapter Seven), boss-employee (Chapter Eight), and teacher-student (Chapter Nine). These latter chapters also attempt to answer the question "How does one reengage in more meaningful interpersonal relationships?" Chapter Ten attempts to extract and articulate a theory of the role of communication in the growth and deterioration of interpersonal relationships.

FIVE

Interpersonal Relationships as Rule-Bound Communication Systems

> Social behavior is rule-bound. . . . If this is so, then it would be valuable to find what the rules are, since they would be a guide to successful performance and key to effective social skills.
>
> M. Argyle and M. Henderson,
> "The Rules of Friendship"

Introduction

When combined with communication skills, rules are important because adherence to them may contribute to relationship growth and breaking them may lead to a disruption or even the destruction of a relationship. Rules provide a valuable guide to the communication skills discussed in Part One. The ability to follow rules such as "should show emotional support" or "should stand up for the other person in his or her absence," which may be essential in one type of relationship but unnecessary or detrimental in another, requires certain communication skills. If these skills are lacking, communication training may be needed before the rules can be successfully applied.

It is the purpose of this chapter to serve as a transition between Chapters One through Four—which lay the foundation for a theoretical approach to the study of why some people remain attached and others leave relationships—and Chapters Six through Nine—which provide a model for reengaging and maintaining a variety of satisfying and meaningful interpersonal relationships, namely, friendship, marriage, supervisor-subordinate, and teacher-student—by articulating a rules approach (Cushman and Whiting, 1972) to the study of the role of communication in reengagement and relational development. Specifically, the key points covered in this chapter deal with (1) relationship rules, (2) relationship stages, and (3) the implications of a rules analysis for the study of relationship satisfaction and growth.

Relationship Rules

Communication students, teachers, and researchers alike are sensitive to the diversity of values, behavioral styles, and thought patterns that are associated with communication activity in different cultures and subcultural groups within a country. Such concerns are motivating a search for an underlying logic consisting of principles that cut across cultural differences and the discovery of cultural variations that create communication gaps between people. A rules approach is designed to serve both of these ends.

A number of researchers have argued that social behavior is rule-governed (e.g., Harre and Secord, 1972). Argyle and Henderson (1984: 213) state it as follows:

> We see relationships, like situations, on the analogy of discrete games, as distinctive social systems. While groups of relationships may share certain features, each has special properties of its own. . . . We postulate that relationships, like games, will be regulated by rules. . . . We are using formal social systems (games) as a model for less formal ones (relationships).

The way in which rules function to create and regulate relationships becomes clearer when comparing different types and stages of relationships in Western culture and when comparing the "same" type of relationship in Eastern cultures, particularly Japan.

Relationship Rules in Western Culture

Among Westerners, while interpersonal communication may play a similar role in each type of relationship (e.g., friendship, love affair, marriage, supervisor-subordinate, parent-child, teacher-student), in general, the specifics involved vary with the uniqueness of each relationship. Argyle and Furnham (1983) found the following:

> Friendship is a major source of rewards; so rules are needed to keep up the rewards and to minimize the conflicts.

> Friends do not usually provide major help, such as lending money or looking after sick children, as kin do.

> Because neighbors are a major source of conflict as well as of rewards, the rules for neighbors deal with the most common annoyances—noise, pets, children, and fences.

Argyle and Henderson (in press) add more unique qualities of particular types of interpersonal relationships.

Marriage usually involves sex, shared property and the production of children, unlike other relationships.

Friendship has its own special properties.

Among family, friends, lovers, receiving benefits does not incur a specific debt to return a comparable benefit, and does not alter the general obligation to aid the other in need.

There are no formal or legal rules for establishing or maintaining friendship in our culture, as there are for marriage, and for parents and children.

In a study of West German and American university students, Kayser, Schwinger, and Cohen (1984) found that three relational types (loving/caring relationships, friend/associate relationships, and work relationships) differed from one another in affective climate, the primary goal of the participants, and the relative importance of various resources exchanged in the relationship. In regards to affective climate, loving/caring relationships were rated by the subjects as the most positive and intense, while work relationships were rated as the least. Loving/caring relationships were rated the most other-oriented, while friend/associate relationships were rated the most unit- (relationship) oriented, and work relationships were rated the most self-oriented. Finally, the resources of value to the relationship ranged from affection and esteem in loving/caring relationships to money and goods in work relationships. These results were interpreted as being consistent with those reported by Davis and Todd (in press) who found that romantic relationships are more likely to involve fascination and exclusiveness than are friendships.

As communication systems, different stages of a relationship also share certain features (function, structure, and process), but each stage has its own unique properties. David and Todd (in press) note that "best friends" and "close friends" differ in intimacy and psychological and emotional support. Moreover, friendships appear to be reliably classifiable into increasing levels of intensity and intimacy as acquaintances, good or close friends, and best friends (Cushman and Cahn, 1985). Similarly, Cushman and Kunimoto (forthcoming) found that casual date, steady date, and fiance/mate function as the semantic markers for discriminating among different levels of the marital relationship development process in America. Each level is a distinctive relationship worthy of study in its own right; or, taken as a whole, each represents stages in relationship growth.

Relationship Rules in Eastern Culture

> We need ... to identify what might be called the "rule books of
> meaning" that distinguish one culture from another. ... Access to the
> world view and the communicative style of other cultures may not only
> enlarge our own way of experiencing the world but enable us to maintain
> constructive relationships with societies that operate according to a dif-
> ferent logic than our own.
>
> D. Barnlund, *Public and Private Self in Japan and the United States*

Not only do types and stages of interpersonal relationships differ
from each other, but cultural perspectives on the "same" type of
relationship or stage differ. This is especially true when one compares
the American and Japanese perspectives on friendship and mateship.
When it comes to predicting the behavior, attitudes, feelings, and
emotions of others, Americans express greater confidence in acquaintances than romantic partners, while the Japanese (and Koreans) report
the reverse (Gudykunst and Nishida, 1984). Moreover, in a study of the
rules of friendship in British, Italian, Hong Kong, and Japanese samples,
Argyle and Henderson (1984) found agreement on only four of forty-
three possible friendship rules. This may be due to the fact that while
some qualities of a type of relationship may be shared between cultures,
others are distinctly unique to cultures such as the Japanese or the
Americans.

Pointing to several differences in communication rules between
Japanese and Caucasians, Johnson and Johnson (1975: 455) describe
Japanese communication as follows:

> (a) an exquisite sensitivity to the social status of the interlocutors; (b) a
> relative lack of assertiveness in comparison to North American speech
> norms; (c) a calculated amount of vagueness inherent in the Japanese
> language (d) a conscious use of indirectness and circumlocution; (e) the
> significance of silence ... during the interaction; and (f) a conspicuous
> focus on the interpretation of nonverbal communication.

FRIENDSHIP. Japanese view friendship differently from Americans. It
is less likely that Japanese have friends who are members of the opposite
sex (Mochizuki, 1981). Takahara (1974) undertook a comparative study
of Japanese and American synonyms for friendship. Thirty subjects from
each culture, evenly divided by sex, listed the following terms with the
highest frequencies:

Japanese	Frequency	American	Frequency
togetherness	25	understanding	29
trust	24	respect	25
warmth	23	sincerity	24
understanding	19	trust	22
		togetherness	22
		helping	22
		caring	22

While there are similarities in the two lists in regard to togetherness, trust, and understanding, there appear to be important differences between American and Japanese views of friendship. Moreover, Gudykunst and Nishida (1983) explored similarities and differences in regard to Japanese and American friendships, focusing on the frequency and depth of their interaction on specific topics. They found that Americans tend to talk about more "intimate" topics such as marriage, love/dating/sex, and emotions, while Japanese tend to talk about more "superficial" topics, such as interests/hobbies, school/work, biographical matters, and physical activities.

MATESHIP. There are also different views between Japanese and Americans with regard to mateship. Although decreasing in frequency, traditional marriages in Japan are arranged in which the time length between initial meeting and the wedding ceremony averages only five months (Mochizuki, 1981). In the comparative study of Japanese and American synonyms cited above, Takahara (1974) reported the following synonyms for marriage with the highest frequency:

Japan	Frequency	America	Frequency
trust	27	love	30
family	20	respect	27
understanding	18	responsibility	24
problem sharing	17	understanding	23
compromise	17	helping each other	22
love	16	problem sharing	22
endurance	16	trust	21
children	16	encouraging	21

Table 8
Qualities Sought in an Ideal Mate

| Japan | | America | |
Males	Females	Males	Females
common values	sound health	sex appeal	sex appeal
easy to talk to	honest	respect	affectionate
sound health	easy to talk to	affectionate	respect
intelligent	common values	supportive	intelligent
affectionate	intelligent	friendship	friendship
honest	affectionate	intelligent	supportive
handles money well	handles money well	attractive	attractive

In regard to their conceptions of marriage, both the Japanese and the Americans appear to share views based on trust, understanding, problem sharing, and love, but they rank the order of these concepts differently. Cushman and Nashida (1984) examined each culture's view of an ideal mate. The following qualities emerged in order of importance by sex:

These findings indicate that both Japanese and Americans share the view that their mates should be intelligent and affectionate. However, Americans also include as important attractions, sex appeal, friendship, supportiveness, and respect, while the Japanese include common values, easy to talk to, handles money well, honest, and sound health.

Relationship Stages

According to Cushman, Valentinsen, and Dietrich (1982), relationships pass through three stages. At the first stage of a relationship, certain causal and normative factors determine one's *field of available* individuals by limiting the range and type of people one meets. Such causal forces as birth and death rates, as well as the age and sexual distributions of a population, serve to constrain the field of availables (Hacker, 1979). Similarly, such normative forces as a society's social, education, religious, and economic structures, as well as socialization processes and role distribution patterns, serve to further constrain whom one is likely to encounter (Booth, 1972). The process of communication in the field of availables and the principles governing these interactions have already been well delineated by Berger and Calabrese (1975) and Duck (1976) in their investigations of initial social interactions.

The literature on initial interaction reveals that there are certain aspects of relationships that increase the likelihood of our making attempts to become friends, lovers, or mates with some rather than other people (Ross and Ross, 1982). Typically the list includes:

proximity (nearness and frequency of exposure)

homophyly and homogamy (similarity in beliefs, attitudes, and values)

physical characteristics (appearance: face, hair, body impression)

status (social standing)

social adjustment (well-adjusted personality)

At the second stage, normative rules delimit one's *field of approachable* persons to those one finds interesting and whom one wishes to approach in order to initiate a closer interpersonal relationship. If one intends to form a friendship, their authenticity, trust, and helping behaviors are key characteristics at this stage of the relationship (La Gaipa, 1977; Crawford, 1977; Gibbs, 1977). If, on the other hand, one intends to form a mate relationship, physical attractiveness, sex appeal, intelligence, affection, and ideal "mateness" are the key defining characteristics of the second stage (Hill, Rubin, and Peplau, 1976; Berscheid and Walster, 1973; Pam, Plutchik, and Conte, 1973; Cavior and Boblett, 1972; Murstein, 1972). These characteristics for both friendship and mateship are defining and are qualitative in nature, for their importance remains constant throughout the later stages of relationship development.

Finally, within this field there exists a subset of individuals who find others interesting and desirable for forming relationships. Such individuals constitute a *field of reciprocals* in which intimacy (Wise and Lowenthal, 1975), self-concept support (Cushman, Valentinsen, and Dietrich, 1982), and feeling understood (Cahn, 1984, 1983) emerge as key characteristics. These characteristics are incremental because their importance grows as the relationship develops.

At each stage of the relationship, some variables continue to be important in relationship development, while others change in relative importance. The former are called marker variables, while the latter are called intensity variables (Cushman, Valentinsen, and Brenner, 1981). Marker variables are defining and are qualitative in nature, for their effects remain relatively constant throughout development; such char-

acteristics as authenticity and helping behavior in friendship and intelligence, physical attractiveness, and sex appeal in mateship function as
marker variables as pairs moved from one stage to the next. An intensity
variable, on the other hand, is incremental; its effects become stronger
as the relationship develops, or weaker as it deteriorates. While people
consider other things initially in interpersonal attraction, it is argued
that the feeling of being understood is an intensity variable, because it is
a key consideration in the continuation of a close relationship, and the
lack of feeling understood is an important reason for a relationship
breaking up.

A high quality, close, intimate interpersonal relationship is subjectively experienced by the participants involved as the eight feelings of
being understood. In positive, growing, close interpersonal relationships
partners share the feelings of satisfaction, pleasure, goodness, acceptance, comfort, relaxation, happiness, and importance. Conversely, a low
quality relationship is subjectively experienced as the eight feelings of
being misunderstood. In negative, empty, and impersonal relationships,
one feels uninteresting, and experiences annoyance, discomfort, insecurity, dissatisfaction, sadness, failure, and incompleteness. While the
feelings of being understood or misunderstood may seem less important
compared to other factors early in the development of an interpersonal
relationship, as the relationship matures, perceive understanding becomes one of the most important factors.

Implications of a Rules Analysis
for Relationship Growth and Deterioration

The role of communication in interpersonal relationships as en-
visioned in this book has important implications for relationship reengagement and growth. The first implication of this analysis for
relational change is that self-concept support via communication skills
produces feelings of being understood that support or alter the structure
of the relationship. This means that, if one is to form significant interpersonal relationships with others, one must first recognize the unique
characteristics of others' preferred self-concepts and manifest recognition and support for them.

When individuals are interdependent and one of the participants
fails to take into consideration the interests, needs, and goals of the
other, the ignored individual may withdraw, which frequently prevents
the other from obtaining desired goals; this, therefore, focuses attention
on the need to achieve consensus as an antecedent to cooperation. The

realization by diverse individuals that they are interdependent provides a pressure for locating and negotiating solutions that are the best they can do if they want the cooperation of others. The thrust of this argument within its interpersonal communication context is that what is an optimal solution to a problem from the individual's point of view may not be optimal from the point of view of the other person or the system. Interpersonal communication involves more than just individuals; it involves others and relationships.

A second implication of a rules approach is that the social relationships obtained between friends, lovers, and mates require the development of a consensus regarding the character of the individual self-concepts involved in such a relationship, as a basis for establishing, maintaining, and terminating that relationship. The peculiar function of interpersonal communication systems (to regulate consensus with respect to individual self-concepts) implies peculiar needs by individuals for a recognition of diversity and interdependence in regard to individual self-concepts, the manifesting of respect for that diversity and interdependence, and then the development of some consensus regarding the character of individual self-concepts. The presentation and validation of individual self-concepts are necessarily involved in establishing, maintaining, or terminating such relationships.

A third implication of a rules approach to interpersonal relationship growth and deterioration is this: The study of any particular type of interpersonal relationship requires knowledge of the unique rules that constitute and govern each type of interpersonal relationship and each stage in its development. To describe the structure of communication that constitutes an interpersonal relationship is to describe the rules that guarantee coordination in defined situations. This means that each type of relationship (friendship, mateship, etc.) is a coordinated affair that is uniquely defined and regulated by a set of rules. For example, self-concept support may contribute positively to all types of relationship development, but the way in which self-concepts are supported varies with the type of relationship. Moreover, any one stage (e.g., casual date, steady date, mate) of a particular kind of a relationship (e.g., friendship or marriage) is also a coordinated affair that is uniquely defined and regulated by a related set of rules that set it apart from other stages of that type of relationship.

Summary

A number of researchers have argued that social behavior is rule-governed. The way in which rules function to create and regulate relationships becomes clearer when comparing different types and stages of relationships in Western culture and when comparing the "same" type of relationship in Eastern cultures, particularly Japan. Among Westerners, while interpersonal communication may play a similar role in each type of relationship (e.g., friendship or marriage), in general, the specifics involved vary with the uniqueness of each type of relationship. Moreover, as a communication system, different stages of a relationship also share certain features (function, structure, and process), but each stage has its own unique properties, and is worthy of study in its own right. Not only do types of relationships differ from each other, but cultural perspectives on the "same" type of relationship or stage differ. This is clear from a comparison of American and Japanese perspectives on friendship and mateship.

The implications of a view of the role of communication in relationship reengagement and growth has important implications for relational development and deterioration. First, self-concept support via communication skills produces feelings of being understood that support or alter the structure of the relationship, which means that if one is to form significant interpersonal relationships with others, one must first recognize the unique characteristics of others' preferred self-concepts and manifest recognition and support for them. Second, the social relationships obtained between friends, lovers, and mates require the development of a consensus regarding the character of the individual self-concepts involved in such a relationship, as a basis for establishing, maintaining, and terminating that relationship. Third, the study of any particular type of interpersonal relationship requires knowledge of the unique rules that constitute and govern each type of interpersonal relationship and each stage in its development. This means that each type of relationship (friendship, mateship, etc.) is a coordinated affair that is uniquely defined and regulated by a set of rules, and that any one stage (e.g., casual date, steady date, mate) of a particular kind of a relationship (e.g., friendship or marriage) is also a coordinated affair that is uniquely defined and regulated by a related set of rules that set it apart from other stages of that type of relationship.

In conclusion, a rules approach as proposed in Part Two is designed to serve as a foundation for a theory that predicts the degree of commitment to and satisfaction with a variety of specific types of ongoing relationships (e.g. friends, lovers, mates, parent-child, supervisor-subordinate) that differ in duration and involvement. The theory propounds that self-concept support via communication skills produces perceived understanding that becomes an increasingly more important determinant of relational satisfaction as a relationship matures. However, as proposed in Part One, commitment to a relationship also includes the availability of alternatives, investment size, and system constraints. In the following chapters, I intend to illustrate in greater detail how one might adapt this theory and its underlying rules approach to specific types of interpersonal relationships of general interest, namely friendship (Chapter Six), marriage and romantic relationships (Chapter Seven), supervisor-subordinate work relationships (Chapter Eight), and teacher-student relationships (Chapter Nine). The specific tenants for a theory of interpersonal communication and relationship development are described in Chapter Ten.

SIX

Friendship

When family ties falter, when love affairs or marriages end, friends relieve our loneliness, fulfill our need for affection, and bolster our morale. Making and keeping friends may be among the most important things you can do for yourself; and relating sensitively and meaningfully to friends is an art you can learn.

> C. Leefeldt and E. Callenbach,
> *The Art of Friendship*

Introduction

Friendships appear to be reliably classifiable into increasing levels of intensity and intimacy as acquaintances, good or close friends, and best friends (Cushman and Cahn, 1985). Americans tend to have numerous acquaintances, some good and close friends, but only a small number of "best friends." Until problem arise, one tends to take friendships for granted. Because most everyone has one or more friends, people forget how difficult it is to establish and to maintain them, and how much loneliness and stress are involved when they end. Researchers report that attempts to initiate friendships are stressful and that 54% of the individuals approached as friends decline such offers. When conflicts threaten the friendship, one may experience feelings of loneliness, self-doubt, and depression (Trower, 1981; Duck, 1981).

Although those with close friends tend to report less physical and psychological illness, live longer, and express greater satisfaction with life than those without good friends (Duck, 1981), one must also be aware of who are one's friends, because friendships are important to one's personal development and social adjustment. There are people serving time in prison, some on drugs, some deep in debt, some without jobs, and others engaged in other forms of self-defeating behavior because of the adverse influence of their friends. Just as one's support group may have beneficial effects, so may another add resistance to one's constructive personal and social development.

In spite of its importance, the nature and process of friendship is not very well understood. Usually, the creation and maintenance of a friendship is left to chance. While the penalties for error are made more clear in mateship and some other types of interpersonal relationships, friendship errors are often less clearly defined. It is the purpose of this chapter to shed light on the nature and process of friendship growth and deterioration. More specifically, this chapter deals with (1) a quality friendship communication environment, (2) friendship self-concept support generally, (3) friendship self-concept support among males and among females, (4) friendship development and communication competence, and (5) friendship reassessment. The key question is this: What should one consider in selecting and relating to others as friends?

A Quality Friendship Communication Environment

People exercise superior judgment in making new friends when they realize and appreciate the role played by a quality communication environment in friendship formation and maintenance. A quality communication environment for a successful friendship is one which facilitates change and promotes personal growth and relational satisfaction. The criteria for assessing the quality of a communication environment are the accurate identification of the unique scope, depth, and configuration of one another's preferred self-concepts; support for each other's preferred identity, evaluative, and behavioral self-concept characteristics; and communication skill.

Positive self-concept support in the form of recognition, acknowledgment, and endorsement (Cissna and Sieburg, 1979) is essential among friends. Any friendship that contains a preponderance of rejection or disconfirmation utterances contributes to a lower self-regard and less satisfaction with the relationship. Competence in interaction also refers to the effective use of messages aimed at objectifying, analyzing, evaluating, and synthesizing one another's self-concepts, the nature of the friendship, and the quality/quantity of friendship communication itself. The specific friendship communication skills include effective listening, self-assertion, and collaboration. When applied to friendship communication problems, this reflection process, which is called friendship reassessment, is aimed at realigning self-concepts, the friendship, and communication patterns.

In sum, self-concept accuracy, preferred self-concept support, and communication skill are criteria for judging the quality of a communication environment in a friendship. These are proposed as the criteria by which one may assess a relationship to determine whether it warrants continuation, change, or disengagement.

Friendship Self-Concept Support in General

Friendship has its own special qualities (Argyle and Henderson 1984). Its distinctive activites include talking, eating, drinking, and joint leisure (Argyle and Furnham, 1983). Based on the work of several researchers, interpersonal trust and a type of liking that manifests itself in helping behavior appear to be the key underlying dimensions of friendship formation and development (Crawford, 1977; Gibbs, 1977). In a summary of four studies on the rules of friendship using data collected from British, Italian, Hong Kong, and Japanese samples, Argyle and Hendersen (1984) report that the following six rules (out of an original list of forty-three are generally endorsed as important for friendship, and that the breaking of these rules contributes to the breakdown of an actual friendship:

—Standing up for the other in his/her absence.

—Share news of success with him/her.

—Show emotional support.

—Volunteer help in time of need.

—Strive to make him/her happy while in each other's company.

—Trust and confide in each other.

If one views the first five rules as indicative of a helping orientation and the last rule as the trust dimension, then trust and helping orientation function as friendship marker variables, because they are essential at all stages of a friendship and distinguish a friendship from other kinds of interpersonal relationships.

A factor that becomes increasingly more important as friendships grow, deepen, and becomes more satisfying is self-concept support (Cushman, Valentinsen, and Brenner, 1981; Cushman, Valentinsen, and Dietrich, 1982) and the underlying feeling of being understood (Cushman and Cahn, 1985). Self-concept support in friendship consists of messages indicating one's support of the other's behavioral, identity, and evaluative self-object relationships. In this section, I intend to discuss the nature of self-concept support in friendships and warn against common problems in friendship self-concept support.

The Nature of Friendship Self-Concept Support

According to Cushman, Valentinsen, and Dietrich (1982), self-concept support may be classified into two roles: confidant and companion. While a confidant is someone who provides evaluative self-concept support, a companion is someone who provides behavioral self-concept support. The same friend may fill both of these roles.

In America, few friends exist by simply supporting one's identity or social self-concept. Americans do not share this type of friendship with the Japanese, who include *tsukiai* as a type of friendship (Atsumi, 1980). An interpersonal relationship cultivated and maintained as a result of social obligation, *tsukiai* are usually tied to work or neighborhood contacts of limited duration. Americans may have colleagues, co-workers, and neighbors, but these categories of people do not include the stronger friendship ties that exist in Japan. In regard to relationship development in the West, Argyle and Furnham (1983), who identified the factors underlying relational satisfaction and interpersonal conflict, found distinctly different patterns of satisfaction and conflict scores for same- and opposite-sex friends, on the one hand, and work associates, superiors, and neighbors, on the other. Same- and opposite-sex friends had a high overall level of satisfaction, especially on shared interests, emotional-support, sharing the same friends, doing things together, and discussing personal problems. Conflict was fairly low, especially in regard to criticism. Meanwhile work associates, superiors, and neighbors typically had a low overall level of satisfaction, especially in doing things together, emotional support, discussing personal problems, being identified with the other, sharing the same friends, and simply being with the other. While work associates and neighbors were fairly low on conflict, work superiors were high in emotional conflict. Thus, friendship has a distinctly different pattern from that of work associates, superiors, and neighbors, suggesting that in the West such social relationships fulfill a different function from that in Japan.

In order to assess one's present or potential friendships, one must know and appreciate the scope, depth, and configuration of one's own and the other's self-concepts, especially the behavioral and evaluative dimensions that form a basis for confidant and companion type friendships. For the purpose of this chapter, let the following self-concepts described in Table Nine serve as examples.

A glance at the self-concepts for the three friends above indicates a strong basis for a companionship between Phil and Gary, a confidant relationship between Phil and Sharon, and little chance of either type of close friendship between Sharon and Gary. In the potential companionship between Phil and Gary, one finds considerable behavioral self-concept support in that both play golf, are competitive, and spend a lot of time out of doors. The fact that they differ greatly on the evaluative dimension of their self-concepts may prevent them from developing a very close relationship, one that is open and trusting. In the potential confidant relationship between Sharon and Phil, a great deal of overlap in the evaluative dimensions of their self-concepts is readily apparent. Both are materialistic, in that they like to shop, spend money, and desire new things. In cases where they are interested in buying the same product, they might enjoy shopping together, suggesting a narrow basis for a companionship, too. If Phil could continue playing golf, Phil and Sharon would find each other's life style more appealing than that offered by Gary. Sharon would probably prefer to be more open and trusting of Phil than of Gary for advice on economics and financial matters.

Having accurately discovered one's own and another's self-concept, two potential friends must negotiate into their friendship those self-concept characteristics that are necessary for personal growth and satisfaction, and negotiate out of the relationship those that interfere with each one's growth and satisfaction. Negotiation that is collaborative in nature requires self-assertiveness, being "upfront" about one's self, and solicitation and effective listening techniques to create an atmosphere in which one's friend or potential friend can also be assertive. These two qualities characterize a unique approach to a friend relationship. Being open and honest with one's friend or potential friend and allowing him or her freedom of expression and room to grow produces feelings of being understood and are important forms of self-concept support, creating a basis for a successful friendship. In the following discussion, an extended example is used to illustrate mutual self-concept support.

Friends since their college days when they played together on the basketball team, Joe and Bob have continued over the years to attend the college basketball games together. After each game, they stop by a local bar to reminisce over the game, past teams, and outstanding players. The problem is that Joe is beginning to loose interest in the college's current athletic program. It occurs to him that he might be outgrowing his friendship with Bob. After giving the matter much thought, Joe decides to try something new for him—ballroom dancing. The next Saturday night, while sitting in the local bar after the college basketball game, Joe tells Bob that he will not be attending next Wednesday night's game because he has decided to spend less time at the games and take up ballroom dancing with his wife. As expected, Bob makes a mild protest and then lets the matter ride. Joe suggests that Bob and his wife join them for dance instruction, but Bob politely declines.

After a couple of weeks of instruction, Joe realizes that he is really enjoying the dancing lessons. He is having a good time with his wife, and after the sessions, they are socializing with other interesting couples. Yet, due to his curiosity about the basketball season and his friend, Bob, Joe decides to phone Bob and meet him in the local bar after the next college game. He is pleased to see that Bob is clearly delighted by the idea. When they meet, each tells the other about some of the events that have occurred since they last got together.

In an effort to achieve a new balance in their friendship, Joe realizes that he wants to pursue ballroom dancing and not fall back into his former routine. Each could try to avoid the other or use unfair tactics to pressure the other to do more with him. Instead, Joe and Bob openly seek separate interests and permit each other the freedom to do so.

Joe's need for a change posed a potential interpersonal conflict that threatened his friendship with Bob, but the two friends were able to resolve the conflict in a collaborative manner that supported one another's self-concepts. The result is that by each pursuing different paths, Joe and Bob seem more interesting to one another. Joe is glad that he took the risk of alienating Bob, and knows that he may do it again if necessary. It is only by becoming more independent and each permitting the other to pursue his own interests that each is able to grow and find the friendship satisfying.

Caveats: Problems in Friendship Self-Concept Support

While one may engage in positive actions that result in self-concept support for one's self and others, there are some strategies that must be avoided. First, friends should not try to expand their friendship into additional areas that neither is able to support. For example, Phil who

Table 9
Self-Concepts: Three Friends

Phil	Sharon	Gary
plays golf	watches TV	plays golf
competitive	accommodating	competitive
physically active	reads a lot	physically active
spends a lot of time out of doors	goes to movies	spends a lot of time out of doors
likes to spend money	likes to spend money	likes to save money
likes to shop	likes to shop	thrifty
desires new things	desires new things	enjoys free concerts
status-conscious	status-conscious	rents an apartment

may enjoy his companionship with Gary, especially when they play golf together, may not desire a confidant type of friendship because of their divergent core values. Since many personal concerns involve financial consideration, Gary's advice may be too conservative, reserved, and thrift-conscious to suit Phil. If Gary tries to confide more in Phil and expect him to reciprocate, each may find that the other is unable to provide the type of self-concept support necessary for a close or best-friend relationship. Gary must be sensitive to the basis for the friendship he has with Phil and not expect that they share all behavioral and evaluative dimensions of their self-concepts.

Secondly, friends should avoid demanding too much from a limited degree of self-concept support. To any individual, some of his or her activities and values are more important than others. In the above example, Phil may enjoy going to a movie on occasion (once a month), while Sharon enjoys going a lot more often (twice weekly). Thus, Sharon's insistence that Phil accompany her to all the movies she wants to attend exceeds Phil's level of interest and may interfere with his desire for personal growth and friendship satisfaction. Sharon needs to discover and respect the scope and configuration of Phil's self-concept to determine the nature of their friendship and not exceed the basis on which it depends.

Third, friends should avoid becoming too dependent on one another. While they may offer considerable self-concept support, some people have an acute need that they try to satisfy through one or more friendships. Frequently, the need is emotional, turning a friendship into a pseudo therapist-client relationship. No one really enjoys a friend who constantly dwells on his or her emotional problems. Such a person should seek professional help and not belabor serious personal problems with friends. In other cases, a friend may be too great a financial burden. Perhaps, Phil is unable to manage his money very effectively and is in debt. In addition, the bank often notifies him that it has returned an overdrawn check. When he needs cash in a hurry, the automated teller refuses to honor his request. Because of his debt, no bank will lend him money. Such a friend can present real problems because he constantly asks to borrow money, or, when one accepts his checks, they bounce. Friends may be expected to help one another, but a dependent person may place demands on a friendship that exceed the usual limits. While self-concept support is essential to the growth of a friendship, other factors may result in friendship deterioration and lack of relational satisfaction.

Fourth, assuming that their relationship is a friendship and nothing more, opposite-sex friends usually find it to their advantage to avoid appearing to be sexually involved. Because male-female friendships have sexual components that may result in difficulties, especially for married persons, some people have only same-sex friends. Unfortunately, this limits the range and depth of available sources of self-concept support. This is particularly unfortunate for women in non-traditional female jobs where more men than women are in positions of authority, and for men in traditionally female-related employment where women may dominate the status hierarchy. Traditionally friendships have been important in one's career advancement. In the business world, the associates with whom one shares interests and activities are usually members of the same sex who may provide some type of job related support when needed. The social sanctions that prohibit male-female friendships in the adult world place some men and women at a disadvantage in career development. Hopefully all this will change, but in the meantime, to succeed in their careers, men and women may need to be very careful not to give the impression that their male-female companionship type friendships involve sex. By meeting with members of the opposite sex in groups rather than individually or in private, by dressing for success rather than physical attraction and sex appeal, by paying one's own way, by providing one's own transportation, and by avoiding after hour or weekend engagements, a cautious man or woman may be able to develop male-female friendships that are useful to one's career goals without sexual complications.

Friendship Self-Concept Support: Males and Females

In *Glamour's* May 1984 issue, Helgesen cites the following instances of female expressions of frustration over male friendships:

She says: He called his closest college friend last night; they hadn't talked in two years. I heard them on the phone: All they did was discuss the scores of different football games for about half an hour. After he hung up, he said how much he liked Bill, and what good friends they still were. How can he tell?

She says: I can't understand him. Last week he went to dinner with his best friend who's in the middle of a really agonizing divorce. So I asked him when he got home how it's going with the divorce, and he said they never got around to discussing it. There's no intimacy in men's friendships.

Is the meaning of friendship the same for both men and women? Research indicates the contrary. Although times are changing, bringing about new definitions regarding male-female roles, men's friendships traditionally differ from women's in terms of the type of self-concept support each sex tends to provide to other people. Women's friendship ties tend toward more confidants whom they relate to intensely and intimately (Caldwell and Peplau, 1982; Fischer and Narus, 1981; Hill and Stull, 1981). Research shows that females tend to engage in intimate conversation, show affection, are emotionally supportive, respect privacy, and blame breakups on lack of support significantly more than males (Argyle and Henderson, 1984). ⚹

Traditionally, men, on the other hand, are socialized to be aggressive, daring, suspicious of both teammates and competitors. The result of the traditional male socialization process is that men's friendships are seen more in terms of utility and purpose, and are associated with business, sports, and hobbies (Tognoli, 1980; Bell, 1981). It is argued that these men have trouble forming and maintaining close friendships and that they have practically no other male friends with whom they can relate in an emotionally open and trusting way. However, in contemporary society, friendship patterns of the two sexes along with social roles and lifestyles have started to converge (Leefeldt and Callenbach, 1979).

Friendship Development and Communication Competence

One's friendships seldom remain constant. In the first place, the nature of the relationship between friends is itself a dynamic process. Moreover, because the average American family moves at least once every three years (Leefeldt and Callenbach, 1979), one can expect to shift from old friendships to new ones. Finally, one may have many friends because one shares only a limited range of interests or values with each one. Leefeldt and Callenbach (1979: 205-6) make the following distinctions:

> While good friends usually share some common interests, it is a mistake to assume from this that any one friend will share all of your interests or, for that matter, your attitudes and values.... Thus, you would instinctively phone different friends to confide upsetting news, to ask for a quick ride to the airport, or to tell about a new job. The friend you would most like to go camping with is probably not the one you'd most like to go to a movie with.... With each of your friends you get the chance to be a somewhat different person, developing and strengthening different sides of your character and providing variety and stimulation for your life.

The problem posed by an interactive, dynamic, process-oriented view of friendship is how to form, change, and maintain friendships in constructive and positive ways that enhance one's personal growth and friendship satisfaction. To prevent relational recidivism, or the tendency to miss an opportunity to improve upon the quality of subsequent friendships, one must better understand the factors that are key to a successful friendship. This understanding enables one to better judge present friendships, to better determine when to renegotiate or let go of them, and to better understand how to form superior ones in the future.

Individuals are expected to change friendships over time. While one's personal growth and relational satisfaction is a key factor in friendship, it is not necessary to reduce the field of potential friends to only one individual, as in the process of mate selection. In other words, one can have several friends, including one or more "best friends," who contribute more or less and in different ways to one's personal growth and relational satisfaction. Since friendship is not likely to involve clearing competitors from the field (as in mateship), it usually does not require intense feelings of affection and commitment. Therefore, the periodic changes that take place in one's social network usually do not involve any symbolic act or ceremony, as in the case of marriage.

The position taken here is that one should expect friendships to change as one's values and activities change. Because friendships are focused (centered on specific behavioral or evaluative dimensions of the self-concept), the companions and confidants needed at an earlier stage of one's personal growth and development may differ from those needed later. For example, three individuals who collaborated on a research project viewed one another as mutually supportive. When one undertook another research project that did not interest the other two, he lost contact with them and found someone new with whom to collaborate. Thus, they outgrew one another and moved on to form new friendships. For a while, one may feel that he or she is learning, improving skills, or becoming stronger. One may feel that one is progressing, achieving greater rank, superior positions, or more authority. One may realize a greater accumulation of property, material goods, or wealth. One may become more popular or increase some other basis of political support. Seeing some desirable goal and observing progress toward it through an association with others constitutes personal growth and relational satisfaction. But when one finds that progress has ceased, one looks to a new environment, or a different social support system that enhances one's progress toward old and new goals. Leefeldt & Callenbach (1979: 158) state that with old friends, however precious, the entire weight of the past is always present. As a result, it is important for you to remain open to establishing new friendships, which allow you to start with a clean slate. New friendships also give you the opportunity to concentrate on the process of "creating yourself." It's up to you to bring whatever you consider relevant from your past into new relationships. What's more, you're free to present yourself as you are *becoming*, not as you have *been*.

Friendship Developmental Stages

Cushman, Valentinsen, and Dietrich (1982) describe a friendship development model that consists of a three-stage filtering process. At the *first* stage, causal and normative factors delimit the range of potential friends to a field of availables or *acquaintances*. While a large number of people may fall into such a category for some individuals, usually is it impossible to seriously consider them all as potential friends due to demographic, geographical, and attitudinal factors. (For summaries, see Duck, 1977, and Huston and Levinger, 1978). Let us first consider the meaning of the demographic factor. In a recent study, Verbrugge (1983) found that the following factors affected one's availability for developing friendships:

1. *Age:* individuals in the 40–49 age bracket are least available for friendship development because of job and family commitments.

2. *Marital status:* individuals who are married are less likely than single and divorced persons to be available for friendship because of spouse or family commitments.

3. *Occupation:* professionals, administrators/managers, and self-employed workers are less likely than students, production workers, and sales personnel to be available for friendships because of less easy access to others and unusual time schedules.

4. *Residential stability:* movers (short length of residence) are less likely than nonmovers (relatively longer length of residence) to be able to develop close, active friendships.

A second key factor in the first stage of friendship development is proximity. The closer individuals are located geographically, the more likely they will interact and the more likely they will become friends. For example, several investigators have found that students tend to develop stronger friendships with those students who share their dormitory or sit near them in class than they do with those located a little further away (Nahemow and Lawton, 1975).

At the *second* stage, normatiave factors that function as antecedent conditions for generating messages aimed at establishing a friendship further delimit the range of acquaintances to a field of approachables or *close/good friends.* The filtering process predicts that the greater an individual's perceived relationship between preferred attributes of one's own self-concept and the perceived attributes of another's preferred self-concept, the greater the likelihood he or she will attempt to engage in communication aimed at initiating a friendship. More specifically, when one thinks there are qualities of another's self-concept that he or she would enjoy because they are similar to qualities the individual prefers in ones' own self-concept, then one attempts to support the other's self-object relationships. Needless to say, the more self-object commonalities people have, the more self-concept support each provides the other (Thompson and Nishimura, 1952; Lundy, 1958).

An important factor at the second stage is attitudinal similarity. The claim here is that proximity (first stage) merely provides the occasion for the discovery of common attitudes (second stage). Numerous studies show that attraction to a hypothetical stranger is directly related to the similarity of attitudes, although it would seem to be the attitudes most *salient* to the situation in which the interactants find themselves that bear upon the interpersonal attraction among strangers (Sykes, 1983).

The filtering process also suggests that the more one perceives that the other will accept one's offer of a friendship, the more likely one will engage in communication aimed at initiating a friendship. That is, when one thinks that another is likely to respond favorably to one's offer of self-concept support, one is more likely to provide such support (Laumann, 1969).

At the *third* stage of the friendship developmental process, there exists within one's field of good/close friends a subset of individuals who will reciprocate one's offer of a mate relationship when the occasion arises. This field is limited to one's *"best friends."* Normative factors influence when people choose to reciprocate an offer of friendship, and these form the basis for the communication factors that lead to establishing and maintaining a friendship. The three-stage filtering process suggests that the more frequently the friends receive from one another messages that manifest an accurate perception of the other's preferred identity, behavioral, and evaluative dimensions of the self-concept, the more likely the friendship will become satisfying. More specifically, the more frequently the interactions among friends reveal the accuracy of their perceptions of the portions of each other's self-concepts that each respects, the greater the likelihood that their friendship will grow (Laumann, 1969; Duck, 1973).

Moreover, the filtering process predicts that the more self-concept support is perceived to be reciprocated (through the roles of confidant or companion), the more likely the relationship will become satisfying. That is, the greater the respect friends manifest for each other's preferred self-concept, the greater the likelihood their friendship will grow (Bailey, Finney, and Helm, 1975; Bailey, Digiacomo and Zinser, 1976).

The factors identified as normative forces that define the field of approachables (good/close friends) at the second stage continue to be important at stage three ("best friends"). Numerous studies show that interpersonal trust and helping orientation are important both in the initiation of a friendship and at later stages of a friendship (Cushman, Valentinsen, and Dietrich, 1982; Cushman and Cahn, 1985). Thus, these factors function as *marker variables* in the friendship development process. In addition, the factors identified as a communicative, which play a role in moving persons from acquaintance and good/close friend levels to the level of "best friends," are also important later on in the friendship. As argued in previous chapters, perceived understanding links self-concept support to interpersonal relationship satisfaction and development (which in this case refers to friendship), and functions as an *intensity variable*.

Friendship Communication Competence

Cook (1977: 320) argues that "making friends with someone is a skilled performance in the same sense (as) driving a car or playing tennis. . . . All have goals or purposes. . . . All depend on knowing what to do next to bring the object or person nearer the desired state, then doing it; then observing the effect." However, like Horowitz and French (1979), I find that among those who describe themselves as lonely the most common type of problem is knowing how to make and keep friends. According to Hays (1984: 76), "From a clinical perspective, such knowledge is vital, for the degree to which one can alter attributes such as physical attractiveness and attitude similarity is limited, while change at a behavioral level, that is, developing social skills . . . is more promising."

Friends also need a set of interactional strategies to repair relationship errors in regard to preferred self-concept support and self-concept accuracy. Unfortunately, some individuals try to dominate others. They may sound dogmatic, as though they expect to get their way all the time. To the extent that one fails to listen to others' needs and interests, one is competitive in one's approach to settling interpersonal conflicts. Therefore, while one may feel like asserting oneself, he or she must avoid over doing it at the expense of others around him or her.

Some nonassertive individuals who do not realize the harm such an approach does to friendships may pursue a passive, accommodating style. Krantzler (1977: 76–78), has identified several personality types that are, for different reasons, essentially nonassertive in self-defeating ways.

The don't make-Wavers. Remaining unassertive, inconspicuous, and conformist is the only way they feel they can be loved since others seem stronger and more capable.

The Martyrs believe they will be loved only if they please and serve everybody.

The Yesterdayers. Their whims were always satisfied and they were never disciplined. Passive response was all that was required to attain love.

The Futurizers. Today is unimportant. It's what will happen tomorrow that counts.

The Erasers grew up escaping problems by erasing them.

Because these personalities are not being emotionally honest, one finds it difficult to negotiate into a friendship those self-concept characteristics important for personal growth and satisfaction.

Friends exercise interpersonal competence when they meet the criteria for a quality communication environment. As argued previously, a quality communication environment for a successful friendship is one that facilitates change and promotes personal growth and relational satisfaction. The skills included in a quality communication environment are positive and accurate self-concept support and collaboration in the form of self-assertiveness and responsiveness to others.

On occasion, a friend makes the error of overstepping the boundaries of friendship by failing to help when asked or committing an act against one's trust. Such behavior seriously threatens the friendship. When such an offense occurs, three courses of action are available to the person who is offended. He or she may ignore the act and treat it as an accidental occurrence (which may be appropriate if it appears unlikely that a minor offense will be repeated), break off the friendship by withdrawing, or confront the friend by indicating the problem and its effect, and ask for an account. If the friend accurately perceives the violation of expectation and its effect, and wants to preserve the friendship, then an account should be forthcoming aimed at realigning the friendship. As a realignment strategy, accounts "sustain the flow of joint action by bringing individuals back into line with one another in problematic circumstances," and "they sustain a relationship between ongoing conduct and culture in the face of a recognized failure of conduct to live up to the cultural established expectation" (Stokes and Hewitt, 1976: 844).

A friendship offers an excellent opportunity for persons to offer accounts and communicate mutual self-concept through the alignment of self-concepts by achieving dyadic consensus on key personal qualities that form a basis for the friendship. Thus, with interpersonal communication competence, friendship satisfaction can be achieved.

Friendship Reassessment: Key Communication Factors in Friendship Development

Why are individuals more satisfied with some of their friendships than they are with others? Why are some persons emotionally committed to their friendships and others are not? Why do some friendships last longer than others? Many researchers assume simply that if people are attracted to each other, they will seek to maintain their friendship (e.g., Duck and Spencer, 1972). Rusbult (1980) questions this assumption by claiming that there is a difference between one's satisfaction with a friendship and his or her commitment to it. The present approach, an interpersonal model of relational development, is designed to extend research in communication (Knapp, 1978; Friedman, Giffin, and Patton, 1978; Cushman, Valentinsen, and Dietrich, 1982) and the exchange tradition within social psychology (Thibaut and Kelley, 1959; Kelley and Thibaut, 1978). The interpersonal communication model assumes that friends are in general motivated to maximize perceived understanding and minimize perceived misunderstanding, and distinguishes between two important characteristics of relationships satisfaction and commitment. As argued in Chapter Four, from the point of view of the interpersonal communication model, persons who intend to maintain their friendship should also feel psychologically linked to it.

Friendship Satisfaction

Friendship satisfaction may be defined as having positive feelings about one's partner and the relationship (Rusbult, 1980). Based on this notion of friendship satisfaction, the interpersonal communication model of friendship development predicts that the more positive one's perceived understanding, the more one is attracted to and satisfied with the friendship; conversely the more negative one's perceived understanding or the greater the misunderstanding, the more one is repelled by and dissatisified with the ongoing relationship.

The interpersonal communication model asserts that one's satisfaction in enduring relationships is a simple function of one's perceived understanding experienced in the relationship. As argued in Chapters Two and Three, self-concept support via communication skills produces perceived understanding. Because research shows that perceived understanding may not be as important initially as other factors in interpersonal attraction but plays a more important role in relational satisfaction during later stages of relationship development, the interpersonal communication model asserts that in latter phases of friendship development individuals are in general motivated to maximize mutual perceived understanding while minimizing perceived misunderstanding. Zakahi and Duran (1984) found that while physical attractiveness may be the primary predictor of initial interaction, it did not appear as important as communication skills once the relationship was underway. Therefore, satisfaction with and attraction to a friendship may be a function of the discrepancy between the individuals' perceived understanding and misunderstanding, based on self-concept support via interpersonal communication skills.

In addition, as discussed in Chapter Four, a neutral point exists where both the feelings of being understood and misunderstood are minimal; this neutral point is determined by the degree of confirmation, rejection, and disconfirmation experienced in other and previous friendships. Thus, individuals evaluate their present friendship in relation to their neutral point in order to assess the degree of satisfaction with and attraction to the present relationship.

Friendship Commitment

Friends may argue greatly, expressing dissatisfaction with their friendship, but remain committed to each other. Why? The answer lies in the nature of commitment and the factors affecting commitment.

According to Rusbult (1980), lack of emotional commitment is a better predictor of disengagements from friendships than relational dissatisfaction alone. Rusbult also defines friendship commitment as the tendency to maintain the friendship and feel attached to it psychologically. Within this view of friendship commitment, the interpersonal communication model predicts the following: While friendship satisfaction is expected to remain unchanged with changes in the value of alternative relationships, investment size, and system constraints, friendship commitment is expected to decrease with increases in the value of alternative relationships, but is expected to increase with increases in investment size and system constraints. This prediction is derived from the interrelationship of the value of alternative relationships, the investment size, and social system constraints.

The *value of alternative relationships* has been shown to be an important comparison level for assessing the attractiveness of the present friendship (Rusbult, 1980). According to the interpersonal communication model, one may predict that the more value one places on an alternative relationship, the less one feels emotionally committed to a friendship.

The *size of investments* has been shown to affect commitment in friendships (Rusbult, 1980; Lund, 1985). The interpersonal communication model predicts that the more one invests in the present interpersonal relationship, the more one feels emotionally committed to it.

System constraints have been shown to influence relational commitment (Argyle and Henderson, 1984; Parks, Stan, and Eggert, 1983). As discussed in Chapter Four, system constraints refer to perceived pressures from one's social networks consisting of relatives, friends, and other persons. For example, La Gaipa (1982) claims that social networks constrain the disengagement process. The model predicts that the more friends perceive system constraints, the more they feel emotionally committed to their friendship.

In summary, to the extent that one is satisfied with a friendship owing to a great deal of perceived understanding at a later stage of development, he or she should remain committed to it. However, commitment is also influenced by other factors. The model predicts that one becomes more committed if one sees poorer alternatives to the present friendship, sizable investments, and system constraints. Thus, in the absence of satisfaction (due to a lack of perceived understanding at a later stage of development), one may remain committed to a friendship due to the perceived lack of alternatives, size of investments, and/or system constraints.

Summary

It is the purpose of this chapter to adapt a general theory of disengagement and reengagement, an interpersonal communication model, to the friend relationship process in order to predict the degree of commitment to and satisfaction with different stages in its development or disintegration. To this end, I proposed that friendship self-concept accuracy, preferred self-concept support, and communication skill are criteria for judging the quality of a communication environment in a friendship, to determine whether such a relationship warrants continuation, repair, or disengagement.

The friendship process differs from other types of relationships by the way in which perception of interpersonal trust and helping orientation enter into the relationship. Also, one perceives self-concept support from companies and confidants that results in feeling understood. Therefore, the more one believes that a potential friend is ideal for one's self and will reciprocate, the more he or she will move from a acquaintance, to close/good friend, to best friend.

Moreover, a comparative factor concerning the availability of alternative friendships that may be more satisfying, along with such extenuating circumstances as the size of investments and system constraints, may affect one's emotional commitment to a friendship. Although the friendship process does not always involve clearing the field of competitors, there may come a time when one is confronted by too many potential friends and not enough time or energy for them all. In such a case, one may spend more time with some than with others. This strategy usually results in one having only one best friend or a few "best friends," some or several good/close friends, and many social contacts or acquaintances, essentially differing in frequency of contact and depth of intimacy.

SEVEN

Marital Relationships:
Marriage, Divorce, and Remarriage

(Marriage forever) does not look as though it is flourishing. We may be witnessing a dying institution. I am not suggesting remarriage as a cure-all for our marriage problems. I'd rather see people learn enough to avoid problems before any marriage. Not all remarriages make it, of course. And not everyone who wants to remarry can find someone. But remarriage seems to be the answer for many who are unhappily married, those who are divorced and who want to be married, those who never imagined that one marriage could last them all their lives.

L. Westoff,
The Second Time Around: Remarriage in America

Introduction

The statistics on marriages, remarriages, and divorce rates are striking. While almost 75% of all marriages are first marriages, 20% are second marriages, and 6% are third marriages. The average age at first marriage is twenty-one for women and twenty-four for men; at second marriages, twenty-five for women and thirty for men. Women take longer than men before remarrying. The average length of second marriages is only five years compared to seven for first marriages (Westoff, 1977). While 17% of first marriages end in divorce, an amazing 35% of second marriages and over 60% of third marriages end in divorce (Hunt and Rydman, 1976).

Few subjects are as emotionally arousing as marriage, divorce, and remarriage. In most attempts to initiate a mate relationship, one declines the other's offer to form such an intimate relationship, resulting in feelings of anxiety, personal stress, and the questioning of one's personal worth (Murstein, 1972). Moreover, in any marital relationship times arise when misunderstandings occur, disruptions take place, or conflicts emerge that threaten the normal flow of information and the relationship itself, which may be associated with feelings of confusion, anger, personal stress, and the questioning of oneself and others. Finally, the disintegration of a marriage may result in loneliness, family breakup, and depression. Researchers claim that as many as half of those recently married may choose to divorce one another in the next five years, producing loneliness, self-doubt, and other serious psychological problems (Trower, 1981; Newcomb and Bentler, 1981; Duck, 1981).

The emotional trauma associated with marital problems and marital termination may be an overriding concern when it comes to remarriage. Many divorced persons remarry, and some undoubtedly give the matter more serious thought the second time around. Unfortunately, they do not always have superior judgment, even though the motivation was there to let go of a detrimental marital relationship and establish a better one. Unhappily, they may remarry blind to the fact that the same or similar marital problems prevail in the new situation or they may experience a whole new set of marital problems for which they are not prepared. In order to overcome the problem of relational recidivism in marriage and remarriage, one must realize that having made a mistake once, one can make it again.

It is the purpose of this chapter to adapt a general theory of disengagement and reengagement—an interpersonal communication model—to the marital relationship process in order to predict the degree of commitment to and satisfaction with different stages in its development or disintegration. Specifically I intend to discuss (1) quality marital communication environment, (2) marital self-concept support generally, (3) self-concept support within traditional and nontraditional marriages, (4) mateship development and communication competence, and (5) marital relationship reassessment. The key question is this: What should one consider in selecting and relating to a member of the opposite sex as one's mate?

A Quality Marital Communication Environment

Communication quality in marital relationships is the subject of scholarly interest (Montgomery, 1981; Miller et al., 1975; Satir, 1964). Although some authors claim that quality communication is central to a quality marriage relationship, they do little to provide a theoretical view of quality communication and to describe its role in marital relationships (Montgomery, 1981: 21). If quality communication is viewed as quantity of communication, one may be surprised to learn that the amount alone has very little bearing on marital satisfaction (Raush et al., 1974). Furthermore, if the quality of marriage is viewed as the length of time married, one should realize that the longevity of a relationship is no longer considered indicative of marital adjustment and satisfaction (Olson, 1972).

Knowledge of how to effectively assess marital relationships with the factors that enhance satisfaction and growth can be among the most important and useful tools of marital communication. What then constitutes quality communication in marital relationships? The view expressed here is that communication quality in marital relationships promotes both individual and relationship growth. The first is reflected by increased marital satisfaction. An application to the subject of marriage of the approach to human communication and interpersonal relationships presented in the first four chapters of this book suggests that a husband's and wife's self-regard and marital satisfaction are the result of the mates' self-concept accuracy, positive self-concept support, and communication skill.

It is the purpose of this section to describe a quality marital communication environment and to locate the appropriate criteria involved in assessing marital relationships and the role of interpersonal communication in the continuation of a satisfying and growing marital relationship. Specifically, this section deals with marital self-concept accuracy, marital preferred self-concept support, marital communication skill, and the usefulness of a quality marital communication environment.

Marital Self-Concept Accuracy

Criterion no. 1: Mates must accurately identify the unique scope, depth, and configuration of one another's preferred self-concept.

Vital to one's self-understanding and relational growth is a capacity to objectify and reflect upon one's self and to pattern the spouse's expectations for one in an accurate and realistic manner. Inaccurate self-presentation or self-perception by either mate in a marriage leads to self-concept and marital relationship disintegration. It is clear that when one mate communicates expectations that are beyond the other's capacity, the results may be perceived as individual or marital failure. Thus, each marital partner has the responsibility of attempting to accurately perceive the other and of helping the other accurately perceive one's preferred self-concept.

Marital Preferred Self-Concept Support

Criterion no. 2: Mates must provide support for each other's preferred identity, evaluative, and behavioral self-concept characteristics.

Self-concept support is an important function of interpersonal communication, if not the most important function in terms of self-concept
support and relational development. I suggest that positive self-concept
support in the form of recognition, acknowledgment, and endorsement
(Cissna and Sieburg, 1979) is essential to mate's feelings of self-worth
and marital satisfaction, and may be communicated through mutual respect, affection, and psychological-emotional support (Cushman and
Cahn, 1985). Any marriage that contains a preponderance of rejection
or disconfirmation utterances will contribute to a lower self-regard and
lower marital satisfaction.

Marital Communication Skills

Criterion no. 3: Mates must be skillful in their marital communication.

The key skill is collaboration, which requires self-assertiveness and
solicitation techniques that produce a communication climate in which
one's mate or potential mate can also be assertive. A truly romantic
relationship rests on a foundation consisting of such collaboration. Being
open in one's expression of feelings and open to those feelings expressed by one's mate provides a couple with room to grow, produces
feelings of being understood, and is an important form of self-concept
support, creating a basis for a successful marriage. Therefore, it is important for a husband and wife to skillfully negotiate into the marriage those
self-concept characteristics that are necessary for personal growth and
marital satisfaction, and negotiate out of the marriage those that interfere with each one's growth and satisfaction.

Competence in interaction also refers to the effective use of
messages aimed at objectifying, analyzing, evaluating, and synthesizing
a wife's and a husband's self-concepts, the nature of the marriage, and
the quality/quantity of marital communication itself. The specific marital communication skills include effective listening, self-assertion, and
collaboration. When applied to marital communication problems, this
reflection process is called marital reassessment and may include marital counseling aimed at realigning self-concepts, the marriage, and communication patterns.

The idea of a quality marital communication environment serves
three useful purposes. First, it presents criteria for the assessment of
one's present marriage. If one is not receiving encouragement or permitted to collaborate in resolving marital conflicts, a husband or wife
probably finds the marriage less than satisfying. Second, it serves as a
goal for the satisfactory renegotiation of one's present marital relationship. One should try to change the marriage to allow for more personal

growth and satisfaction before considering divorce. Thirdly, the idea of a quality communication environment provides the divorced person with what ought to be an important consideration in the selection of a subsequent romantic and/or marital partner. Since some spouses do not change because to give a partner more self-concept support or to attempt to collaborate more in the resolution of marital problems interferes with that spouse's satisfaction or growth (which has been at the other's expense), in a subsequent marriage or romantic relationship the partners need to select someone who is more supportive and more collaborative in his or her approach to resolving marital problems. Therefore, with the prerequisite knowledge and skill, one can attempt to repair a deteriorating marriage, or, failing that, one can attempt to form a superior marital relationship the next time around.

In sum, marital self-concept accuracy, preferred self-concept support, and marital communication skill are criteria for judging the quality of a communication environment in a marital relationship. These are proposed as the criteria by which one may assess a marital relationship to determine whether such a relationship warrants continuation, counseling, or divorce.

Marital Self-Concept Support in General

The significance of marital self-concept support is seen in the following example:

> I couldn't play tennis with my previous husband. We'd lose a point and he'd almost throw the racket at me. Now I love tennis. My new partner is very different from my first husband. He is more in tune with me. He reinforces what feels good (Westoff, 1977: 137).

Thus, without accurate and positive self-concept support, each partner's attempts to initiate and maintain a successful marital relationship may produce a less than satisfying marriage and stymie one another's personal growth.

During early marriage for a man, a woman's clothes consciousness, his own masculinity, her cheerfulness, and her seeing her husband as he sees himself are important determinants of marital success. For a woman, a man's thriftiness and emotional support for her, along with dyadic consensus and accuracy in regard to marital roles and affection are important to successful marital relationships (Bentler and Newcomb, 1978; Luckey, 1960; Christensen and Wallace, 1976). During the later stages of marriage, both male and female support and accuracy in regard to a spouse's preferred self-concept, consensus and accuracy in regard to affection, perception of role delegation and consensus on friends they have in common are important to successful marital relationships (Luckey, 1960; Christensen, L. and Wallace, 1976). In short, in order to assess one's present or prospective marital relationship, it is necessary to know and appreciate the scope, depth, and configuration of each partner's preferred self-concept, which forms a basis for the marital relationship in order to discover the appropriate self-concept characteristics to support. Without self-assertiveness and responsiveness to others, attempts to resolve marital conflicts have the potential to harm either or both of the spouses' self-concepts and the marriage.

The purpose of this section is to explain the role of sex in self-concept support, encourage the use of paradigm tests as marital communication techniques, discuss legitimate versus fake self-concept support, distinguish mateship from friendship, discuss the problem of uncooperative partners, and describe two survival strategies, namely, productive ambiguity and redefinition of the self-concept.

Differences in Sexual Arousal and Self-Concept Support

As suggested above, a mate's or potential mate's ability to communicate self-concept support is an important factor in the satisfaction of a marriage or a romantic relationship. However, substantial male-female differences in sexual arousal greatly complicates the problem of communicating self-concept support and aligning emotional and sexual intimacy. First, differences in sexual arousal between males and females may be attributed to differences in physical attractiveness and sex appeal (MacCorquodale and DeLamater, 1979). Second, males tend to be attracted to the physical characteristics of the female and tend to idealize and fantasize about past and current love and sexual experiences, while females tend to be attracted to relational characteristics of the dyad and tend to idealize and fantasize about current and imagined love and sexual experiences (McCauley and Swann, 1978; Peplau, Rubin and Hill, 1977). Third, males tend to reach orgasm before women do, unless foreplay is used to help increase female responsiveness or techniques are used to delay male orgasm (Butler, 1976).

These gender differences in sources and rates of sexual arousal are further complicated by differences in the effects of intensity on self-concept support experienced by males and females. Tests of the effect of sexual arousal on the accurate perception of another's self-concept indicate the following for males: Males who are high on sexual arousal tend to be very inaccurate in perceiving the self-concepts of the females they are with; moderate-arousal males are the most accurate; low-arousal are more accurate than high-arousal males but less accurate than moderate-arousal males. Similar tests yield the following results for females: High-arousal females tend to be the most accurate in perceiving the male's self-concept; moderate-arousal females are second; and low-arousal females are last. Therefore, from the standpoint of self-concept support, the ideal male-female romantic relationship or marriage is a moderate-arousal male and a high-arousal female. The worse match is a high-arousal male and a low-arousal female, which is a highly likely occurrence given the gender differences in arousal sources, rates, and intensity (Murstein, 1976).

Using Paradigm Tests

My friend Linda told me that she prefers to socialize more than does her fiancé, Bill. When she approaches him about the subject, he may even agree with her, but it is another matter if and when Bill takes *concrete* steps toward a more balanced social and intellectual life. As noted in Chapter Three, a paradigm test goes beyond a verbal acknowledgement to include behavioral change such that both partners can see what effect the commitment has on them. Although Linda's fiancé, Bill, may have thought that it is an easy matter to cut back on his hours at the office, perhaps he finds that he cannot enjoy his evenings out with Linda because there is work left undone. Thus, a successful test shows that one can commit oneself to the other, while an unsuccessful test reveals that two people cannot provide self-concept support in one or more crucial areas. If these areas are judged to be very important to both individuals, then they have reason not to marry. This is why paradigm tests must be undertaken prior to marriage—to see whether self-concept support can be elicited in areas that are important. The key idea behind a paradigm test is that it requires more than a verbal agreement; one must try to behave differently and monitor the effect of this behavioral change on him or her. While one thinks one knows one's self, the paradigm test frequently provides even greater insight when one tries to cope with change that calls into question his or her core values.

Legitimate Versus Fake Self-Concept Support

In one's efforts to seek out self-concept support, one must learn to tell what is legitimate from what is fake. Some people who initially provide unconditional self-concept support later attempt to negotiate differences. For example, some sexually appealing individuals promote a great deal of freedom in sexual expression early in a relationship, giving their partners a lot of self-concept support, and then implant restrictions that become increasingly more limiting and hence less supportive of one's self-concept. Or, some people may talk about how divorced dates hid their children, parents, or other relatives until after a relationship developed, and then gradually worked them into the relationship to the point that the relatives become the overriding consideration. In other situations, women frequently complain that their dates treated them first class before marriage and second class thereafter. Common to all these examples is the fact that one of the relational partners is using self-concept support strategically, knowing what the partner's sensitive areas are and avoiding confrontation until it appears too late to do anything about it. From the point of view of this book, it is usually better to be "up front" (self-assertion), keep the problem out of the picture permanently, or prevent the problem from becoming an overriding consideration, rather than to initiate a relationship on false pretenses.

Mateship Versus Friendship

Individuals should avoid confusing mateship and friendship. To grow personally and gain greater satisfaction in life, one needs to develop a variety of interests and participate in numerous activities. These interests and activities are expected to change over time. Since there is less expectation that friendships have to be long-term arrangements, friends are an excellent source of self-concept support as one moves in to and out of many interests and activities. Marriage, on the other hand, involves a long-term commitment in which both wives and husbands are expected to grow together and remain satisfied over time. This means that, unlike friendship, a marriage should not have as its basis a narrow range of self-concept support such as a single value, interest, or activity. Spouses need to develop a broader range of shared interests that can survive the ravages of time.

In addition, unlike friendship, a mate relationship should not limit each partner's growth only to those areas the two share in common or can mutually support. A person is a multifaceted, complex set of potentials. If one or both spouses believe that each mate "should be everything to the other," in a short time they may find that such demands exceed the basis of mutual support necessary for a long-term relationship. Consider the case of Phil and Sharon, where husband and wife confuse mateship with friendship. Phil told me that he has a strong interest in outdoor activities, especially golf. His wife, Sharon, decided to play golf because she did not like the idea that he would do something that she did not also do. The problem now is that her accommodating approach to the game lacks the challenge Phil is used to do with his friends, who are a lot more competitive (and she will not play with a handicap); as a result, he does not enjoy golf any more. Both husband and wife need to realize that there are ways in which people outside their marriage are in a better position than they to support each spouse's self-concept in some areas. To restrict the other's source of self-concept support to one's self places an unfair burden on each and limits the range and depth of the self-concept support one may experience.

The Problem of Uncooperative Partners: Survival Strategies

In one's attempts to negotiate a relationship that permits self-concept characteristics that are necessary to personal growth and marital satisfaction and eliminates those that are not, one may encounter the problem of having a partner who does not change or permit one to change because such changes threaten the partner's core values, interests, or needs. In other words, permitting another the freedom to grow may be viewed as self-destructive by one's partner. Such a person desires to maintain a particular situation because he or she finds it personally satisfying, even though it prevents personal growth and interferes with the personal satisfaction of others. Thus, he or she may not see any alternatives as more desirable, while his or her partner finds many alternatives more desirable.

In general, this book favors self-assertion, but there are times when it is best not to take a stand on an issue or to assert one's needs, interests, goals, or values. When such instances occur, strategies of accommodation are useful in the maintenance of an otherwise successful marital relationship or when one has no alternative at present. Two useful accommodation strategies are productive ambiguity and the reorganization of one's self-concept.

PRODUCTIVE AMBIGUITY. Consider the situation in which Linda enjoys sailing more than her partner, Bill, and he chooses to accommodate and overlook this difference between them. There are three instances in which such a strategy may be most useful and productive. First, the issue may involve a characteristic essential to Linda's self-concept. In such a case, if Bill were to criticize Linda's sailing interests, she might get very upset, find Bill less attractive, and withdraw from further contact. Second, the issue may not be very important to Bill. If Bill does not object to a few sailing artifacts around the house, and a sailing trip once a year or so, perhaps Linda will feel satisfied. Third, the issue may be tolerated if it does not require action by both partners. If Bill thinks that Linda's sailing interests have little likelihood of involving him because they do not have a sailboat, they do not live near water, or Linda gets seasick, then Bill may simply humor Linda or let the matter ride. While this strategy is not completely honest, in that Bill fails to make an issue out of their differences in regard to sailing, it results in self-concept support on a matter that may be best left alone. Therefore, it is not enough to identify one's needs, interests, and values, one must also see them in perspective, realizing the depth of his and her key concerns.

REORGANIZATION OF ONE'S SELF-CONCEPT. There are times when it is best to change, eliminate, or reorder one or more of one's own self-concept characteristics. One must realize that one can have more or less of a need, value, or interest. When Bill says that he is a researcher and teacher-scholar, he means that he sees himself spending all day and part of almost every night in the library or in his office reading, researching, analyzing data, and word processing. Linda who enjoys going out to eat, dance, and socialize may feel abandoned if Bill only takes a break for lunch and dinner. In this case, Bill may need to cut back some on his work schedule or rearrange his schedule to make himself more available in the evenings for socializing. Obviously, if Bill views himself as a playboy prior to marrying Linda, he may have to totally eliminate that aspect of his self-concept once married. At any rate, a relationship is most likely to survive when marital partners strive for balance, attempt to be reasonable, and try to proportionate key self-concept characteristics in a manner that fits one another's expectations.

A reorganization of one's self-concept is not necessarily bad. Following divorce, for example, there is a need for a new self-definition. As they find themselves more open to new interests and different people, some individuals develop new personalities and become more interesting as persons. According to Westoff (1977: 137), as one makes new friends, dates, or remarries

> one develops tastes and activities never before dreamed of. A sedentary wife becomes a whirlwind on the tennis courts; a portly husband sheds pounds while munching his new wife's natural-food dinners. He discovers he really likes opera, and she reads her first novel in years and actually enjoys it. A lot of dormant interests come alive, a lot of new ones take root and flower.

Self-Concept Support in Traditional
and Nontraditional Marriages

Assessing a marital relationship is no easy task. Yet, such assessments are necessary if mates are to exert any measure of control over the growth and decay of their self-concepts and the marriage itself. The search for a quality communication environment and a sense of personal worth and relational satisfaction depends on both one's self-concept accuracy and preferred self-concept support. In addition to the general considerations discussed above, there are specific factors that are key in American marriages because of the fact that there are different marital arrangements available. In this section, I describe two different marital patterns in the United States, traditional and contemporary, and self-concept support relevant to each marital pattern.

American Marital Patterns

While every American marital relationship is at least to some extent unique to the mates involved, there are recognizable patterns or marriage types. Two of the more popular patterns are labeled traditional and contemporary alternatives (Blood and Blood, 1979). Each type has its own symbolic acts, including communication styles, social expectations, and rituals. Whereas at one time the traditionally style was by far the most common in America, today only a little over one-half of the marriages tend toward this type, while the rest tend toward the contemporary alternative or a mixture of the two (Hacker, 1979).

The traditional pattern consists of idealized cultural duties and obligations that guide mates' understanding of their marital relationships. Typically this kind of marriage is symbolized in the selfless wedding vow to marry for better or worse, "until death do us part," and defines ideal mates as the husband being the economic provider and the wife being the obedient servant and caretaker (Blood and Blood, 1979).

Unlike the traditional pattern, the contemporary alternative pattern consists of idealized individual development and personal relationship satisfaction. Here, the wedding vows are more conditional in nature and are frequently devised at least in part by the particular mates who are expected to live up to them. The vows are also more self-oriented, and the relationship is intended to last only "so long as we both shall love." In this arrangement, the ideal mate and relationship satisfaction depends on individual and relational development. "Increasingly individuals are seeking a relationship that will provide growth for them as individuals and as a couple . . . Ideally, the successful marriage is seen as a relationship context in which growth and development of both partners is facilitated to a greater extent than it could be for either of these individuals outside the relationship" (Olson, 1972: 390).

The traditional and contemporary alternative marital patterns have their own rituals representing the successful attainment of their ideals. According to Tamashiro (1978), the traditional marriage is successful if it completes the following four stages. The first is magical, in that the newlyweds attempt to adhere to the idealized cultural duties and obligations involved in getting married, the wedding, and the honeymoon. The second stage is "idealized conventional," as husband and wife attempt to perform and perfect the traditional cultural roles of husband as breadwinner and family head and of wife as caretaker and obedient servant. The third stage, which is "individualistic," prevails when each mate begins to accept and appreciate his or her own interests, values, and needs, even if these differ from those of his or her partner. Finally, the fourth stage is "affirmational," as husband and wife learn to accept and appreciate the other's unique self-concept and no longer rely solely on social conventions to guide interactions.

If successful, the contemporary alternative follows a different pattern from that of the traditional marriage. The first phase is typically self-centered, in that each partner idealizes the relationship in terms of his or her own interests. Since this pattern was probably emphasized in the premarital phase, it is not surprising to learn that many marriages today are undertaken with the assumption that each person has more to gain by getting married than by going it alone. In the second phase, husband and wife discover that there are important differences that must be negotiated and some self-sacrifice is necessary for the marriage to continue. In the third phase, they begin to accept and appreciate the other's unique interests, values, and needs. In the final phase, they devise rules of the relationship for avoiding marital problems (Cushman and Cahn, 1985).

The successful progression through the four phases of each marital pattern depends on the husband's and wife's ability to accurately perceive one another's ideals, to accurately perceive changes that occur as the discrepancy between the real and ideal self-concepts decrease, to positively support continually changing self-concepts, and to effectively convey these perceptions through communication skill.

When unsuccessful, the two dominant marital patterns have their own unique forms of disengagement. The dissolution of traditional marriages by divorce "as a last resort" typically emphasizes violations of the marriage vows as a legal basis for the divorce or fault on the grounds of breach of contract. The offended mate and children are seen as victims of criminal acts such as adultery, squandering communal property on drink or riotous living, or being disobedient and rebellious. The offended party is usually hurt and angry, and the offender is condemned by the courts, leaving a feeling of guilt and making the divorce a bitter and painful experience. Typically, the parent and children involved and the violator completely sever the primary relationship and deal with each other indirectly through an attorney and later through the friend of the court. The public and the court see to it that the violator pays for his or her evil deeds in payment of property and loss of child custody (Blood and Blood, 1979).

Unlike the traditional marital pattern, the disengagement ritual for the contemporary alternative may not be as punishing, because it is normally more amicable and no-fault in nature. Because both partners are committed to one another's personal growth—meaning that personal changes are expected—a divorce due to such an occurrence is not blamed on the mate who changes. The usual conditions for ending such relationships without fault are as follows: First, mates who are initially compatible become incompatible because one partner changes in a way that the other can or will not support. Second, sometimes the change is not in one partner's values but in his or her physical location, as when one mate relocates in a distant foreign land. Third, sometimes people have a conflict before marriage that becomes more severe after. In each case, staying together produces strain on the individual, requiring one partner to sacrifice a significant aspect of self, and divorce offers a solution to the problem by allowing room for personal growth. The divorcing partners perceive the marriage as "having meaning as long as it lasted." Because there is no victim to feel angry nor an offender or criminal to feel guilty, those involved may redefine the relationship from mate to close friend, date, or even lover. Where each retains individual property and where communal property is split or shared, children are allowed equal access to both parents, who may accept a shared responsibility for their children's development and finances. One result of a more amicable arrangement is that both parents are more likely to create stronger ties with their children since the single-parent time is often considered higher quality time (Blood and Blood, 1979).

Self-Concept Support: Traditional and Contemporary Mates

Differences in traditional and contemporary self-concept characteristics have been found to affect a variety of communication variables: persuasibility (Montgomery and Burgoon, 1977), dominance and submissiveness (Putnam and McCallister, 1980; Isenhart, 1980; Brown, 1980; Berzins, Welling and Wetter, 1976), self-disclosure (Greenblatt, Hasenauer, and Freimuth, 1980), touching behavior (Eman, Dierks-Stewart, and Tucker, 1978), communication apprehension (Greenblatt et al., 1980), and communication competence (Brunner and Phelps, 1980; Wheeless and Duran, 1980).

A widely used measure of masculine and feminine self-concept characteristics is Bem's (1974) Sex-Role Inventory (BSRI), a Likert-type self-report. Bem's list of male-female characteristics, as modified by Wheeless and Dierks-Stewart (1981), are expressive in nature for traditional females and instrumental for traditional males.

Traditional Self-Concepts

Females	*Males*
gentle	acts as a leader
tender	has leadership abilities
understanding	dominant
warm	aggressive
sensitive to needs of others	willing to take a stand
compassionate	forceful
sincere	assertive
helpful	strong personality
eager to sooth hurt feelings	competitive
friendly	independent

Among traditionalists, the adoption of one sex's self-concept characteristics by members of the other sex is discouraged.

While traditionally males are viewed in terms of instrumental characteristics and females in terms of expressive characteristics, contemporary males and females are defined as androgynous. Androgyny is a third type of gender orientation in which males and females manifest both instrumental and expressive characteristics. While this may seem like a contradiction in terms, the possession of instrumental self-concept characteristics does not prevent one from also possessing expressive ones (Montgomery and Burgoon, 1977; Eman, Dierks-Stewart, and Tucker, 1978; Ellis and McCallister, 1980).

The gender differences among traditional and contemporary (androgynous) mates may result in conflicts over the meaning of love, commitment, sex, and marriage. *Love* is an integrating force in a relationship that exerts its effect through

> socialization to the beliefs that one's concern for the welfare of the other, one's helping the other, one's concern for being with the other, one's pain in the absence of the other, and one's dependency on the other are key attributes of an intimate relationship (Krain, 1977: 250).

Although most everyone may feel comfortable with this statement about love, in keeping with their traditional self-concepts, traditional spouses may define love quite differently from contemporary marrieds. In the extreme, traditionalists are more likely to view love as more conditional, demanding, and possessive than contemporary mates (O'Neill and O'Neill, 1972). The point here is not which type of love is superior but rather to raise the issue of loss of self-concept support that may occur when one partner subscribes to one view of love while his or her mate takes the opposing view. From the standpoint of communicative alignment and self-concept support, traditional mates share one view of love, while contemporary spouses share another.

Traditionalists define *commitment* differently from nontraditionalists. In an extreme form, traditionalists view commitment as a focusing force in a relationship that directs one's interest in and affection toward a particular person to the exclusion of competitors (Karp, Jackson, and Lester, 1970). Contemporary mates view commitment personally and individually as a focusing force on the individual that directs one's interest in and affection toward a particular person because he or she contributes more than others to one's personal growth (Olson, 1972). Again, the point here is not which type of commitment is superior but rather to raise the issue of misalignment and lack of self-concept support that occurs when one partner subscribes to one view of commitment while his or her mate takes the opposing view. Like love, both mates need to share a similar view of commitment, which is more likely to happen when both mates are either traditional or contemporary.

Partially due to different understandings of the meaning of love and commitment, traditionalists may view *sex* differently from nontraditionalists (Turner, 1970). Extreme traditionalists view sex as inseparable from love and strong relational commitment, while contemporary mates view it as a more casual and recreational activity distinctly separate from love and relational commitment (Peplau, Rubin, and Hill, 1977; D'Augelli and D'Augelli, 1977). Clearly, when two people engage in sex and hold the same meaning for love, commitment, and sex, less difficulty should occur in communicating self-concept support than when they hold different views.

Traditionalists differ from nontraditionalists in their definition of *marriage*. According to O'Neill and O'Neill (1972), pure traditionalists ascribe to a "closed marriage" that involves adherence to a rigid set of traditional social expectations in which the husband is the head of the family, provider, and protector. In contrast, contemporary mates expect an "open marriage" in which the mates share duties and sometimes reverse roles. Although the O'Neills advocate open over closed marriages, the important point here is to draw attention to the problems of communicative alignment and lack of self-concept support in a marriage where one partner idealizes an open marriage while his or her mate envisions a closed marriage. To maximize self-concept support, both mates need to share a similar view of marriage.

Mateship Development and Communication Competence

The relationship between a woman and a man rarely remains constant. A couple is always changing. The changes may be subtle—hardly noticeable—or they may be dramatic, even explosive. Sometimes they may require much attention and work from each person, while, at other times, changes may flow easily and effortlessly. Whatever the situation, there is a continual dynamic interaction. Each partner's attitudes, goals, and decisions affect her/his behaviors. The quality of the relationship depends upon the sum of the interactions between the two partners, as well as with other persons who may be involved in the life situation of the couple.

R. Hunt and E. Rydman, *Creative Marriage*

The problem posed by an interactive approach to marriage is how to change in constructive and positive ways that promote intimacy, love, and commitment. To prevent repeating errors of judgment, one must better understand the facts that are key to a successful marriage for that person and his or her mate. This understanding enables one to better judge how to attempt improving a present marriage, when to let go of it, and how to form a superior one the next time around.

Defining the term mateship as any opposite sex relationship for which one clears competitors from the field, Cushman and Kunimoto (forthcoming) found that casual date, steady date, and fiancé/mate function as the semantic markers for discriminating among different levels of the marital relationship development process in America. Each level is itself a type of relationship worthy of study in its own right, but taken together, they represent developmental steps toward marriage and may contain some public component, a symbolic act, such as an exchange of rings or pins, the establishment of a common household, or a marriage ceremony.

Because the marital relationship process is different from that of other interpersonal relationship formation processes (such as friendship), the factors that define and govern the steps are unique to it. Based upon the work of several researchers, marital relationships appear to differ from other types of interpersonal relationships by the manner in which intelligence, physical attraction, sex appeal, affection, and ideal mateness affect the relationship (Pam, Plutchik, and Conte, 1973; Cushman and Kunimoto, forthcoming).

Mateship Developmental Stages

Cushman et al. (1982) describe a marital relationship development model that consists of a three-stage filtering process. At the *first* stage, causal and normative factors delimit the range of potential mates to a field of availables or *first dates and casual dates*. While a large number of people may fall into such a category for some individuals, usually it is impossible to seriously consider them all as potential mates due to geographical, physical, and social considerations.

At the *second* stage, normative factors that function as antecedent conditions for generating messages aimed at establishing a mate relationship further delimit the range of casual dates to a field of approachables or *steady dates*. The filtering process predicts that the more one perceives that an opposite-sex other is about as physically attractive, intelligent, and sexually appealing as one perceives one's self to be, the more likely one will engage in communication aimed at initiating a mate relationship. Research has found that if one's previous communications with another member of the opposite sex indicate that the other person is about as good-looking, intelligent, and sexually attractive as one perceives one's self to be, then he or she feels both at ease with the other person and sufficiently attracted to that individual to attempt to establish a mate relationship (Hill, Rubin and Peplau, 1976; Berscheid and Walster, 1978; Murstein, 1972; Cavior and Boblett, 1972).

The filtering process leads one to expect that the more one perceives an opposite-sex other's self-concept as being similar to one's ideal for a mate, the greater the likelihood of engaging in communication aimed at initiating a mate relationship. One may ideally prefer as a mate someone who is thoughtful, easygoing, and athletic. After meeting another who has these characteristics, one may see that the other's real self-object relationships are very similar to what one ideally wants (Bailey and Helm, 1974; Murstein, 1972; Luckey, 1960).

The filtering process indicates that the more one perceives that an opposite-sex other's real-ideal self-concept discrepancy is small, the more likely one will engage in communication aimed at initiating a mate relationship. Previous research provides greater support for this prediction for males than for females. More specifically, it is usually when a male is very close to what he would like to be that he seriously considers marriage. Meanwhile, it is only when a female also believes that her perspective mate is what he would like to be that she considers him sufficiently stable and clears the field of competitors. However, past research suggests that a similar requirement of a low real and ideal self-concept discrepancy may not appear essential for females (Luckey, 1962; Murstein, 1971; 1972).

The filtering process suggests that the more one perceives that the other will accept one's offer of a relationship, the more likely one will engage in communication aimed at initiating a mate relationship. Previous research indicates the retarding effect of one's perception that he or she might be turned down on the initiation of such a relationship (Shantean and Nagy, 1979; Huston, 1974; Murstein, 1972).

At the *third* stage of the mateship developmental process, there exists within one's field of steady dates a subset of individuals who will reciprocate one's offer of a mate relationship when the occasion arises. This field is limited to one's *fiancé or spouse,* depending on whether or not there is an engagement period prior to the marriage. Normative factors influence when people chose to reciprocate an offer of mateship, and these form the basis for the communication factors that lead to establishing and maintaining a mate relationship. The three-stage filtering process suggests that the more frequently both mates receive from one another messages that manifest an accurate perception of the mate's real and ideal self-concept, and indicate a perceived lack of discrepancy between the mate's real and ideal self-concept, the more likely the relationship will become satisfying. The more each mate's perceptions of self-object relationships in regard to mateship for one another are accurate, and the more each mate conveys self-concept support, the more the relationship will develop (Luckey, 1960; Murstein, 1971, 1972; Shafer, Braito, and Bohlen, 1973). Moreover, the filtering process predicts that the more self-concept support is perceived to be reciprocated (through the communication of respect, affection, and psychological-emotional support), the more likely the relationship will become satisfying (Cushman, Valentinsen, and Dietrich, 1982; Cushman and Cahn, 1985).

The factors identified as normative forces that define the field of approachables (steady dates) at the second stage continue to be important at stage three (fiancé/mate). Numerous studies show that physical attraction, intelligence, sex appeal, and real and ideal self-concept discrepancy are important both in the initiation of a marital relationship and later in the marriage itself (Cushman, Valentinsen and Dietrich, 1982; Cushman and Cahn, 1985). Thus, these factors function as *marker variables* in the mateship development process. In addition, the factors identified as communicative, which play a role in moving couples from casual and steady dating levels to fiancé/mate, are also important later in the marriage. Several studies show that the accuracy of one's perceptions of the mate's real and ideal self-concepts, the discrepancy between the two, and perceived self-concept support are all strongly related to marital satisfaction (Cushman, Valentinsen, and Dietrich, 1982; Cushman and Cahn, 1985). As argued in previous chapters, perceived understanding links self-concept support to interpersonal relationship satisfaction and development (which in this case refers to marriage), and functions as an *intensity variable.*

Marital Communication Competence

Navran (1967) explored when and how marital communication can contribute to relational growth and satisfaction, and he concluded that happily married couples differ from unhappy ones in the following ways:

1. talk more to each other

2. convey the feeling that they understand what is being said to them

3. have a wider range of subjects available to them

4. preserve communication channels and keep them open

5. show more sensitivity to each other's feelings

6. personalize their language symbols

7. make more use of supplementary nonverbal techniques of communication

Similarly, several studies report a strong relationship between communication behaviors similar to those listed above and marital adjustment, while the absence of such behaviors leads to marital disintegration (Margolin, 1978). In addition, the best predictors of relational discord in marriage is still a lack of consensus between spouses on the desired levels of affection, love, and sex, as well as weak or inaccurate self-concept support (Christensen and Wallace, 1976; Luckey, 1960).

Landis (1946) reports on the length of time it takes couples to achieve relational consensus in various marital coordination areas, such as spending, friends, marital roles, and affection. The most problematic area for married couples is the area of affection—in particular, sex. This is particularly true when the couple lacks the communication skills necessary to resolve such conflicts (Rim, 1979).

Marital interaction offers an ideal opportunity for couples to communicate mutual self-concept support through the alignment of self-concepts by achieving dyadic consensus on key concepts like love, commitment, sex, and type of marital pattern. With interpersonal communication competence, marital satisfaction can be achieved.

Marriage Reassessment:
Key Communication Factors in Marital Development

Why are some partners more satisfied with their marriages than others? Why are some partners more emotionally committed to their marriages? Why do some marriages last longer than others? Most research designed to evaluate the theoretical predictions of marriage and romantic involvements is limited to a single point in relational development. In the absence of research that has utilized more of a developmental approach, it is difficult to answer these important questions. The present interpersonal model of relational development is designed to extend research in communication (Knapp, 1978; Friedman, Giffin, and Patton, 1978; Cushman, Valentinsen, and Dietrich, 1982) and the exchange tradition within social psychology (Thibaut and Kelley, 1959; Kelley and Thibaut, 1978). Assuming that marital partners are in general motivated to maximize perceived understanding and minimize perceived misunderstanding, the interpersonal communication model distinguishes between two important characteristics of relationships satisfaction and commitment. As discussed in Chapter Four, persons who intend to maintain their marriage should also feel psychologically attached to it.

Marital Satisfaction

Rusbult (1980; 1983) defines marital satisfaction as marital attraction or having positive feelings about one's partner and the relationship. In line with this conception of marital satisfaction, the interpersonal communication model of marital development predicts that the more positive one's perceived understanding, the more one is attracted to and satisfied with the marriage; conversely, the more negative one's perceived understanding, the more one is repelled and dissatisfied.

According to the interpersonal communication model, one's satisfaction in mature stages of a romantic relationship is a simple function of one's perceived understanding experienced in the relationship. As argued in Chapter Two and Three, self-concept support produces perceived understanding. Because research shows that perceived understanding may not be as important initially as other factors in interpersonal attraction but plays a more important role in relational satisfaction during later stages of relationship development, the interpersonal communication model argues that partners are in general motivated to maximize mutual perceived understanding while minimizing perceived misunderstanding in latter phases of marital development. Therefore, satisfaction with and attraction to a marriage may depend on the degree of difference between the individual partner's perceived understanding and misunderstanding.

Furthermore, as described in Chapter Four, there is a neutral point determined by the degree of confirmation, rejection, and disconfirmation experienced in previous relationships where both the feeling of being understood and misunderstood are minimal. Therefore, individuals evaluate their marriage in relation to their neutral point in order to assess the degree of satisfaction.

Marital Commitment

Marital commitment may be defined as the tendency to maintain the marriage and feel attached to it psychologically (Rusbult, 1980; 1983). Within this view of marital commitment, the interpersonal communication model predicts the following: While marital satisfaction is expected to remain unchanged with changes in the value of alternative relationships, investment size, and system constraints, marital commitment is expected to decrease with increases in the value of alternative relationships, such as extramarital affairs, but is expected to increase with increases in investment size and system constraints. This prediction is derived from the interrelationship of the value of alternative relationships, the investment size, social system constraints, and emotional commitment.

Rusbult (1980; 1983) has shown that the *value of alternative relationships* is an important comparison level for assessing the attractiveness of the present romantic relationship. The interpersonal communication model predicts that the more value one places on an extramarital affair, the less one feels emotionally committed to a marriage. When an alternative relationship is perceived as more attractive than one's present marriage, "it is then that dissolution, such as separation or divorce becomes a possibility" (Galvin and Brommel, 1982, p. 66). Until this value is reached, any marriage is likely to continue simply because the marital satisfaction ratio is, at least, "barely tolerable," and in some cases may even range into the "acceptable," or perhaps on into the "very favorable" (Scanzoni, 1972).

Furthermore, researchers (Rusbult, 1980; 1983 Lund, 1985) have shown that the *size of investments* affects commitment in romantic relationships. According to the interpersonal communication model, the more one invests in the present interpersonal relationship, the more one feels emotionally committed to it.

Finally, Parks, Stan, and Eggert (1983) have shown that *system constraints* influence relational commitment. Recall from Chapter Four that system constraints refer to perceived pressures from one's social networks, consisting of relatives, friends, and other persons. It is suggested that the more marital partners perceive system constraints, the more they feel emotionally committed to their marriage.

Summary

In this chapter, a general theory of disengagement and reengagement, in the form of an interpersonal communication model, was adapted to the marital relationship process in order to predict the degree of commitment and satisfaction at different stages of development or disengagement. It was argued that marital self-concept accuracy, preferred self-concept support, and marital communication skill are criteria for evaluating the quality of a communication environment in a marital relationship to determine whether such a relationship needs counseling.

Compared to friendship and other types of relationships, the mateship process is unique in the way partners' perceptions of intelligence, physical attraction, sex appeal, affection, and ideal mateness enter into the relationship. Also, one perceives from opposite sex others who reciprocate their expressions of respect, affection, and psychological-emotional support self-concept support that results in feeling understood. Therefore, the more two individuals believe that a potential mate is ideal for one's self and will reciprocate, the more they will move from the level of casual date, to that of steady date and fiancé/spouse.

Research reveals that one of the most important factors in a successful marriage is comparative in nature. The process of elimination as one clears the field of competitors by moving from one stage to the next involves frequent comparisons to determine whether the prospective mate is more or less desirable than the available alternatives. Even after marriage, comparison remains an important factor. If a marriage has only minor problems, it is unlikely that either mate will make a serious effort to find someone who is more compatible. Even if the marriage becomes more troublesome, it is not likely that one will find an alternative more desirable owing to investments that have accumulated and to social system constraints. However, when a marriage is a disaster, practically any alternative may appear more desirable.

EIGHT

Supervisor-Subordinate Work Relationships

I have become concerned about the *quality* of interaction between and among people—not so much about the accurate transfer of information from source to destination, but rather with the emotional impact that people have on one another. In the course of pursuing this concern I have come to believe that there is considerable potential for damage in the most ordinary garden–variety conversations between supervisor and subordinate, among co-workers, or even among well-meaning friends.

E. Sieburg, "Confirming and Disconfirming Organizational Communication"

Introduction

Supervisor-subordinate communication is defined as verbal and nonverbal exchanges of information between organizational members, of whom one has formal authority to direct and evaluate the activities of others in the organization (Jablin, 1979). Katz and Kahn (1966) list downward communications from superior to subordinates as job instructions, job rationale, organizational procedures and practices, feedback about subordinate performance, and indoctrination of goals. Communication upward from subordinate to superior includes information about the subordinate, co-workers and their problems, information about organizational practices and policies, and information about what needs to be done and how it can be done.

The nature of supervisor-subordinate communication appears to be a factor in employee satisfaction and job performance, which in turn influences organizational effectiveness (Baird and Diebolt, 1976). Stogdill (1974) reviews studies that found two basic dimensions of supervisor-subordinate communication that affect an employee's satisfaction and performance: consideration and the initiation of structure. While consideration refers to friendship and warmth, mutual trust, rapport and tolerance, and two-way communication, the initiation of structure refers to how one organizes and redefines group activities and one's relation to the group. Elsewhere, these basic dimensions are referred to as "employee orientation" and "production orientation" (Katz, Maccoby and Morse, 1950). Studies found that high employee absenteeism, turnover, grievance rates, and low supervisor-subordinate evaluations are associated with high initiating structure when accompanied with low consideration (Bass, 1981). In general, high initiating structure contributes most to organizational effectiveness when combined with high consideration.

In terms of organizational effectiveness, supervisor-subordinate communication involves sharing. Supervisors and subordinates may share ideas, feelings, and information; they may share experiences; they may share trust and respect; but perhaps most importantly, they share the feeling that each understands the other (Cahn, 1986). While research indicates that overall organizational effectiveness depends at least partially on consideration and initiating structure, Weissenburg and Kavanagh (1972) report that most studies using the Leadership Behavior Description have found a positive correlation (.52) between consideration and initiating structure, suggesting that there may be an even more fundamental factor accounting for this overlap. The position taken here is that both consideration and initiating structure depend to a great extent on the supervisor and subordinate sharing perceived understanding or the feeling of being understood. One is less willing to follow closely another's instructions and directions unless mutual perceived understanding occurs. In addition, one is unable to communicate consideration to another unless perceived understanding is mutual. In the early stages of relationship development, one does not expect a great deal of perceived understanding; later, however, such expectations may become overriding concerns that in the case of organizational effectiveness influence employee satisfaction and job performance (Cahn, 1986).

In contrast, empty, distant, impersonal supervisor-subordinate relationships are based on a lack of feeling understood. As a major source of anxiety and despair, such treatment contributes to perceived social injustice and leads to employee absenteeism, turnover, grievances, and low evaluations. Where social contexts are lacking in perceived understanding—as in some public, private, and industrial organizations—the problem of a lack of feeling understood erodes organizational effectiveness. Barnlund (1968: 613) states it as follows:

> People do not take time, do not listen, do not try to understand, but interrupt, anticipate, criticize, or disregard what is said; in their own remarks they are frequently vague, inconsistent, verbose, insincere, or

dogmatic. As a result people often conclude conversations feeling more inadequate, more misunderstood and more alienated than when they started them.

The emotional trauma associated with job related problems and employment termination may be an overriding concern when it comes to finding another job. Many seek another job, and some undoubtedly give the matter more serious thought the next time around. Unfortunately, they do not always have a superior judgment, even though the motivation was there to let go of a detrimental supervisor-subordinate relationship and establish a better one. Unhappily, they may move into a new situation blind to the fact that the same or similar problems prevail or they may experience a whole new set of problems for which they are not prepared. In order to overcome the problem of relational recidivism in supervisor-subordinate relationships, one must realize that having made a mistake once, one can make it again.

It is the purpose of this chapter to adapt a general theory of interpersonal communication and relationship development to the work place. Specifically, I intend to (1) describe the criteria underlying quality work communication environments, (2) discuss the role of self-concept support generally in work environments, and (3) specify self-concept support in traditional and contemporary organizations, (4) present key communication factors in supervisor-subordinate relations reassessment, and (5) discuss two paradigm tests, namely, the employment interview and employee appraisal. The key question is this: What should one consider in selecting and relating to a supervisor or subordinate at work?

A Quality Work Communication Environment

Several studies have corroborated with the common sense notion that effective communication is one of the top, if not *the* top, requirements of a successful manager (Alpander, 1974; Tubbs and Widgery, 1978; Cahn and Tubbs, 1983). Some communicative behaviors contribute to a "climate" or atmosphere within which work is performed. In his well-known categories of supportive and defensive behaviors, Gibb (1961, 1965) claims that a defensive "climate" makes for a greater distortion in communicating, while a supportive "climate" makes for a greater accuracy in communication. Gibb then proceeds to list and describe behaviors that are perceived as threatening and those that are perceived as supportive. Thus, Gibb provides one answer to the question: How can a supervisor communicate in such a way as to have a more positive influence on a subordinate?

Another answer to this question takes one away from the "climate" and focuses on the supervisors' and subordinates' feelings toward themselves, each other, and the relationship. It is the purpose of this section to describe a quality work communication environment, as well as to locate the appropriate criteria involved in assessing supervisor-subordinate relationships and the role of interpersonal communication in the continuation of a satisfying and growing relationship. Specifically, this section deals with worker self-concept accuracy, worker preferred self-concept support, interpersonal communication skill, and the usefulness of a quality work communication environment.

Supervisors and subordinates must accurately identify the unique scope, depth, and configuration of one another's preferred self-concept. Vital to one's self-understanding and relational-growth is a capacity to objectify and reflect on one's self and to pattern the other's expectations for one in an accurate and realistic manner. Inaccurate self-presentation or self-perception by either worker leads to self-concept and relationship disintegration. It is clear that when one communicates expectations that are beyond the other's capacity, the results may be perceived as individual or relational failure. Thus, each worker has the responsibility of attempting to accurately perceive the other and of helping the other accurately perceive one's preferred self-concept.

Workers must provide support for each other's preferred identity, evaluative, and behavioral self-concept characteristics. Self-concept support is an important function of interpersonal communication, if not the most important function in terms of self-concept support and relational development. According to Sieburg (1976), positive self-concept support in the form of recognition, acknowledgment, acceptance, and involvement is essential to workers' feelings of self-worth and job satisfaction, and any supervisor-subordinate relationship that contains a preponderance of utterances showing indifference, imperviousness, and disqualification will contribute to a lower self-regard and job satisfaction.

Workers must be skillful in interpersonal communication. Having accurately discovered one's own and the other's self-concept, a supervisor and a subordinate must negotiate into their relationship those self-concept characteristics that are necessary for personal growth and job satisfaction and negotiate out of the supervisor-subordinate relationship those that interfere with each one's growth and satisfaction. Negotiation that is collaborative in nature requires self-assertiveness, being "up front" about one's self, and solicitation and effective listening techniques to create an atmosphere in which one's employer or employee also can be assertive. These two qualities characterize a unique approach to a supervisor-subordinate relationship. Being open and apest with one's boss or employee and allowing him or her freedom of expression and room to grow are important forms of self-concept support that produce feelings of being understood, thereby creating a basis for a successful relationship.

Competence in interaction also refers to the effective use of messages aimed at objectifying, analyzing, evaluating, and synthesizing supervisor's and subordinate's self-concepts, the nature of the relationship, and the quality/quantity of communication itself. The specific communication skills include effective listening, self-assertion, and collaboration. When applied to supervisor-subordinate communication problems, this reflection process—which is called relational reassessment—is aimed at realigning self-concepts, the relationship, and communication patterns.

In general, there are undoubtedly numerous ways to achieve a quality communication environment in the work place beyond good pay and strong benefits. The results of a series of studies describe effective supervisors as "communication-minded," "willing, empathic listeners," who "ask" or "persuade" rather than tell or demand, who are "sensitive to subordinate's feelings," and who tend to be more "open" as communicators (Redding, 1972). More recently, Moskowitz (1985) found that the following traits were typical of the best companies to work for:

1. Supervisors and subordinates are made to feel part of a team.

2. Open communication is encouraged by supervisors and subordinates.

3. Supervisors and subordinates stress quality and are made to feel good about what they are doing.

4. Distinctions in rank are reduced.

Moskowitz concludes that such efforts on the part of supervisors and subordinates result in employees identifying their interests with those of the company.

The idea of a quality work communication environment serves three useful purposes. First, it presents criteria for the assessment of one's present supervisor-subordinate relationship. If one is not receiving encouragement or permitted to collaborate in resolving work-related conflicts, a supervisor or subordinate probably finds the job less than satisfying. Second, it serves as a goal for the satisfactory renegotiation of one's present working relationship. One should try to change the relationship to allow for more personal growth and satisfaction before considering termination. Thirdly, the idea of a quality communication environment provides the terminated person with what ought to be an important consideration in the selection of a subsequent employee or employer. Since some workers do not change because to give the other more self-concept support or to attempt to collaborate more in the resolution of problems at work interferes with that person's satisfaction or growth (which is at the other's expense), in a subsequent situation or relationship one needs to select someone who is more supportive and more collaborative in his or her approach to resolving work-related problems. Therefore, with the prerequisite knowledge and skill, one can attempt to repair a deteriorating supervisor-subordinate relationship, or, failing that, one can attempt to form a superior relationship the next time around.

In sum, worker self-concept accuracy, preferred self-concept support, and interpersonal communication skill are criteria for judging the quality of a work communication environment. These are proposed as standards for assessing a supervisor-subordinate relationship to determine whether such a relationship warrants continuation, change, or termination.

Supervisor-Subordinate Self-Concept Support in General

Growing out of earlier work by Reusch (1961) and Watzlawick et al. (1974), Sieburg and Larson (1971) theorize about the self-confirming aspects of communication. They divide communication patterns into four types:

1. explicit rejection

2. implicit rejection

3. explicit acceptance

4. implicit acceptance

Both explicit and implicit rejection are disconfirming, which refers to communicative behavior that causes another person to value himself or herself less. Explicit rejection involves either a negative evaluation or an overt dismissal of the other person. For example, person A says: "I can't understand how they can just sit on their duffs and not do anything about it. Time is running out." But person B answers: "Oh yeah? Well I don't see you doing anything about it." Implicit rejection involves four more subtle types of disconfirmation: (a) interruptions—When a communicator cuts you off in mid-sentence; (b) imperviousness—when a communicator ignores what you say as if you had never said it; (c) irrelevant response—when a communicator starts off on a totally unrelated topic in response to your initial comment; and (d) tangential response—when a communicator gives some acknowledgement to your initial comment but immediately launches off on a new irrelevant topic.

By contrast, both explicit and implicit acceptance refer to communicative behavior that results in another person valuing himself or herself more. Explicit acceptance involves a positive evaluation of the person. For example, person A says: "So I just told him straight out that he wasn't going to pull that kind of stuff on me." And person B says: "That took guts." Implicit acceptance involves either a direct acknowledgment of a person's remark, an attempt to clarify the remark by asking for more information, or an expression of positive feeling. For example, person A says: "What I meant to say was that I've known him for a long time and I've never seen him do anything like that." And person B responds: "Oh, well, now I understand."

The importance of the literature on self-concept support lies in the specific identification of communication patterns that seem to promote relationship growth and deterioration. Cissna (1976)—who summarized studies in widely differing situations, including supervisors-subordinates—found that the only factor that consistently appeared in these studies was the self-concept support or confirmation-disconfirmation factor. Therefore, this factor may be one of the most pervasive dimensions in interpersonal communication.

Self-Concept Support in Traditional and Nontraditional Organizations

Supervisor-subordinate relationship assessment is not easy. Such assessments are useful, however, when workers wish to exert some measure of control over the improvement and deterioration of their self-concepts and their working relationships. The search for a quality work communication environment, one that enhances feelings of personal worth and relationship satisfaction, depends on both one's self-concept accuracy and preferred self-concept support. There are specific factors that are key in American employment because of the fact that there are different supervisor-subordinate relationships available, traditional and contemporary. In this section, I discuss the type of self-concept support relevant to each pattern.

The Traditional Supervisor-Subordinate Relationship

Supervisor-subordinate interaction offers an ideal opportunity for workers to communicate mutual self-concept support through the alignment of self-concepts by achieving dyadic consensus on key concepts related to work. The nature of what constitutes appropriate self-concept support depends on whether the supervisor-subordinate relationship is traditional or contemporary. Traditionally, boss-employee relationships were geared to the centralized factory model of the industrial age. An obvious example would be Ford Motor Company's huge plant at River Rouge, where 100,000 people worked in the 1920s. Ford and other manufacturers required large concentrations of material, capital, plant, and labor, which meant that thousands of workers might have to convene daily at the same place of work (Cahn, 1985).

Large numbers of laborers worked more efficiently when organized vertically or hierarchically with a one-way communication system in which a top person sent information in one direction downward. Hierarchical organization included high specialization on the assembly line, differentiation, clear separation of duties and responsibilities, close supervision of subordinates, respect for authority and loyalty to supervisors, elaborate rules and controls, and impersonality (Goldhaber, 1983). Such industries were known for their pressures on workers to conform to expectations of the organization and for encouraging an assembly-line mode of thinking. They were also known for upward movement, stress and tension, defensive behavior, and anxiety. The top-down organization chart and the chain of command were symbols of boss-employee interpersonal relationships in the industrial age.

A Contemporary Model of Supervisor-Subordinate Relationships

The distinguishing feature of the contemporary model is networking (almost a synonym for decentralization) which fosters equality and informality in worker and boss-employee interpersonal relationships (Cahn, 1985). Networking describes people sharing information with each other. This new management style is lateral, diagonal, bottom up, and interdisciplinary (Naisbitt, 1982). In contrast to traditional organizations, networks provide the horizontal link. According to Hine (1977), a network may be characterized as "a badly knotted fishnet," but this fails to capture the three dimensional nature of networks that make them even more complex. Whether one is in business for one's self, stays at home and works for someone else via a telecommunications network, or is employed in an information industry, one may find one's self embedded in a network where everyone serves everyone else. Networking captures the essence of the postindustrial society that is based on services and is a transaction between people.

Relationship Reassessment:
Key Communication Factors in Relational Development

Why are some workers more satisified with their jobs than others? Most research designed to evaluate the theoretical predictions of supervisor-subordinate communication is limited to a single point in relational development. In the absence of research that has utilized more of a developmental approach, it is difficult to answer these important questions. As noted in earlier chapters, the interpersonal model of relational development extends research in communication (Knapp, 1978; Friedman, Giffin, and Patton, 1978; Cushman, Valentinsen, and Dietrich, 1982) and the exchange tradition within social psychology (Thibaut and Kelley, 1959; Kelley and Thibaut, 1978). In employment contexts, the model assumes that supervisors and subordinates are in general motivated to maximize perceived understanding and minimize perceived misunderstanding, and it distinguishes between two important characteristics of relationships job satisfaction and commitment. The model assumes that persons who intend to maintain their working relationships should also feel psychologically attached to them.

Job Satisfaction

Job satisfaction, according to Smith, Kendall, and Hulin (1969), consists of one's positive or negative feelings toward supervision, work, pay, promotions, and co-workers. Falcione, McCoskey, and Daly (1977) found that the first factor, satisfaction with supervisor, accounted for 77% of the variance in job satisfaction among Federal employees. Supervisor-subordinate satisfaction may be defined as interpersonal attraction or having positive feelings about one's supervisor or subordinate and the relationship (Farrell and Rusbult, 1981). Based on this notion of supervisor-subordinate satisfaction, the interpersonal communication model of relational development predicts that the more positive one's perceived understanding, the more one is attracted to and satisfied with the job; conversely the more negative one's perceived understanding, the more one is repelled by and dissatisfied with an ongoing supervisor-subordinate relationship.

According to the interpersonal communication model, one's job satisfaction depends on one's perceived understanding experienced in working relationships. It may be recalled from Chapters Two and Three that self-concept support produces perceived understanding. Because research shows that perceived understanding may not be as important initially as other factors in interpersonal attraction but plays a more important role in relational satisfaction during later stages of relationship development, the interpersonal communication model suggests that in latter phases of relational development persons are in general motivated to maximize mutual perceived understanding while minimizing perceived misunderstanding. Therefore, satisfaction with and attraction to a job is a result of the disparity between the individuals perceived understanding and misunderstanding in their working relationships.

Moreover, as presented in Chapter Four, a neutral point also plays an important role in relationship satisfaction. This point exists where both the feelings of being understood and misunderstood are minimal and is determined by the degree of confirmation, rejection, and disconfirmation experienced in previous work-related experiences. Therefore, to assess the degree of satisfaction with and attraction to the present job, workers evaluate their present working relationships in relation to their neutral point.

Job Commitment

Farrell and Rusbult (1981) argue that lack of emotional commitment is a better predictor of disengagements from employment than relational dissatisfaction alone. They define job commitment as the tendency to maintain one's employment situation and feel attached to it psychologically. Within this view of job commitment, the interpersonal communication model predicts that while job satisfaction is expected to remain unchanged with changes in the value of alternative relationships, investment size, and system constraints, job commitment is expected to decrease with increases in the value of alternative relationships, such as alternative jobs, but is expected to increase with increases in investment size and system constraints. This expectation is derived from the interdependency among the value of alternative relationships, the investment size, and social system constraints.

The *Value of alternative relationships* has been shown to be an important comparison level for assessing the attractiveness of the present job (Farrell and Rusbult, 1981). According to the interpersonal communication model, one may predict that the more value one places on another job opportunity, the less one feels emotionally committed to the present job. When an alternative relationship is perceived as more attractive than one's present relationship, termination, such as quitting or being fired, becomes a possibility. Until this value is reached any job is likely to continue simply because the job satisfaction ratio is, at least, "barely tolerable," and in some cases may even range into the "acceptable," or perhaps on into the "very favorable."

The *size of investments* (Farrell and Rusbult, 1981) and *system constraints* (Pascale, 1985) have been shown to affect commitment in supervisor-subordinate relationships. The interpersonal communication model predicts that the more one invests in the present interpersonal relationship, the more one feels emotionally committed to it. Viewing system constraints as perceived pressures from one's social networks, the model also predicts that the more supervisors and subordinates perceive system constraints, the more they feel emotionally committed to their relationship.

Paradigm Tests

While organizations require a certain amount of order and consistency, the precise combination of behaviors and attitudes that "work" in one company are likely to be different from those in another organization (Redding, 1972). To achieve a necessary level of coordination, an organization uses procedures and controls in a manner that may be described as a socialization process (Pascale, 1985). Thus, some degree of socialization is an inescapable necessity for organizational effectiveness. The aim of socialization is to develop attitudes, habits, and values that encourage cooperation, integrity, and communication.

The adaptation of a general theory of interpersonal communication and relational development to supervisor and subordinate relationships provides a useful and practical understanding of how formal work organizations socialize employees through interaction with individual self-concepts and by influencing the development of one's interpersonal relationships (Cushman and Cahn 1985). In the following two subsections, I intend to examine supervisor-subordinate relationship development in the context of two common paradigm tests involving relational assessment and reassessment: the employment interview and employee appraisal.

Assessment: Employment Interview

Recruitment is the organizational equivalent of "romance." Hiring someone is like marriage—and a broken engagement is preferable to a

messy divorce. Recruiters are expected to get deeper than first impressions. Their skill and intuition are developed by intensive training. A
great deal of thought is given articulating precisely and concretely the
traits that count.... The screening process causes one to reveal
oneself....

                    R. Pascale, "The Paradox of Corporate Culture:
                    Reconciling Ourselves to Socialization"

The employment interview is interesting because it represents the
first opportunity for the development of a subordinate-supervisor
relationship (Cahn, 1976). The interview is a time in which those
involved consciously explore behavioral, identity, and evaluative preferred self-concepts, and form a potential relationship based on the
nature and extent of self-validation. The interviewer may or may not be
a potential supervisor of the job applicant. Although the interviewer
may not be the prospective supervisor, he or she serves to reinforce the
organization's expectations in a manner similar to the role served by the
supervisor. In addition, at some point in the interviewing process, an
applicant eventually meets his or her prospective supervisor. Therefore,
for our purposes, the prospective employer and interviewer are one and
the same.

At the first stage of the interpersonal communication process, interviewer meets applicant. The purpose of communication at this stage is to
present and receive information regarding one another's behavioral,
identity, and evaluative real and ideal self-concepts. Each should realize
that the scope, depth, and configuration of their self-object relationships
constrain the number and type of employers or applicants who can
effectively relate to them. This is another way of looking at the maxim,
"right person, right job."

At the second stage of the process, both the interviewer and the
applicant compares his or her own self-concept with that of the other
person. Each ascertains an impression that he or she makes on the other,
and compares it to his or her own self-concept. If either finds a significant difference, he or she should determine the reasons for the disparity
and work to create a better foundation for future interviews.

At the third stage, both interviewer and applicant form an interpersonal relationship based on each person's comparison of his or her self-
concept and the impression created. In actually, this realization may
only take a few minutes (Zunin and Zunin, 1973). At this stage, the interviewer and applicant may experience the mutual realization that they
are both being understood. Since a goal of most employment interviews
is to develop a favorable interpersonal relationship between the inter-

viewer and applicant, presumably they will attempt to disclose favorable self-concepts, which are then received as intended. However, experienced people know that this is not always the case. The interview can result in an unfavorable relationship if either of the following two problems occurs: The interviewer or applicant fails to intend to present a favorable self-concept, or the interviewer or applicant intends to display a favorable self-concept, but it is not received by the other as intended.

Tschirgi (1972) found that recruiters are more impressed with how well job applicants communicate with them in the interview than they are with impressive dossiers, unless such information is particularly noteworthy. Therefore, the interpersonal communication process is useful because it emphasizes the importance of listening, assertion, and collaborating skills in the employment interview. As described in Chapter Three, these skills improve one's ability to understand others and enable others to make themselves more clearly understood. First, if their primary purpose is to determine one another's self-object relationships, the interviewer and applicant must be very clear on the type of information they are providing, be it a thought, feeling, intention, or action. It is important that each assert symbolic information that clarifies his or her relationship to concepts or objects that are important to the other. Second, each must listen effectively to determine whether one another's statements are asserting or denying relationships to objects. Third, the interviewer and applicant have available at least two strategies for clarifying their understanding of each other's statements. They can check out each other's statements in order to assist self-concept presentation. In addition, one may feed back to the other what he or she heard or observed. Assertion and listening skills enable both the interviewer and applicant to avoid erroneous assumptions and thereby to enhance accurate perception of the other's self-concepts.

Having described the role of interpersonal communication in the employment interview, I next turn to a subsequent task, employee appraisal.

Reassessment: Employee Appraisal

Employee appraisal refers to more or less formal occasions in which supervisors feed back to subordinates an evaluation of their task performance, including attitude potential, and interpersonal relations. From the supervisor's standpoint, employee evaluation may serve to correct employee deficiencies and increase productivity. From the employee's standpoint, the evaluation may serve to motivate, guide, reward, and please. At a minimum, subordinates hope to avoid being discouraged, confused, punished, or offended. Because employee evaluation presents a challenge to supervisor-subordinate relationships, it represents a serious area of concern for students of interpersonal communication (Cahn, 1979; Cahn and Tubbs, 1983). If handled improperly, the appraisal may cause the subordinate to feel apathetic toward the job, resulting in lack of cooperation and perhaps in the eventual termination of one's employment. Tactful handling, however, offers opportunities to motivate subordinates, direct their energies toward company goals, and build favorable supervisor-subordinate relationships (Kindall and Gatza, 1976).

At the first stage of the interpersonal communication process, the supervisor initiates an appraisal of the job performance of a particular subordinate. Each brings to the appraisal interview behavioral, identity, and evaluative real and ideal self-concepts. At the initial stage of the process, the supervisor and subordinate disclose information regarding these self-concepts.

At the second stage, the supervisor and subordinate compare their own self-conceptions with the concept each finds the other has formed of him or her. Each needs to know what impression he or she has made on the other, and each compares that impression with his or her own self-concept. These comparisons are based primarily on past and present symbolic information.

At the third stage of the process, the nature of the existing supervisor-subordinate relationship may change as a result of each person's comparison of his or her self-concept and the impression created. It is at this stage that the participants may experience the mutual feeling that they are both being understood.

As for the employment interview, the application of a theory of interpersonal communication to employee appraisal is a paradigm test that emphasizes the importance of listening, assertion, and collaborating skills. These skills better enable the supervisor and subordinate to understand one another and to make themselves understood. The process involves the following steps. First, they must assert what they think, feel, want, and do. Second, they must determine whether these statements are instances of an identity, behavioral, or evaluative self-object relationship. Third, they must use two strategies to clarify each person's understanding of statements made by the other: They can each check out the other's statements to assist self-concept presentation, and they can feed back to the other what he or she heard or observed.

Summary

In Chapter Eight, a general theory of disengagement and re-engagement, an interpersonal communication model, was adapted to the supervisor-subordinate relationship process in order to predict the degree of job commitment and job satisfaction at different stages of development or deterioration. The view expressed here is that communication quality in work relationships promotes both individual and relationship growth. The first is reflected by increased feelings of self-regard, while the latter is realized by increased job satisfaction. An application to the subject or work of the approach to human communication and interpersonal relationships presented in the first four chapters of this book suggests that a supervisor's and subordinate's self-regard and job satisfaction are the result of their self-concept accuracy, positive self-concept support, and communication skill. These are the criteria for judging the quality of a communication environment in a supervisor-subordinate relationship to determine whether such a relationship warrants continuation, change, or termination.

It is clear that a key factor in a successful employment is comparative in nature. Job commitment involves frequent comparisons to determine whether the supervisor-subordinate relationship is more or less desirable than the available alternatives. If a working relationship has only minor problems, it is unlikely that either person will take major steps to rectify the situation. More troublesome working relationship may not motivate one to view an alternative as being more desirable because of investments that have accumulated and social system constraints. When a working relationship becomes a disaster, however, watch out, since practically any alternative may appear more desirable.

NINE

Teacher-Student Relationships

If the creation of an atmosphere of acceptance, understanding, and respect is the most effective basis for facilitating the learning which is
called therapy, then might it not be the basis for the learning which is
called education? If the outcome of this approach to therapy is a person
who is not only better informed in regard to himself, but who is better
able to guide himself intelligently in new situations, might a similar outcome be hoped for in eduation? It is questions of this sort which plague
the counselor who is also a teacher.

C. Rogers, *Client-Centered Therapy*

Introduction

Rogers recommends that teachers trust students to learn. By so
doing, the teacher creates a classroom climate that respects the students' integrity and that is personally meaningful to each and every student. Instead, many teachers believe that they must act as the source of
students' motivation to learn. They see themselves as sources and
organizers of information about a given field of knowledge. They use
examinations to coerce the student toward the teacher's goals.

Branan (1972) and Silberman (1970) report that there is increasing
student alienation toward school and learning. This dissatisfaction may
be the result of teacher training programs that emphasize primarily subject matter competency. Wittmer and Myrick (1974) estimate that
teachers respond to students' feelings either positively or negatively less
than 1% of the time. Even worse is the discovery that in their classroom
behaviors, teachers frequently have a negative impact on students' self-
concepts. Students report cases that involve "humiliation in front of a
class, unfairness in evaluation, destroying self-confidence, personality
conflicts, and embarrassment" (Branan, 1972: 82). In addition, "actual
prescriptive models involving interpersonal variables and effects on the
teacher-student relationship are noticeably absent from teacher training objectives" (Sorensen, 1981: 1).

There are at least two trends in teacher education that are of special
interest to teachers and students of communication and interpersonal
relationships. The first trend is toward increasing recognition that com-

munication variables function in the instructional environment as they do in a broader social context (Sorensen, 1981). At least three constructs from interpersonal communication research have been linked with the student evaluation of their teachers: self-disclosure (Sorensen, 1981), communicator style, and interpersonal solidarity (Andersen, Norton, and Nussbaum, 1979). According to Scott and Nussbaum (1981: 51), some researchers take the position that, in spite of its unique features, the instructional environment is also a "microcosm of the larger, interpersonal communication environment." The realization that the role of communication in the teaching process is similar to the role of communication in other social relationships necessitates the investigation of what a teacher says and does, along with students' perception of these words and actions.

The second trend is toward an increasing awareness that some therapeutic and counseling variables, which also happen to be of interest to communication scholars, operate in teacher-student relationships as they do in professional helping relationships. In the teaching of any subject, according to Wittmer and Myrick, (1974), it is important that the teacher's role be that of a helper and facilitator of personal growth. They go on to say that facilitative teaching includes "the reflection of feeling response," in which the teacher conveys to the student the feeling of being understood. Presumably teachers can learn how to communicate caring, respect, and understanding to their students through the skillful use of words and actions. The resultant feeling of being understood, as a positive teacher-student orientation, functions as a mediating variable in the process of interpersonal growth and subject matter learning.

It is the purpose of this chapter to adapt a general theory of interpersonal communication and relationship development to the classroom. Specifically, I intend to (1) describe the criteria underlying quality communication environments surrounding teacher-student relationships, (2) discuss self-concept support in traditional and contemporary educational institutions, and (3) discuss the role of perceived understanding in teacher evaluation by students. The key question is this: What do students consider when evaluating a teacher?

Quality Teacher-Student Communication Environment

It is the purpose of this section to describe a quality communication environment and to locate the appropriate criteria involved in assessing teacher-student relationships and the role of interpersonal communication in the continuation of a satisfying and growing relationship. Specifically, this section deals with self-concept accuracy, preferred self-concept support, interpersonal communication skill, and the usefulness of a quality communication environment.

Teachers and students must accurately identify the unique scope, depth, and configuration of one another's preferred self-concept. Vital to one's self-understanding and relational growth is a capacity to objectify and reflect on one's self and to pattern the other's expectations for one in an accurate and realistic manner. Inaccurate self-presentation or self-perception by either the teacher or the student leads to self-concept and relationship disintegration. It is clear that when one communicates expectations that are beyond the other's capacity, the results may be perceived as individual or relational failure. Thus, each person has the responsibility of attempting to accurately perceive the other and of helping the other accurately perceive one's preferred self-concept.

Students and teachers must provide support for each other's preferred identity, evaluative, and behavioral self-concept characteristics. In education, some researchers refer to this as interpersonal functioning (Berenson, 1971). Positive self-concept support in the form of recognition, acknowledgment, acceptance, and involvement is essential to one's feelings of self-worth and satisfaction, and any teacher-student relationship that contains a preponderance of utterances showing indifference, imperviousness, and disqualification will contribute to a lower self-regard and relational satisfaction.

Teacher-student relationships are enhanced by skillful interpersonal communication (Carkhuff, 1971). Having accurately discovered one's own and the other's self-concept, a teacher and a student must negotiate into their relationship those self-concept characteristics that are necessary for personal growth and relational satisfaction, and negotiate out of the relationship those that interfere. Negotiation that is collaborative in nature requires self-assertiveness, being honest about one's self, solicitation techniques, and effective listening to create an atmosphere in which a teacher and a student can be assertive. These two qualities characterize a unique approach to teacher-student relationships. Being open and honest with one another and allowing each other freedom of expression and room to grow are important forms of self-concept support that produce feelings of being understood, thereby creating a basis for a successful relationship.

Competence in interaction also refers to the effective use of messages aimed at objectifying, analyzing, evaluating, and synthesizing a teacher's and a student's self-concepts, the nature of the relationship, and the quality/quantity of communication itself. The specific com-

munication skills include effective listening, self-assertion, and collaboration. When applied to teacher-student communication problems, this
reflection process, which is called relational reassessment, is aimed at
realigning self-concepts, the relationship, and communication patterns.

In teacher-student interaction, the idea of a quality communication
environment serves three useful purposes. First, it presents criteria for
the assessment of one's present relationship. If one is not receiving
encouragement or permitted to collaborate in resolving course-related
conflicts, a teacher or student probably finds the relationship less than
satisfying. Second, it serves as a goal for the satisfactory renegotiation of
one's present relationship. One should try to change the relationship to
allow for more personal growth and satisfaction before considering termination. Third, the idea of a quality communication environment provides the dissatisfied student with what ought to be an important
consideration in the selection of a subsequent teacher. Some teachers
do not change because to give the student more self-concept support or
to attempt to collaborate more in the resolution of problems in class
interferes with that teacher's satisfaction or growth (which may be at the
student's expense). In a subsequent situation or relationship, the student
needs to select a teacher who is more supportive and more collaborative
in his or her approach to resolving course-related problems. Thus, with
the prerequisite knowledge and skill, one can attempt to repair a
deteriorating teacher-student relationship, or, failing that, one can
attempt to form a superior relationship the next time around.

In sum, self-concept accuracy, preferred self-concept support, and
interpersonal communication skill are criteria for judging the quality of
a teacher-student communication environment. These are proposed as
standards for assessing a teacher-student relationship to determine
whether such a relationship warrants continuation, change, or termination.

Self-Concept Support in Traditional
and Nontraditional Classrooms

How does one assess a teacher-student relationship? If teachers
and their students are to exert any measure of control over their self-
concepts and the nature of their relationships, such assessments are
necessary. The quest for conditions that promote a sense of personal
worth and relational satisfaction leads to both self-concept accuracy and
preferred self-concept support. It is my position that there are specific
factors that are key in American education, because, while some

teachers operate on a traditional model of teacher-student relationships, more successful teachers strive for a more contemporary model. In this section, I describe the self-concept support relevant to two different models of teacher-student relationships, traditional and contemporary.

Traditional Teacher-Student Relationships

The traditional model for teacher-student relationships was geared to the traditional manufacturing industry (Cahn, 1985). Everyone who recalls his or her school days remembers vividly the invariant organizational structure of the teacher-led class. As they moved up, grade by grade, students remained in this rigid scheme, gaining no experience with fluid, rapidly changing organizational systems or with substituting one type of organizational form for a different type. In addition, the pattern of movement conformed to the upward mobility in industry and to the "assembly line mode of thought." In a system based on authority, teacher-student relationships were one of dominance versus submission, informed versus naive, and active (teacher) versus passive (students). Thus, in the traditional learning model, one person was viewed as a high-ranking teacher of facts and skills, while the other persons were viewed as a class of low-ranking, naive students there to be taught. While in the past successful teachers may have adhered to the traditional model, I believe that many will find greater success today by adopting a more contemporary model of teacher-student relationships.

Contemporary Teacher-Student Relationships

A new model of teacher-student relationships is emerging in contemporary American educational institutions (Toffler, 1970). This model is especially designed to meet the needs of students who are potential workers in high tech and service-oriented industries. These needs are to learn how to cope with rapid change, how to think, how to make decisions, how to solve problems, how to develop insights, and how to be more creative. Usually, these needs are not met by the traditional model of the teacher-student relationship, which is based on obedience to authority and encourages assembly line thinking.

To teach students how to cope with rapid change, the new model uses variable methods of instruction in a variety of "classroom" settings. While the traditional model relied heavily on the lecture method, which permitted only vertical unidirectional communication and hierarchical organization, the new model emphasizes networking—in that it features more horizontal communication, which is interactive and participatory (Hogrebe, 1981). The "classroom" is a mixture of inside and outside

learning activities, a combination of lectures, class and small group discussions, case studies, on site visits, guest lectures, films or videotapes, a
variety of structured and some unstructured games and simulations, and
a combination of opportunities to speak and write. In contrast to the
traditional model in which students were expected to sit, take notes, and
be taught, the contemporary model emphasizes more equality and informality as the teacher occupies more of a role of facilitator of change and
of helper in adapting to this change (Cahn, 1985).

To teach students how to think, make decisions, and solve problems,
the contemporary model avoids the traditional practice of basing grades
primarily on recall tests. One of the interesting outcomes derived from
computer technology is the realization that humans think differently
from machines. The computer can store facts, manipulate them logic-
ally, and transmit them, but it cannot make decisions as can humans.
When people perceive facts, store them, and recall them for a test, they
are thinking like a computer and may some day be replaced by one if
they continue to think that way. Humans have the unique capacity to
abstract and concretize, use variable logics, manipulate facts and symbols, and persuade others in a way that a computer cannot. The contemporary model exploits this capability by encouraging students to learn
how to think, make decisions, and solve problems.

The Role of Perceived Understanding in
Teacher Evaluation by Students

Why are some students more satisfied with their teachers than
others? Why are some more emotionally committed to their classes?
Why do some students finish their studies while others do not?

Effective teaching requires an understanding of the "nature of the
relationship between the teacher and the student" (Krypsin and Feldhusen, 1974: 2). According to Coombs (1959), effective teaching
involves effecting relating. An effective teacher is one "who elicits positive orientations from students" (Kearney and McCroskey, 1980: 533).
Although knowledge about subject matter is important, teachers "cannot force the pupil to learn; what she (he) can do is produce a situation
which the pupil will find conducive to learning" (Guba and Getzels,
1955: 335). While education researchers have shown that affective
orientations toward the academic subject (Crosswhite, 1972), school
(Lunn, 1969; Shepps and Shepps, 1971), self (Brookover, Thomas and
Paterson, 1964), and even specific instructional units (Bloom, 1976) are
related to student learning outcomes, only recently has the concept of

"affect toward instructor" received attention by communication researchers (Scott and Wheeless, 1977). Andriate (1982: 792) states the following:

> Investigations of the relationship implied in teacher-student interactions should specify ways in which teachers contribute to student orientations and motivations toward learning and generate specific criteria for establishing professionally appropriate classroom relationships.

The present approach, an interpersonal model of relational development, is designed to extend research in communication (Knapp, 1978; Friedman, Giffin, and Patton, 1978; Cushman, Valentinsen, and Dietrich, 1982; Cushman and Cahn, 1985) to the process of teacher-student relationship development, measured by teacher evaluation by students. The interpersonal communication model assumes that teachers and students are in general motivated to maximize perceived understanding and minimize perceived misunderstanding. Presumably, the role played by perceived understanding in the development of positive teacher-student relationships contributes to a situation that students find conducive to learning.

The interpersonal communication model of relational development predicts that the more positive students' perceived understanding, the more they are attracted to and satisfied with their teachers; conversely, the more negative their perceived understanding, the more students are repelled by and dissatisfied with their ongoing teacher-student relationships. The purpose of this section is to describe the background, method, and results of a study designed to test this hypothesis.

Background of the Study

Intuitively, expertness and character are important traits associated with members of the teaching profession. Researchers suggest that near the end of the course, students evaluate a teacher's "expertness" using global judgments about his or her personality (McGlone and Anderson, 1973; Cooper, Stewart, and Gudykunst, 1982). Some evidence exists that perceived understanding plays a role in a student's perceptions of another person's expertness and character. Cahn and Frey (1982) randomly paired sixty college students and allowed them twenty minutes to discuss and advise one another regarding their choice of topics for a persuasive speech. Immediately following the discussion, the subjects were instructed to complete the perceived understanding instrument (Cahn and Shulman, 1984) and the expertness and character scales of Giffin's

(1968) Trust Differential. Students who scored high in perceived understanding differed significantly on the trust measure and its two subscales from subjects with low perceived understanding scores. Cahn and Frey concluded that the feeling of being understood or misunderstood contributed significantly to the development of perceived expertness and character. Thus, the more one feels understood, the more likely one perceives the other as high on the expertness and character scales of Giffin's Trust Differential.

Teacher evaluation is of interest in many educational institutions. At some colleges and universities, teaching evaluation is a factor in such personnel decisions as hiring, tenure, and promotion. Although its use is widespread, teacher evaluation has been the subject of little systematic research (Meeth, 1976). Yet, one of the most prevalent means of measuring teacher effectiveness is through student evaluations (Cooper, Stewart, and Gudykunst, 1982).

At least one study indicates that perceived understanding plays a role in the evaluation of teachers by students. Cahn (1982) asked fifty-three undergraduate students enrolled in a public speaking course to complete the perceived understanding instrument (Cahn and Shulman, 1984) and to evaluate the teacher (who remained anonymous) of the course immediately preceding the public speaking class. The student evaluations of the teacher consisted of eleven questions pertaining to four different aspects of teaching: the teacher's handling of the students, students' attitude toward the class, students' perceptions of teaching/lecturing techniques, and students' perceptions of the teacher's level of knowledge and attitudes toward the subject. Statistical analysis of the data (using student's t-test for independent samples with a .05 confidence level) showed that the subjects who scored highest in perceived understanding gave the teacher significantly more favorable ratings on all four aspects than did the students who scored lowest in perceived understanding.

While it appears that perceived understanding is a factor in the development of positive teacher-student relationships as reflected in teacher evaluation, it is not clear whether this is one of the more important factors. Moreover, it is not clear what specific teacher communication behaviors contribute to students' perceived understanding. Therefore, a study (Cahn, 1984) was conducted to answer these research questions.

Method

Seventy-nine university students (forty-two males and thirty-seven females) who were enrolled in an introductory communication course participated as subjects. With a grade point average of 2.9 (out of 4), they consisted of thirty-four freshmen, twenty-five sophomores, ten juniors, and ten seniors. A survey consisting of a set of measuring instruments was administered to the subjects during a regularly scheduled class hour near the end of the semester. The subjects were instructed to fill out the rating scales in reference to the professor of the last class period attended prior to the present class hour. This approach was taken to add generalizability to the results; while the evaluation of a single target instructor suggests greater control, the findings are more difficult to generalize beyond that one teaching personality or type of course. The evaluations were anonymous, and the time spent on the survey was twenty minutes.

First, the survey consisted of a standardized students' instructional rating form used to evaluate teachers throughout the New York State system of higher education. According to Kulik and McKeachie (1975), students' evaluations of teachers on commonly used rating forms tend to be reliable. Second, the survey included the perceived understanding instrument (Cahn and Shulman, 1984). Third, the survey contained five-point rating scales for seven additional variables considered relevant to the evaluation of teachers:

1. Was the teacher well prepared for class?

2. Did the teacher communicate course content clearly?

3. Did the teacher stimulate interest in the course?

4. Did the teacher challenge students intellectually?

5. Was the teacher available outside of class?

6. Did the teacher hold students to high standards?

7. What was the students' expected course grade?

Finally, unlike some studies that used more global types of teacher communication behavior (e.g., Scott and Nussbaum, 1981), the survey consisted of a twenty-five item questionnaire of four categories of specific communication behaviors:

Type 1: Classroom-platform behavior (use of eye contact, voice, gesture/ movement, facial expressions, distance between teacher and students, and confidence)

Type 2: Student-centered instructional strategies (listening, treating students as individuals, stating expectations, giving feedback, learning students' names).

Type 3: Democratic-participatory teaching style (democratic classroom procedures, effective questioning techniques, group projects, student discussion, putting students in class at ease).

Type 4: Self-disclosure (information imparted by the teacher to the students about his/her family, educational experiences, relationship with other faculty, personal beliefs, and future plans).

Statistical analyses were conducted in two stages. First, to describe the degree of contribution of perceived understanding and the seven other factors thought relevant to the development of teacher-student relationships, a mutliple regression analysis was incorporated in which all eight factors were treated as independent variables and were brought to bear in predicting scores on the dependent variable, that is, students' evaluation of teachers. Second, to identify specific teacher communication behaviors that contribute to the students' perception of being understood or misunderstood by their teachers, Pearson product-moment correlations were computed between students' perceive understanding scores and the students' perceptions of each of the four types of teacher communication behavior. As an additional item of interest, a correlation was also computed between the students' expected course grade and both their evaluation of the teacher and their perceived understanding scores.

Results and Discussion

Of the eight variables thought to be relevant to teacher evaluation by students, the most potent variable to emerge at step one of the regression analysis was perceived understanding, which accounted for 44% of the total variance. At step two, high standards emerged as the next highest predictor (7% of the variance). At step three, "stimulating" appeared as the third most influential variable (4% of the variance). The remaining five variables typically believed to be relevant to teacher evaluation accounted for only 3% of the variance, when the first three (perceived understanding, high standards, and "stimulating") were controlled. Together, the eight variables accounted for 58% of the total variance.

Moreover, three of the four categories of teacher communication behaviors correlated at least moderately with perceived understanding (and were statistically significant at $p < .01$). They were classroom/platform behavior ($r = .45$), student-centered behavior ($r = .42$), and democratic-participatory teaching style ($r = .44$). The fourth category, teacher self-disclosure, correlated very slightly ($r = .08$) and was nonsignificant at p>.05. The correlation between students' expected grades and perceived understanding was .23 (p<.05), and between the expected grade and the overall instructor rating it was .24 (p<.05).

This study is not without its limitations. First, the use of a single introductory communication class of students at a university may limit generalizability of the results to every type of teacher-student relationship imaginable. However, since the students were primarily freshmen and sophomores who represented a variety of majors or were undecided, and since the university was a state-supported (public) institution, the above limitation may not be as severe as it might seem. Second, some of the concepts were measured by one-item scales, which may be less reliable than multiple-item scales. However, with the exception of the instructor rating, the single-item scales dealt with specific, concrete factors typically believed to be relevant to teacher evaluation (i.e., was the teacher well-prepared for class?). Moreover, the instructor rating was an overall or general rating that followed several more specific rating scales, which suggests that in some way it represents them. Third, the present approach, which maximized the number of teachers and types of classes being evaluated, failed to control for the differences in personalities, class size, teaching methods (i.e., lecture versus discussion or lab), and course content. While it might be interesting to focus on one method of instruction, the present approach was taken to add generalizability to the results.

To the extent that the findings of this study are generalizable, the results help to clarify the role of perceived understanding in teacher evaluation as a measure of the quality of teacher-student relationships. While an earlier study (Cahn, 1982) suggested that perceived understanding plays an important role in the development of positive teacher-student relationships as measured by student evaluation of teachers, the present study supports the claim that it is *the most important variable.* Other variables considered important in the teacher evaluation process contribute *less* to the overall evaluation of teachers than perceived understanding. Holding students to high standards of performance and stimulating interest in the course were considered more important by the students than course-grade expectations, availability of the teacher outside of class, and the clear communication of course content. Challenging the students intellectually has little impact, and being well-prepared for class has practically none.

In the present study, the students filled out a survey in reference to the professor of the last class period attended prior to the present class hour. Since the students included a diversity of undergraduate majors and some who were undecided, the procedure resulted in the evaluation of many professors teaching a wide variety of courses. In spite of this diversity, it appears that the subjects in this study tended to view the teacher's preferred role less as the source of factual information (content) and more as a facilitator of learning (process). They generally preferred teachers who created a situation conducive to learning, set high standards of performance, and stimulated their interest in the course. Thus, *what* the teachers taught tended to have less impact than *how* the subject was taught.

When it comes to developing positive teacher-student relationships, the students indicated that grades were not one of the more important considerations. In fact, student grade expectations correlated very low with both the students' evaluation of teachers and the students' perception of being understood or misunderstood by teachers. While it may be difficult to convince teachers of the fact (Armour, 1979), the results of this study were consistent with those of other recent studies that found that grade expectations did not affect students' evaluations of teachers (Abrami, Perry, and Leventhal, 1980; Cooper, Stewart, and Gudykunst, 1982). Moreover, the nonfacilitation style embedded in the predominently task-oriented professor who emphasized knowledge, thoroughly prepared and organized the lecture, clarified ideas, maintained regularly scheduled and convenient office hours, graded students very high, and challenged the students intellectually did *not* fare well when evaluated by students in this study.

Additional results revealed that specific teacher communication behaviors enhanced perceived understanding, which in turn promoted the development of more positive teacher-student relationships as measured by teacher evaluation. Three types of teacher verbal and nonverbal communication behaviors clearly contributed to the students' perception of being understood by the teachers. Correlating at least moderately with perceived understanding, *classroom/platform behaviors* include use of eye contact, voice, gesture/movement, facial expressions, distance between teacher and students, and confidence. Obviously, a dull lecturer not only loses student interest but also conveys to the students a lack of respect for them as listeners. Anyone who presents a monotone with no variety in gestures, movement, or enthusiasm/dynamism has forgotten what it is like to be a student attending a dull lecture.

The second type of teacher communication behavior, which also correlated moderately with perceived understanding, consisted of the following *student-centered instructional strategies:* listening to the students, expressing interest in them as individuals, clearly stating what he or she expects from them, providing frequent and immediate feedback on their progress, and learning students' names. Thus, social and emotional (affect) variables, such as being personable, treating students as individuals, and facilitating rather than dictating or impeding the students' learning efforts are essential features of the instructional process. While the approach is clear, the size of many undergraduate courses makes it difficult to deal with students on a personal basis. More individualized instructional strategies that are useful in large classes are needed.

The third type, which correlated moderately with perceived understanding, consisted of a *democratic and participatory teaching style,* including the use of democratic classroom procedures, feedback from students (such as effective questioning techniques), group projects, student discussion, and efforts to put students at ease in class. Again, class size may make it difficult for some teachers to rely on more participatory forms of instruction; however, democratic procedures in which students have input into the nature of the course and the learning process enhances the development of positive teacher-student relationships.

With regard to the development of positive interpersonal relationships between teachers and students, as measured by student evaluation of teachers, self-disclosure *failed* to emerge as effective teacher behavior in this study. Teacher self-disclosure was measured by seven rating scales covering information imparted by the teacher to students about his or her family, education experiences, relationships with other faculty, personal beliefs, and future plans. Defined in this way, there was only a very slight correlation ($r=.08$) between self-disclosure and perceived understanding. Owing to the way in which self-disclosure was operationalized in this study, the possibility remains that some statements that manifest care, respect, and understanding may have a positive effect on teacher-student relationships. Such statements are "I care about my students," "I go out of my way to help students," "I don't believe in punishing students." Poorly evaluated teachers, on the other hand, presumably self-disclose attitudes and opinions that do not impress some students or may even offend them.

It would seem reasonable to assume that having discovered some of the teacher communication behaviors that make students feel understood, instructional training might improve teacher's communication skills. Berenson (1971) showed that after twenty-five hours of training in such interpersonal skills as accurate empathy, positive regard, genuiness, concreteness, immediacy, significant other references, and confrontation, student teachers used significantly more positive reinforcing behaviors in their teaching and were rated by their teaching supervisors as more competent in the classroom. It seems likely that a similar training program in communication skills designed to make students feel understood would have similar results.

In general, the implications of this study are three-fold. First, primarily task-oriented teachers who ignore the social and emotional aspects of the teaching process tend to fail to convey to students the perception of being understood, tend to miss opportunities to develop more positive teacher-student relationships, and tend to do poorly on teacher evaluations by students. This instructional environment may not be conducive to learning, and runs contrary to the notion of the "teacher-helper." Second, primarily socio-emotionally oriented teachers who place very little emphasis on the task aspects of the teaching process tend to fail to challenge students intellectually and to lack adequate preparation for class. Third, a balance between task and socio-emotional orientations may be the preferable instructional strategy. Certainly, teachers should spend some class time and effort analyzing the needs and interests of the students, learning about them, learning their names, and conveying caring, respect, and understanding to them throughout the course. In addition, teaches should devote time and energy to clearly communicating course content, objectives, and grade expectations, intellectually challenging students, and thoroughly preparing for class.

Summary

In teacher-student relationships, the quality of the relationship rather than the content of the course may be the most important factor determining the effectiveness of teachers. Self-concept accuracy, preferred self-concept support, and interpersonal communication skill are proposed as standards for assessing a teacher-student relationship to determine whether such a relationship warrants continuation, change, or termination.

Assessing a teacher-student relationship is no easy task. Yet, such assessments are necessary if teachers and their students are to exert any measure of control over the growth and decay of their self-concepts and their relationships. The search for a quality teacher-student relationship depends on self-concept accuracy and preferred self-concept support, but the nature of what constitutes accurate and preferred self-concept support has changed as teacher-student relationships moved from a traditional model of teacher-student relationships to a more contemporary model.

Because the traditional model for teacher-student relationships was geared to industry, the pattern of movement conformed to the pattern of upward mobility in industry and to the "assembly line mode of thought." In a system based on authority, teacher-student relationships were one of dominance versus submission, informed versus naive, and active (teacher) versus passive (students). Thus, in the traditional learning model, one person was viewed as a high-ranking teacher of facts and skills, while the other persons were viewed as a class of low-ranking, naive students there to be taught.

A new model of teacher-student relationships is emerging in contemporary American educational institutions. This model is especially designed to meet the needs of students who are potential workers in high tech and service-oriented industries. These needs are to learn how to cope with rapid change, how to think, how to make decisions, how to solve problems, how to develop insights, and how to be creative. These needs are met by variable methods of instruction in a variety of classroom settings, by emphasizing networking—which features more horizontal communication that is interactive and participatory—and by stressing more equality and informality as the teacher occupies more of a role of facilitator of change and of helper in adapting to this change.

Avoiding the traditional practice of basing grades primarily on recall tests, the contemporary model encourages students to learn how to think, make decisions, and solve problems. While successful teachers of another era may have adhered to the traditional model, many will find greater success today by adopting a more contemporary model of teacher-student relationships.

Why are some students more satisfied with their teachers than others? Why are some more emotionally committed to their classes? Why do some students finish their studies while others do not? Effective teaching requires an understanding of the "nature of the relationship between the teacher and the student." The present approach, an interpersonal model of relational development, is designed to extend research in communication to the process of teacher-student relationship development, as measured by teacher evaluation by students. The interpersonal communication model assumes that teachers and students are in general motivated to maximize perceived understanding and minimize perceived misunderstanding. Presumably the role played by perceived understanding in the development of positive teacher-student relationships contributes to a situation which students find conducive to learning.

Intuitively, expertness and character are important traits associated with members of the teaching profession. One line of research found that the feeling of being understood or misunderstood contributed significantly to the development of perceived expertness and character. Therefore, the more one feels understood, the more likely one perceives the other as high on the expertise and character scales of Giffin's Trust Differential.

Teacher evaluation is of interest in many educational institutions. At some colleges and universities, teaching evaluation is a factor in such personnel decisions as hiring, tenure, and promotion. Although its use is widespread, teacher evaluation has been the subject of little systematic research. Yet, one of the most prevalent means of measuring teacher effectiveness is through student evaluations.

While it appears that at least one study indicates that perceived understanding is a factor in the development of positive teacher-students relationships as reflected in teacher evaluation, it is not clear whether this is one of the more important factors. Moreover, it is not clear what specific teacher communication behaviors contribute to students' perceived understanding. Therefore, a study was conducted to answer these research questions. The hypothesis of this study was as follows: The more positive students' perceived understanding, the more they are attracted to and satisfied with their teachers; conversely the more negative their perceived understanding, the more students are repelled by and dissatisfied with their ongoing teacher-student relationships. The hypothesis of this study was confirmed by the findings. To the extent that the findings of this study was generalizable, the results indicated that perceived understanding is *the most important variable* in the development of positive teacher-student relationships, as measured by student evaluation of teachers. Other variables considered important in the teacher evaluation process contributed *less* to the overall evaluation of teachers than perceived understanding. It appears that the subjects in this study tended to view the teacher less as the source of factual information (content) and more as a facilitator of learning (process). They generally preferred teaches who created a situation conducive to learning, set high standards of performance, and stimulated their interest in the course. Thus, *what* the teachers taught tended to have less impact than *how* the subject was taught.

When it comes to developing positive teacher-student relationships, the students indicated that grades were not one of the more important considerations. Moreover, the nonfacilitation style embedded in the predominently task-oriented professor who emphasized knowledge, thoroughly prepared and organized the lecture, clarified ideas, maintained regularly scheduled and convenient office hours, graded students very high, and challenged the students intellectually did *not* fare well when evaluated by students in this study.

Additional results revealed that specific teacher communication behaviors enhanced perceived understanding, which in turn promoted the development of more positive teacher-student relationships, as measured by teacher evaluation. Three types of teacher verbal and non-verbal communication behaviors clearly contributed to the students' perception of being understood by the teachers: *classroom/platform behaviors, student-centered instructional strategies,* and *democratic and participatory teaching style.* Self-disclosure *failed* to emerge as effective teacher behavior in this study.

In general, the implications of this study are three-fold. First, primarily task-oriented teachers who ignore the social and emotional aspects of the teaching process tend to fail to convey to students the perception of being understood, tend to miss opportunities to develop more positive teacher-student relationships, and tend to do poorly on teacher evaluations by students. Second, primarily socio-emotionally oriented teachers who place very little emphasis on the task aspects of the teaching process tend to fail to challenge students intellectually and to lack adequate preparation for class. Third, a balance between task and socio-emotional orientations may be the preferable instructional strategy.

TEN

The Renegotiation of Interpersonal Relationships: A Theory of Reengagement and Relationship Development

A good deal of recent research indicates that a disordered, nonlogical, or unpredictable world is dissatisfying to people. Inconsistency, at least in gross amounts, is aversive, and the person strives to avoid such conditions.... After all, it is the ordered and consistent world that best allows the person to maximize his returns.... If the environment is capricious, his capacity to make a "correct" choice is destroyed.

K. Gergen, *The Psychology of Behavior Exchange*

Introduction

When individuals engage in social interaction that contributes to the development of deterioration of an interpersonal relationship, they are interested in predictability. If interpersonal behavior had no rhyme or reason, there would be no point in reflecting on one's previous experiences (what went wrong?) and contemplating future courses of action (what should I do now?) to improve or disengage from some relationships. Rather, according to Chapter One, one chooses to take steps toward changing some relationships and toward maintaining others to improve, alter, or continue one's situation in life.

Because of a general interest in predicting and controlling interpersonal behaviors, social scientists have developed theories, identified key factors, manipulated them in laboratory and field studies, and report research findings that lend some predictability to the development of interpersonal relationships. Unfortunately, they tend to focus on the study of interpersonal attraction and its antecedents (Aronson and Linder, 1965; Byrne and Nelson, 1965; Gerard and Mathewson, 1966; Insko and Wilson, 1977). While helpful in understanding initial attraction

toward strangers, the findings are not generalizable to later developments in long-term relationships.

A few communication researchers have proposed models of interpersonal attraction in ongoing relationships (Knapp, 1978; Friedman,
Giffin, and Patton, 1978; Cushman, Valentinsen, and Dietrich, 1982).
Each researcher has attempted to identify stages of development and
factors that account for the growth or deterioration. The theory proposed in this book, a rules-based interpersonal communication model, is
in this general tradition. As discussed in Chapters One and Five, rules
function as criteria for choice among goals that define and guide social
behavior. The primary goal of the model is to predict the degree of commitment to and satisfaction with a variety of types of ongoing relationships (e.g., friends, mates, parent-child and supervisor-subordinate) that
differ in duration and involvement. In this chapter, I intend to present a
more concise version of a theory of relationship reengagement and
relationship development by (1) presenting an integrated approach to
the study of human communication; (2) describing an interpersonal
communication model of relationship development derived from the
integrated perspective; and (3) identifying the key communication factors in relationship development and communication competence,
along with hypotheses for future research. The key question with which
this chapter deals is this: What should one consider in selecting another
person for a significant interpersonal relationship?

An Integrated Approach to the
Study of Human Communication

In the fields of human communication and psychology, much of the
research on interpersonal communication and human relationships has
borrowed heavily from social and behavioral research. Since many social
science researchers belong to one of two research orientations—
behaviorists and phenomenologists—they tend to be influenced by one
or the other perspective on research. Unfortunately for the study of
human communication, the division in social and behavioral research
between behaviorists and phenomenologists is problematic and coun-
terproductive. The rift between these "rival camps" contributes to considerable misunderstanding regarding the nature and scope of the
subject matter of human communication and appropriate research
methodology.

Behaviorists, in their application of method to the subject matter,
may give students the impression that every human movement per-

ceived by another communicates something (i.e., one cannot *not* communicate).

> Communication does not refer to verbal, explicit, and intentional transmission of messages alone.... The concept of communication would include all those processes by which people influence one another.... This definition is based upon the premise that all actions and events have communicative aspects, as soon as they are perceived by a human being (Ruesch and Bateson, 1961: 5-6).

Meanwhile, phenomenologists may focus on meanings, interpretative experience, and symbols, but in their application of method to subject matter, they may give some students of communication the impression that the actual method should be of little concern, or that rigor, measurement, and validity are unimportant considerations. Thus, the opposing approaches contribute to confusion as to the proper subject matter and appropriate methods for the study of human communication.

Surprisingly, few resources adhere to an articulated combination of the behaviorists and phenomenological approaches. One notable exception is Jesse Delia and his colleagues at the University of Illinois (1977). Others claim to be eclectic, which usually translates into merely citing the findings and claims of both types in one's review of the literature, without actually integrating the two perspectives into a unified view.

In this section, I intend to reopen the question of whether a combination of perspectives is possible by arguing for integration. To achieve this goal, I will compare and contrast the subject matter and methodology of the behaviorists and phenomenologists, and I will suggest how they may be integrated into a comprehensive approach to the study of human communication.

Behaviorism

The roots of behaviorism's methodology, that is, empiricism, are found in 1674, when John Locke claimed that knowledge is obtained mainly or only through observation. Empirical is a very broad term, referring to data obtained from and based on sensory experience. To be empirical one must employ a means for obtaining objective facts from experience. Observation, an empirical means for acquiring knowledge, is controlled and quantified.

To implement the behavioral orientation, there are typical steps toward research; generally these include stating the problem, anticipating the obstacles to the solution of the problem, and devising ways and means to overcome the difficulties in order to provide a sound answer to the problem of research. More specifically, these characteristic functions include constructing careful designs to facilitate objective observation, refining measurements to classify and describe the data, and using statistics to analyze and interpret the findings.

The behaviorists' use of operationalism—i.e., use of terms that can be measured (quantified)—places dominant consideration on method in the researcher's effort to be objective. Hence, the behaviorist frequently expresses greater concern for the method than for the subject matter. Since behavior is observable and inner experience is not, there is an inherent tendency to reduce any and all experience to behavior. In psychology, behaviorism is so preoccupied with behavior alone that there is inadequate consideration of the less visible elements of personal experience, including the psyche or the self. This preoccupation results in the predicament of a "psychology without a psyche."

The reduction of experience to behavior has carried over from psychology into other fields. In the study of human communication, behaviorists have attempted to reduce the meaning of human communication to the objective dimensions of verbal behavior (Skinner, 1957) or to discriminatory responses of an organism to a stimulus (Stevens, 1950). These definitions are as informative about human communication as the medical definition (a flat EEG) is for the meaning of death.

Behaviorists in psychology, communication, and other fields have attempted to reduce the subjective to the objective. Because objectifying a person converts the human subject into an object, behaviorists have dealt solely with observable behavior, without sufficient caution that the person might be better viewed as a subject. When behaviorists deal exclusively and dogmatically with behavior, they have failed to consider the subjective, experiential side of human life.

Basically, the behavioral approach is productive because it uses the most rigorous methods, such as experimentation, objective data collection, measurement, and statistics. While these were incorporated from the past, behavioral psychologists also have eliminated the least rigorous of methods, such as purely subjective introspection. Yet, as methods are refined and more rigorously designed, behaviorists in communication, psychology, and other disciplines also tend toward reductionism of subject matter.

Phenomenology

Phenomenologists stress consciousness, an awareness of thoughts and feelings. If consciousness causes behavior, then behavior cannot be reduced to a stimulus-response model, nor its causes to sensation or to bodily changes. Consciousness and mental activity are irreducible, aver the phenomenologists. That knowledge is reducible to sense experience is a major assumption of the empirical orientation, which the phenomenologists do not accept. William James (1902), as a tacit phenomenologist, insisted that there must be something more than merely sensory experience. Since there is something more—such as meaning, intention, self-awareness, and intuition—determinism cannot be a valid assumption. Consciousness is a better assumption according to phenomenologists. They ask: Can anyone deny one's own consciousness? Even to doubt one's consciousness requires consciousness. In a similar vein, Franz Bretano spoke of intention and self-consciousness as being characteristic of the psychological (Chisholm, 1960). He distinguished this psychological from the physiological, which could be studied from the assumption of determinism and experimental causation.

An emphasis on self-understanding is also significant, for the force of the phenomenologists through consideration of the self is to place additional value on the person. One of the most important points in phenomenology is its attempt to do justice to the uniqueness of the individual and the uniqueness of the individual's world view.

In contrast to the behaviorists, the phenomenologist attempts to experience the meaning of the subject by granting priority to the subject matter. Such phenomenological experiencing is excluded from strict behaviorists' operationalism. The phenomenological experience is the subject's perception, interpretation, and awareness of phenomena. Thus, phenomenology advocates experientialism as opposed to empirical operationalism. A similar distinction is that the behaviorist observes the object, while, in contrast, the phenomenologist allows the object to appear and present itself before him or her, the perceiver or interpreter.

Phenomenologists are more willing to be influenced by the mystery of the subject matter, while behaviorists are determined to master the subject matter. Mastery often requires elimination of mystery. Phenomenology provides a fresh perception to feelings. It is more trustful of feelings and experiences, which includes an aesthetic awareness of the world that is related to human communication. Therefore, in their study of human communication, implicit and explicit advocates of the phenomenological approach tend to adhere to broad, rich definitions of the subject matter. Martin Buber (1947) defines human communication as genuine dialogue expressed, in I-Thou relationships. Maslow (1967: 195) claims that

> communication between the person and the world ... depends largely
> on their isomorphism ... I include all the processes of perception and of

learning, and all the forms of art and creation. And I include primary process cognition . . . as well as verbal, rational, secondary process communication. I want to speak of what we are blind and deaf to as well as
what gets through to us; of what we express dumbly and unconsciously as
well as what we can verbalize or structure clearly.

According to Stewart (1978: 184), communication is "the dynamic, complex, context dependent communicative 'transaction,' 'reciprocal bond,'
'between,' or 'relationship.'" Johannesen (1971) defined communication as "a two-way dialogic transaction." Unlike the behaviorists' definitions of human communication, the phenomenologists' definitions
seem more significant and broader in scope.

In psychology, speech communication, and other disciplines, the
phenomenologist embraces all experience, not just that which is observable. The phenomenologist intends to broaden the horizon of the researcher to include the whole world, not just that confined to the
laboratory.

The predominant weakness of the phenomenological orientation is
that its methodology fails to contain a means for validating results. Its
constructs and measuring instruments have been described as chaotic
(Wylie, 1961). Without valid constructs, valid and reliable measurement
is impossible. These obstacles are inherent in the orientation. As
phenomenologists persistently deal with personal and private constructs, such as self-regard and self-acceptance, their definitions in-
evitably vary. Operational definitions appear impossible. Because there
are significant differences in the ways people disclose themselves to
others, there is no sufficient consistency from one person to another and
from their responses to various investigators. Also, the problem of
measurement in phenomenology centers on the difficulty of identifying
the subject's self-concept. What is there to measure and in relation to
what standards of measurement? How is the measurement free from
other unknown variables, even unconscious or nonphenomenal factors?
Another obstacle is to distinguish between the phenomenological and
the nonphenomenological determinants of behavior. This obstacle is
related to the difficulty of drawing the boundaries of the phenomenal
field. This construct, the phenomenal field, is so inclusive that it does
not discriminate. The result is that variables are not defined or measured
and explanations abound without adequate plausibility.

An Integrated View of Human Communication

The brief comparison and contrast of two orientations within
human communication research suggest that behaviorism includes both

a subject matter (observable behavior) and an empirical method (operationalism, measurement), just as phenomenology includes a subject matter (subjective experience, meaning) and a hermeneutical method (interpretation). An integrated approach is based on (1) a fusion of subject matters, behavior and meaning, into human action; (2) a fusion of methods, the behaviorists' criteria of reliability and validity and the phenomenologists' criterion of subjectivity, into a unified criterion involving the operationalism of intersubjective experience; (3) a fusion of the major concerns, the behaviorists' concern for method and the phenomenologists' concern for subject matter, into a unified concern for the proper fitting of the method to the problem; and (4) a fusion of goals, the behaviorists' goal of explanation-prediction-control and the phenomenologists' goal of understanding, into a unified goal of prediction through explanation and understanding involving interpretive processes. Figure Four illustrates these propositions. Thus, an integrated view meets the meta-theoretical concerns for the conduct of research on the role of human communication in the formation, maintenance, and disintegration of interpersonal relationships.

In summary, an integrated view holds behaviorism and phenomenology simultaneously in tension. A critical perspective on assumptions underlying research, an integrated view allows diversity of methods and maximizes perspective to render meaningful judgments. It is broad enough to deal with the study of the role of human communication in the development and disintegration of interpersonal relationships, yet flexible enough to give priority to the problem of study over the method

Figure 4

Meta-Theoretical Concerns	Behaviorism	Phenomenology	Integrated Approach
1. Subject matter	Behavior	+ Meanings	= Human action
2. Method	Operationalism	+ Interpretation	= Operationalism of inter- subjective experience
3. Major concern	Method	+ Subject matter	= Subject matter's fit to method
4. Goal	Explanation, prediction, and control	+ Understanding	= Explanation and understanding

of study. It broadens without losing definition, it diversifies without losing objectivity, and it increases flexibility without sacrificing rigor. A
stimulating way of viewing humans and research, the integration of
phenomenology and behaviorism has significant potential for studying
the role of communication in interpersonal relationships.

An Interpersonal Communication Model
of Relationship Development

The integrated view described in the foregoing section forms the
basis for an interpersonal communication model of relationship development. Basically the model depicts an interpersonal relationship as
each partner experiences a conception of self that is confirmed or disconfirmed by the other, resulting in degrees of perceived understanding. To a limited extent, the model resembles one on reciprocal perspectives described by Laing, Phillipson, and Lee (1966). Figure Five is
a pictorial representation of the model in a dyadic situation.

Components of the Model

The model has several key components. First, communicator self-
concepts are important. Suppose persons A and B in the model see or
know one another. Each person has a direct perspective of the other
and himself or herself. The direct perspective of one's self is a self-
concept, defined as the information one has regarding his relationship
to objects, people, and places (Cahn, 1976; Cushman and Cahn, 1985).
As argued in Chapter Two, the self-concept of primary interest in interpersonal relationship development is the one *preferred* by the individuals involved and consists of those real and ideal (behavioral, evaluative,
and identity) self-object relationships that each thinks are assets in
interaction. As argued in the Overview of Part Two, attempts to reengage and develop superior interpersonal relationships must focus on a
better understanding of the entity one calls the self.

A second key component, self-concept support, consists of verbal
and nonverbal messages that assert, affirm, or deny one's own or
another's self-concept. Such support depends on one's accurate identification of the unique scope, depth, and configuration of the other's
preferred self-concept and possession of the communication skills for
producing self-concept support (Cushman and Cahn, 1985). Wylie
(1979) reports studies that show that the accurate perception and perceived support of self-concepts not only function to validate others' self-

Figure 5

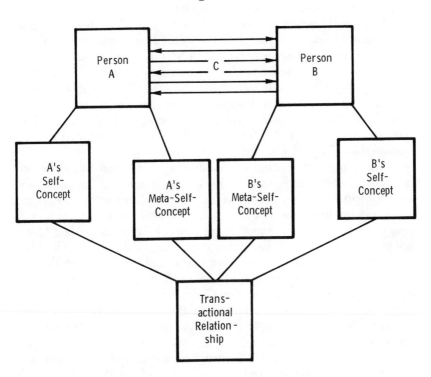

concepts but also function as important message variables for creating and sustaining interpersonal relationships. The relationship development process, then, involves the accurate perceptions and mutual support of the preferred self-concepts by those involved in interpersonal relationships.

The preferred self-concept is conveyed to others and confirmed, rejected, or disconfirmed by them through communication defined as "the transmission of information by means of symbol manipulations which are understood as intended" (Cushman and Whiting, 1972: 225). By stressing the intentional nature of communication, the model may be distinguished from that of Goffman (1959), who includes unintentional behaviors (cues "given off") as well as intentional behaviors (cues "given"). In the model, the transfer of symbolic information (C) represents the intentional expressions and/or confirmation of the preferred self-concepts of A and B, and their responses to these messages. As noted in the Overview of Part Two, some communication behaviors facilitate the development of superior interpersonal relationships and enhance one's self-regard and relationship satisfaction.

Third, each person creates a "meta-self-concept" (Cahn, 1976), or a conception of one's self based on the symbolic information he or she receives from the other about himself or herself. Although intended for a different purpose, self-attitude research lends support to this idea (Bergin, 1962). While self-concepts and meta-self-concepts both concern the self, sometimes they appear to one as incongruent. For example, a young man may depart from his date feeling good about himself (a favorable self-concept) but feeling that he somehow offended her (an unfavorable meta-self-concept).

According to the model, each individual is in communication with the other to confirm himself or herself by comparing the meta-self-concept with his or her preferred self-concept. Meta-self-concepts are produced by the process of role-taking, in which one imaginely constructs the attitudes and expectations others have of him or her. Meta-self-concepts are at least partially distorted because it is difficult, if not impossible, to completely construct the attitudes and expectations of others. Presumably error in one's meta-self-concept increases as one decreases role-taking. As argued in Chapter Two, inability to advance to higher levels of role-taking limits one's ability to accurately perceive and support other's self-concepts (Lauer and Boardman, 1971; Cushman and Craig, 1976; Cushman and Cahn, 1985).

Fourth, as described in Chapter Two, the information individuals have regarding who they are is not limited solely to what others think they are, nor is it determined primarily by what the individuals think of themselves. Rather, a real self-concept (one tried and tested in social interaction) is by definition an interactively determined construct created and sustained in interaction with others. To conceive of one's self, one must "get outside of one's self" by taking the role and perspective of others, through which one imaginatively constructs the attitudes and expectations others have of him or her. To influence other's perceptions of them, individuals may decide to assert various aspects of their preferred conceptions of themselves. Conversely, individuals need to recognize (through interaction) others' self-concepts and recognize the role their self-concepts play in either supporting or limiting others' presentation of self. This means that one's ability to create and sustain a vision of self depends on the room others provide for one and the room one creates in interaction to establish and sustain one's self-concept.

Lastly, self-concept support in the form of self-confirmation, rejection, or disconfirmation produces different kinds of interpersonal relationships. These relationships are transactional in nature because they depend on the assertion, listening, and negotiation (collaboration) skills discussed in Chapter Three, which result in different degrees of feeling understood or misunderstood. The extent to which feeling understood or misunderstood plays a role in the development of interpersonal relationships depends on the phase of relational development.

Developmental Phases

As discussed in Chapter Five, according to Cushman and his colleagues (Cushman and Cahn, 1985; Cushman, Valentinsen, and Dietrich, 1982), relationships pass through three phases. In the first phase of a relationship, certain causal and normative factors determine one's *field of available* individuals by limiting the range and type of people one meets. In the second phase, normative rules delimit one's *field of approachable* persons to those one finds interesting and whom one wishes to approach in order to initiate a closer interpersonal relationship. This suggests the following hypotheses:

H_1: The more one perceives that another's real self-concept is similar to one's own real self-concept, the more likely one will engage in communication aimed at initiating a relationship.

H_2: The greater an individual's perceived relationship between attributes of his/her preferred self-concept qualities and the perceived attributes of another's real self-concept, the greater the likelihood that communication aimed at forming a relationship will be initiated.

H_3: The more one perceives that another's real-preferred self-concept discrepancy is small, the more likely one will engage in communication aimed at initiating a relationship.

H_4: The greater an individual's perceived likelihood that the other will accept an offer of a relationship (friends, lovers, mates, boss-employee), the greater the likelihood that communication aimed at forming a relationship will be initiated.

H_5: The more frequently an individual provides messages that support some preferred identity, evaluative, or behavioral self-object relationships of another's self-concept, the greater the likelihood that the other individual will perceive those messages as an attempt to initiate a relationship.

Finally, in the third phase, within the second field there exists a subset of individuals who find others interesting and desirable for forming relationships. Such individuals constitute a *field of reciprocals*. This suggests the following hypotheses:

H_6: The more frequently both individuals receive from one another messages which manifest an accurate perception of one another's real and
preferred self-concepts, the greater the likelihood that interpersonal
communication will be perceived as mutually supportive of one another's self-concept.

H_7: The greater an individual's perceived accuracy with regard to the
relationship between one's preferred and another's real self-concept,
the greater the likelihood that interpersonal communication will be perceived as mutually supportive of one another's self-concept.

H_8: The more self-concept support is perceived to be reciprocated, the
more likely the relationship will become satisfying.

In each phase of the relationship, marker variables continue to be
important in relationship development, while intensity variables change
in relative importance. Marker variables in general include attitudinal
similarity (Byrne and Nelson, 1965), physical attributes (Walster et al.,
1966), and self-esteem (Aronson and Linder, 1965). As argued in the
Overview of Part Two, a different set of characteristics mark the growth
at each stage of the relationship. This means that each type of relationship (friendship, mateship, etc.) is a coordinated affair that is uniquely
defined and regulated by a set of developmental rules that represent the
consensus of those involved in the relationship. Moreover, any one stage
(e.g., casual date, steady date, mate, etc.) of a particular kind of a
relationship (e.g., marriage) is also a coordinated affair that is uniquely
defined and regulated by a related set of rules that set it apart from other
stages of that type of relationship. Thus, the study of any particular type
of interpersonal relationship requires knowledge of the unique features
of that type and of each stage in its development. In other words, while
interpersonal communication may play a similar role in each type of
relationship (e.g., friendship, marriage, supervisor-subordinate, parent-
child, teacher-student) in general, the specifics involved vary with the
uniqueness of each relationship. For example, self-concept support may
contribute positively to all types of relationship development, but the
way in which self-concepts are supported varies with the type of
relationship. Chapters Six through Nine identified and discussed marker variables for different types of relationships.

According to the Overview of Part Two, the communication that
fulfills the other's self-referent motives and encourages the relevant
characteristics for a particular type of interpersonal relationship is not
enough for the development of a superior relationship. One must also
communicate in a manner that facilitates intimacy. The intimate relationship is personal, free of formality, and involves a high degree of

closeness, spontaneity, emotional commitment, responsibility, and mutuality. Intimacy is facilitated by perceived understanding that is produced by self-concept support in the form of similarity, reciprocity, compatability, and respect. A comparison of the findings of two studies suggests that perceived understanding may provide an index of intensity, since it appears to be more important later on in longer-term relationships (Cahn, 1983; 1984).

Interpersonal Communication Competence

From the perspective of the model, *competence* in interpersonal communication and relationship development refers to the effective use of interpersonal communication that objectifies, analyzes, evaluates, and synthesizes individual self-concepts, the nature of the interpersonal relationship, and the quality/quantity of interpersonal communication, with the aim of changing and improving self-concepts, relationships, and communication patterns. How does interpersonal communication function to redefine self-concepts and bond individuals together? According to Katriel and Philipsen (1981), the terms "self," "relationship," and "communication" represent conceptual phenomena that people objectify and reflect on. Thanks to communication, these concepts may be analyzed, taken apart, evaluated, and put back together in an improved form. This process of self and relational reflection is enhanced by communication competence, which is judged by the quality of communication characteristic of one's interpersonal relationship. When one's competence is low, relational breakdowns occur, and when high, communication is more successful, individuals grow, and relationships become more satisfying.

Although appealing, it would be difficult to find an interpersonal relationship completely free of problems or conflicts. In the United States, competent relationship partners may employ a common repair ritual that consists of a specific set of expectations and sequences involved in "sitting down to talk" (Katriel and Philipsen, 1981). Since *the norm of interaction* includes attaching significance to the process of communication and recognition that the partners should "sit down and talk," the *setting* is normally private and free of distractions. The participants are the two partners involved. Because the *topic* is the initiator's self-definition, the *purpose* of the ritual is to seek self-confirmation from a significant other.

The ritual unfolds as follows. First, one partner initiates the ritual by *announcing the existence of a problem* that may be worked out in communication. Second, there is an *acknowledgement step* where the relevant other indicates a willingness to discuss this problem, thereby acknowledging its legitimacy. Third, there is a *negotiation step* where the problem is stated and explored from several points of view. As the initiator of the ritual, one would engage in self-disclosure with an attitude of acceptance toward both feedback and suggestions for change, while the other would indicate cooperation by listening with nonjudgmental, noninquisitive empathy. Finally, there is a *reaffirmation step* in which the uniqueness of the individual is affirmed and the solution is found to be consistent with some valued principle of the initiator's self-concept, thus mitigating any threat to the initiator's identity. The fact that conflict resolution is not always possible is seen as threatening to a relationship. Both persons must clarify for each other and examine together the discrepant positions, personal needs, and individual interpretations, but they must reaffirm their relationship to lessen the interpersonal threat posed by the differences.

If the other person accurately perceives the violation of expectation and its effect, and wants to preserve the relationship, then an account should be forthcoming aimed at realigning the relationship with the initiator of the repair ritual. As discussed in Chapter Three, accounts are socially acceptable vocabularies that may effect interpersonal alignment in two ways. First, "they sustain the flow of joint action by bringing individuals back into line with one another in problematic circumstances," and second, "they sustain a relationship between ongoing conduct and culture in the face of a recognized failure of conduct to live up to the cultural established expectation" (Stokes and Hewitt, 1976: 844). As argued in Chapter Three, excuses, justifications, concessions, and refusals are all socially acceptable vocabularies for neutralizing an act or its consequences when one or both are called into question by the initiator of the repair ritual. As a communication skill, the use of accounts is essential to a quality communication environment in that such skill enables an individual to repair interactional errors in regard to positive self-concept support and self-concept accuracy.

Relationship Reassessment: Key Communication Factors in Relationship Development

Most research designed to evaluate the theoretical predictions of interpersonal relationships is limited to a single point in relational development. In the absence of research that has utilized more of a developmental approach, it is difficult to answer these important questions. Based on the rules approach, an interpersonal communication model of relational development extends research in communication (Knapp, 1978; Friedman, Giffin, and Patton, 1978; Cushman, Valentinsen, and Dietrich, 1982) and the exchange tradition within social psychology (Thibaut and Kelley, 1959; Kelley and Thibaut, 1978). The Overview of Part One suggested that the interpersonal communication model assumes that individuals are in general motivated to maximize perceived understanding and minimize perceived misunderstanding, and it distinguishes between two important characteristics of relationships: satisfaction and commitment. As stated in Chapter Four, persons who wish to remain in their relationships should also feel psychologically committed to them.

Relational Satisfaction

H_9: The more positive one's perceived understanding, the more one is attracted to and satisfied with an ongoing interpersonal relationship: conversely the more negative one's perceived understanding, the more one is repelled by and dissatisfied with an ongoing interpersonal relationship.

Briefly, the interpersonal communication model asserts that one's *satisfaction* in mature relationships is influenced by one's understanding as perceived in the relationship. According to Chapters Two and Three, self-concept support increases the feeling of being understood. A's or B's perceived understanding in any relationship X is measured by the feeling understood (FU) and feeling misunderstood (FM) dimensions of the Perceived Understanding Instrument (Cahn and Shulman, 1984). By subtracting FM from FU, a composite perceived understanding (FUM) score that represents the extent of perceived understanding one experiences in social interaction may be computed. As discussed in Chapter Four, research shows that *perceived understanding may not be as important initially as other factors in interpersonal attraction but plays a more important role in relational satisfaction during later stages of relationship development.* The interpersonal communication model based on perceived understanding assumes that in latter phases of ongoing relationships individuals are in general motivated to maximize mutual perceived understanding while minimizing perceived misunderstanding. Therefore, relationship satisfaction may be a function of the discrepancy between the individual partner's perceived understanding and misunderstanding.

In addition, as discussed in Chapter Four, a neutral point exists where both the feelings of being understood and misunderstood are minimal (FM − FU = 0); and it is determined by the degree of confirmation, rejection, and disconfirmation experienced in previous relationships. Therefore, individuals evaluate their present relationship in relation to their neutral point in order to assess the degree of satisfaction with and attraction to the present relationship.

Relational satisfaction (SAT_x) can be represented as follows:

$$SAT_x = W(FUM_x) - NP$$

where FUM_x represents the degree of perceived understanding each person experiences in this particular relationship, W represents the importance of feeling understood or misunderstood, and NP stands for a neutral point or standard against which the attractiveness of any relationship is measured. This notion of neutral point is similar to that of a comparison level in interdependence theory (Thibaut and Kelley, 1959; Kelley and Thibaut, 1978).

Relational Commitment

H_{10}: Relational commitment increases with increases in investment size, system constraints, and relational satisfaction.

H_{11}: Relational satisfaction remains unchanged with changes in the value of alternative relationships, investment size, and system constraints.

H_{12}: Disengagements increase as relational commitment decreases.

H_{13}: Relational commitment predicts disengagements more accurately than relational satisfaction.

H_{14}: The more value one places on an alternative interpersonal relationship, the less one feels emotionally committed to the present one; conversely, the less value one places on an alternative interpersonal relationship, the more emotionally committed one is to the present one.

Research shows that compared to measures of relational dissatisfaction lack of *commitment* is a superior predictor of disengagements (Rusbult, 1980; Farrell and Rusbult, 1981; Rusbult, 1983). Commitment represents identification with and involvement in a relationship, psychological attachment, congruence between one's real and ideal relationship, and system constraints. Commitment exists to the extent that one perceives that he or she is connected to a relationship. Emotional commitment, as discussed in Chapter Four, is a function of satisfaction derived from the relationship (SAT_x), the comparative quality of available alternative relationships (ALT_y), the magnitude of one's investments in the relationship (INV_x), and one' perceived system constraints

(SYS$_x$). Thus, person A's or B's commitment to relationship X (COM$_x$) may be defined as follows:

$$COM_x = SAT_x + INV_x \ SYS_x - ALT_y$$

The following discussion shows how each of the commitment factors may be explained, controlled, and predicted.

It is clear that the *value of alternative relationships* is an important comparison level for assessing the attractiveness of the present relationship in interdependence research (Thibaut and Kelley, 1959; Blau, 1967; Kelley and Thibaut, 1978). The value of an alternative relationship (ALT$_y$) is defined in the same manner as is satisfaction with the present relationship X:

$$ALT_y = W(FUM_y) - NP$$

where FUM$_y$ stands for the degree of perceived understanding each person experiences in an alternative relationship, W represents the importance of feeling understood or misunderstood in that relationship and NP stands for a neutral point or standard against which the attractiveness of all relationships is evaluated.

H$_{15}$: The more one invests in the present interpersonal relationship, the more one feels emotionally committed to it; conversely, the less one invests in the present interpersonal relationship, the less emotionally committed one is to it.

Researchers have also shown that the *size of investments* affects relational commitment (Becker, 1960; Blau, 1967; Rubin, 1975; Rusbult, 1980). The value of one's investments (INV$_x$) in the present relationship X is defined as follows:

$$INV_x = WI$$

where I represents the size of the investment of resources in the relationship X, and W refers to the importance of these resources.

H$_{16}$: The more one perceives system constraints, the more one feels emotionally committed to the present interpersonal relationship; conversely, the less one perceives system constraints, the less emotionally committed one feels to the present interpersonal relationship.

Finally, *system constraints* have been showned to influence relational commitment (Parks, Stan, and Eggert, 1983). The factor of system constraints (SYS_x) is defined as follows:

$$SYS_x = WS$$

where S refers to one's perception of the pressures exerted by one's own social network, consisting of relatives and friends, and W stands for the importance or significance of these persons to the individual.

Summary

Depending on the type of relationship involved, certain features are generally considered to be essential initially. In this chapter, these are called marker variables. In studies of initial interaction and interpersonal attraction, these factors emerge as the key consideration for the formation of a relationship. Over time, however, other features of the relationship, called intensity variables, become increasingly more important. Research has shown that perceived understanding is an intensity variable that may be most important after the initial formation of an interpersonal relationship. Self-concept support in the form of verbal and nonverbal messages that confirm one's preferred self-concept produces feelings of being understood.

Because of a general interest in predicting and controlling interpersonal behavior, social scientists have attempted to develop theories, identify key factors, manipulate them in laboratory and field studies, and report research findings that lend some predictability. Unfortunately, they tend to focus on the study of interpersonal attraction and its antecedents. While helpful in understanding initial attraction toward strangers, the findings are not generalizable to later developments in long-term relationships.

The theory of relationship reengagement and relationship development proposed in this book, a rules-based interpersonal communication model, is derived from an integrated view that combines the strengths of behavioral and phenomenological approaches to the study of human communication. It predicts the degree of commitment to and satisfaction with a variety of forms of ongoing relationships (e.g., friends, mates, supervisor-subordinate, and teacher-student) that differ in duration and involvement. In the application Chapters Six through Nine, I described how to adapt this theory to specific interpersonal relationships of general interest.

References

Overview of Part One

Bernstein, W., and M. Davis. 1982. Perspective-taking, self-consciousness, and accuracy in person perception. *Basic and Applied Social Psychology* 3: 1–19.

Bienvenu, J. 1970. Measurement of marital communication. *The Family Coordinator* 19: 26–31.

Blau, P. 1967. *Exchange and Power in Social Life.* New York: John Wiley & Sons.

Cahn, D. 1976. Interpersonal communication and transactional relationships: Clarification and application. *Communication Quarterly* 24: 38–44.

Cahn, D. 1983. Relative importance of perceived understanding in initial interaction and development of interpersonal Relationships. *Psychological Reports* 53: 923–929.

Cahn, D. 1984. Teacher-Student relationships: Perceived Understanding. *Communication Research Reports* 1: 65–67.

Christensen, L., and L. Wallace. 1976. Perceptual accuracy as a variable in marital adjustment. *Journal of Sex and Marital Therapy* 2: 130–35.

Cissna, K. 1975. *Facilitative Communication and Interpersonal Relationships: An Empirical Test of a Theory of Interpersonal Communication.* Unpublished dissertation. University of Denver.

Clark, F. 1973. *Interpersonal Communication Variables as Predictors of Marital Satisfaction-Attraction.* Unpublished dissertation. University of Denver.

Corsini, R. 1956. Understanding and similarity in marriage. *Journal of Abnormal Psychology* 52: 327–332.

Cushman, D., and D. Cahn. 1985. *Communication in Interpersonal Relationships.* New York: SUNY Press.

Cushman, D., and R. Craig. 1976. Communication systems: Interpersonal implications. In G. Miller, ed., *Explorations in Interpersonal Communication,* 5: 37–58. Beverly Hills: Sage Publications.

205

Farrell, D., and C. Rusbult. 1981. Exchange variables as predictors of job satisfaction, job commitment, and turnover: The impact of rewards, costs, alternatives, and investments. *Organizational Behavior and Human Performance* 28: 78–95.

Frank, E., and D. Kupfer. 1976. In every marriage there are two marriages. *Journal of Sex and Marital Therapy* 2: 137–43.

Gottman, J. 1979. *Marital Interaction: Experimental Investigations.* New York: Academic Press.

Green, R. 1983. The influence of divorce prediction variables on divorce adjustment: An expansion and test of Lewis' and Spanier's theory of marital quality and marital stability, *Journal of Divorce* 7: 67–81.

Green, R., and M. Sporakowski. 1983. The dynamics of divorce: Marital quality, alternative attractions and external pressures. *Journal of Divorce,* 7: 77–88.

Homans, G. 1961. *Social Behavior: Its Elementary Forms.* New York: Harcourt: Brace & World.

Kelley, H.H., and J.W. Thibaut. 1978. *Interpersonal Relations: A Theory of Inter dependence.* New York: Wiley-Interscience.

LaGaipa, J. 1977. Interpersonal attraction and social exchange. In S. Duck, ed., *Theory and Practice in Interpersonal Attraction.* New York: Academic Press.

Laing, R., H. Phillipson, and A. Lee. 1966. *Interpersonal Perception.* New York: Springer Publishing Co.

Larson, C. 1965. *Interaction, Dogmatism, and Communication Effectiveness.* Unpublished dissertation. University of Kansas.

Lewis, R., and G. Spanier. 1979. Theorizing about the quality and stability of marriages. In W. Burr, R. Hill, F. Nye, and I. Reiss, eds., *Contemporary Theories about the Family.* 268–94. New York: Free Press.

Miller, S., R. Corrales, and D. Wackman. 1975. Recent progress in understanding and facilitating marital communication. *The Family Coordinator 24:* 143–52.

Montgomery, B. 1981. The form and function of quality communication in marriage. *Family Relations* 30: 21–30.

Olson, D. October, 1972. Marriage of the future: Revolutionary or evolutionary change? *The Family Coordinator* 21: 383–393.

Rusbult, C. 1980. Commitment and satisfaction in romantic associations: A test of the investment model. *Journal of Experimental Social Psychology* 16: 172–86.

Rusbult, C. 1983. A longitudinal test of the investment model: The development (and deterioration) of satisfaction and commitment in heterosexual involvements. *Journal of Personality and Social Psychology* 45: 101–17.

Sprenkle, D., and D. Olson. 1978. Circumplex model of marital systems: An empirical study of clinic and non-clinic couples. *Journal of Marriage and Family Counseling* 4: 59–74.

Thibaut, J., and H. Kelley. 1959. *The Social Psychology of Groups*. New York: John Wiley & Sons.

Thompson, W. 1972. *Correlates of the Self-concept: Studies on Self-Concept and Rehabilitation.* Nashville, TN: Nashville Counselor Recording Tests.

Watzlawick, P., J. Beavin, and D. Jackson. 1967. *Pragmatics of Human Communication: A Study of Interactional Patterns, Pathologies, and Paradoxes.* New York: W.W. Norton & Co.

Witkin, S., and S. Rose. 1978. Group training in communication skills for couples: Preliminary report. *International Journal of Family Counseling* 6: 45–56.

Chapter One

Berger, C., and R. Calabrese. 1975. Some explorations in initial interaction and beyond. *Human Communication Research* 1: 99–112.

Berscheid, E., and E. Walster. 1978. *Interpersonal Attraction* (2nd edition). Reading, MA: Addison-Wesley.

Cahn, D. April, 1981. Feeling understood as a research concept. Unpublished paper, Central States Speech Association Annual Conference, Chicago.

Cahn, D. 1984. Relative importance of perceived understanding in students' evaluation of teachers. *Perceptual Motor Skills* 59: 610.

Cahn, D., and L. Frey. 1982. Interpersonal attraction and trust: The effects of feeling understood/misunderstood on impression formation processes. Unpublished paper, Speech Communication Association Annual Conference, Louisville, KY.

Cahn, D., and G. Shulman. 1984. The perceived understanding instrument. *Communication Research Reports* 1: 122–125.

Coombs, R. May, 1966. Value consensus and partner satisfaction among dating couples. *Journal of Marriage and the Family,* 166–173.

Cushman, D., and D. Cahn. 1985. *Communication in Interpersonal Relationships.* New York: SUNY Press.

Cushman, D., and Whiting G. 1972. An approach to communication theory: Toward consensus on rules. *Journal of Communication* 2: 217–38.

Driscoll, R., K. Davis, and M. Lipetz. 1972. Parental interference and romantic love: The Romeo and Juliet effect. *Journal of Personality and Social Psychology* 24: 1–10.

Hacker, A. Divorce á la mode. May 1979. *New York Review of Books,* 23–30.

Hatfield, E., and G. Walster. 1978. *A New Look at Love.* Reading, MA: Addison-Wesley.

Laing, R., H. Phillipson, and A. Lee, 1966. *Interpersonal Perception.* New York: Springer Publishing Company.

Langford, G. 1971. *Human Action.* New York: Doubleday.

Levinger, G., and J. Breedlove. 1966. Interpersonal attraction and agreement. *Journal of Personality and Social Psychology* 3: 367–372.

Luft, J. 1969. *Of Human Interaction.* Palo Alto, CA: Mayfield Publishing Co.

Olson, D. October, 1972. Marriage of the future: Revolutionary or evolutionary change? *The Family Coordinator* 21: 383–393.

O'Neill, N., and G. O'Neill. 1972. *Open Marriage.* New York: Avon Books.

Taylor, C. 1964. *The Explanation of Behaviour.* New York: Humanities Press International.

Townsend, P. 1968. The structure of the family. In E. Shanas et al., eds., *Old People in Three Industrial Societies.* New York: Atherton.

Van Kaam, A. 1959. Phenomenal analysis: Exemplified by a study of the experience of "really feeling understood." *Journal of Individual Psychology,* 15: 66–72.

von Wright, G. 1971. *Explanation and Understanding.* Ithaca, NY: Cornell University.

Walster, E., E. Berscheid, and G. Walster. New directions in equity research. *Journal of Personality and Social Psychology* 25(1973): 151–176.

Walster, E., G. Walster, and E. Berscheid. 1971. The efficacy of playing hard-to-get. *Journal of Experimental Education* 39: 73–77.

Yolton, J. 1973. Action theory as the foundation for the sciences of man. *Philosophical Social Science,* 3: 81–90.

Chapter Two

Blumer, H. 1966. Commentary and debate. *American Journal of Sociology* 71: 535–45.

Cahn, D. 1976. Interpersonal communication and transactional relationships: Clarification and application. *Communication Quarterly* 24: 38–44.

Cahn, D., and S. Tubbs. December 1983. Management as communication: Performance evaluation and employee self-worth. *Communication* 12: 46–54.

Cissna, K. 1980. What is interpersonal communication? *The Communicator*, 52–63.

Cissna, K., and S. Keating. Winter 1979. Speech communication antecedents of perceived confirmation. *Western Journal of Speech Communication* 43: 48–60.

Cooley, C. 1902, 1922. *Human Nature and The Social Order.* Charles Scribner's Sons.

Craig, R. Summer 1981. A preliminary investigation of role-taking in descriptions of self and others in the twenty statements test. *Communication Quarterly* 29: 187–195.

Cushman, D., and D. Cahn. 1985. *Communication in Interpersonal Relationships.* New York: SUNY Press.

Cushman, D., and R. Craig. 1976. Communication systems: Interpersonal implications. In G. Miller, ed., *Explorations in Interpersonal Communication*, 5: 37–58. Beverly Hills: Sage Publications.

Cushman, D., and T. Florence. 1974. Development of interpersonal communication theory. *Today's Speech* 22: 11–15.

Cushman, D., and G. Whiting. 1969. Human action, self-conception and cybernetics. Unpublished paper, Annual Convention, International Communication Association, Cleveland, OH.

Cushman, D., and G. Whiting. 1972. An approach to communication theory: Toward consensus on rules. *Journal of Communication* 22: 217–38.

Dance, F., and C. Larson. 1976. *The Functions of Human Communication.* New York: Holt, Rinehart, & Winston.

Fromm, E. 1956. *The Art of Loving.* New York: Harper & Row.

Gauthier, D. 1963. *Practical Reasoning.* Oxford: Oxford University.

Kuhn, M., and T. McPartland. February 1954. An empirical investigation of self-attitudes. *American Sociological Review* 19: 68–76.

Lauer, R., and L. Boardman. January 1971. Roll-taking: Theory, topology and propositions. *Sociology and Social Research* 55: 137–148.

Mead, G. 1934. *Mind, Self and Society.* Chicago: University of Chicago Press.

Miller, G., and M. Steinberg. 1975. *Between People.* Palo Alto, CA: SRA.

Rogers, C. 1951. *Client-Centered Therapy.* Cambridge, MA: Riverside Publishing Co..

Sieburg, E. 1976. Confirming and disconfirming organizational communication. In J. Owen, P. Page, and G. Zimmerman, eds., *Communication in Organizations:* 129–149. New York: West Publishing Co.

Smith, T. 1977. *The Development of Self Through Interaction: A Test of a Communication Paradigm.* Dissertation. Michigan State University.

Spitzer, S., C. Couch, and J. Stratton. 1969. *The Assessment of the Self.* Iowa City: Sernoll.

Thompson, W. 1972. *Correlates of The Self-Concept: Studies on Self-Concept and Rehabilitation.* Nashville, TN: Nashville Counsellor Recording Tests.

Tubbs, W. Fall 1972. Beyond perls. *Journal of Humanistic Psychology* 12: 5.

Turner, R. January 1956. Role-taking, role standpoint, and reference group behavior. *American Journal of Sociology* 61: 316–328.

Watzlawick, P., J. Beavin, and D. Jackson. 1967. *Pragmatics of Human Communication.* New York: W.W. Norton & Co.

Yoshikawa, M. 1982. Japanese and American modes of communication and implications for managerial and organizational behavior. Paper, presented at the Second International Conference on Communication Theory: Eastern and Western Perspectives, Yokahama, Japan.

Chapter Three

Argyle, M. and A. Furnham. 1983. Sources of satisfaction and conflict in long term relationships. *Journal of Marriage and the Family* 45: 481–93.

Bach, G., and P. Wyden. 1968. *The Intimate Enemy.* New York: Avon Books.

Brown, C., and P. Keller. 1979. *Monologue to Dialogue: An Exploration of Interpersonal Communication* (2nd edition). Englewood Cliffs, NJ: Prentice-Hall.

Cahn, D. 1984. Teacher-student relationships: Perceived Understanding. *Communication Research Reports* 1: 65–67.

Cole, C., and R. Ackerman. 1981. A change model for resolution of stress. *Alternative Lifestyles* 4: 134–41.

Cushman, D., and D. Cahn. 1985. *Communication in Interpersonal Relationships.* New York: SUNY Press.

Cushman, D., and D. Cahn. 1986. A study of communicative realignment between parents and children following the parents' decision to seek a divorce. *Communication Research Reports* 3: 80–85.

Derr, C. 1978. Managing organizational conflict. *California Management Review* 21: 76–83.

Deutsch, M. 1973. *The Resolution of a Conflict: Constructive and Destructive Processes.* New Haven: Yale University Press.

Eiseman, J. 1977. A third-party consultation model for resolving recurring conflicts collaboratively. *Journal of Applied Behavioral Science* 13: 303–14.

Fry, W., I. Firestone, and D. Williams. 1983. Negotiation process and outcome of stranger dyads and dating couples: Do lovers lose? *Basic and Applied Social Psychology* 4: 1–16.

Gibb, J. 1961. Defensive communication. *Journal of Communication* 11: 141–48.

Holmes, T., and R. Rahe. 1967. The social readjustment rating scale. *Journal of Psychosomatic Research* 11: 213–18.

Kressel, K., N. Jaffee, B. Tuchman, C. Watson, and M. Deutsch. 1980. A typology of divorcing couples: Implications for mediation and the divorce process. *Family Process* 19: 101–16.

Laing, R., H. Phillipson, and A. Lee. 1966. *Interpersonal perception.* New York: Springer Publishing Co.

McClelland, D., C. Coleman, K. Finn, and D. Winter. 1972. Motivation and maturity patterns in marital success. *Social Behavior and Personality* 6: 163–71.

Menaghan, E. 1982. Measuring coping effectiveness: A panel analysis of marital problems and coping efforts. *Journal of Health and Social Behavior,* 23: 220–34.

Miller, S., R. Corrales, and D. Wackman. 1975. Recent progress in understanding and facilitating marital communication. *The Family Coordinator* 24: 143–52.

Miller, S., E. Nunnally, and D. Wackman. 1975. *Alive and Aware: Improving Communication in Relationships.* Minneapolis: Interpersonal Communication Programs.

Montgomery, B. 1981. The form and function of quality communication in marriage. *Family Relations* 30: 21–30.

Rogers, C. 1961. *On Becoming a Person.* Boston: Houghton Mifflin.

Scott, M., and S. Lyman. 1968. Accounts. *American Sociological Review* 33: 46–62.

Satir, V. 1964. *Conjoint family therapy.* Palo Alto: Science & Behavior Books.

Ting-Toomey, S. 1983. An analysis of verbal communication patterns in high and low marital adjustment groups. *Human Communication Research* 9: 306–19.

Chapter Four

Albert, E. 1968. Value systems. In *International Encyclopedia of the Social Sciences:* 287–91. New York: MacMillan.

Brown, C., and P. Keller. 1979. *Monologue to Dialogue: An Exploration of Interpersonal Communication* (2nd Edition). Englewood Cliffs, NJ: Prentice-Hall.

Burr, W. 1973. *Theory Construction and the Sociology of the Family.* New York: John Wiley & Sons.

Cahn, D. April 1981. Feeling understood as a research concept. Unpublished paper, Central States Speech Association Annual Conference, Chicago.

Cahn, D., and L. Frey. 1982. Interpersonal attraction and trust: The effects of feeling understood/Misunderstood on impression formation processes. Unpublished paper, Speech Communication Association Annual Convention, Louisville, KY.

Chelune, G., F. Sultan, and C. Williams. 1980. Loneliness, self-disclosure, and interpersonal effectiveness. *Journal of Counseling Psychology* 27: 462–68.

Cimbalo, R., V. Faling, and P. Mousaw. 1976. The course of love: A cross-sectional design. *Psychological Reports* 38: 1292–94.

Cultrona, C. 1982. Transition to college: Loneliness and the process of social adjustment. In L. Peplau and D. Perlman, eds., *Loneliness: A Sourcebook of Current theory, research, and therapy:* 291–309. New York: John Wiley & Sons.

Cushman, D., and D. Cahn. 1985. *Communication in Interpersonal Relationships.* New York: SUNY Press.

Driscoll, R., K. Davis, and M. Lipetz. 1972. Parental interference and romantic love: The Romeo and Juliet effect. *Journal of Personality and Social Psychology* 24: 1–10.

Farrell, D., and C. Rusbult. 1981. Exchange variables as predictors of job satisfaction, job commitment, and turnover: The impact of rewards, costs, alternatives, and investments. *Organizational Behavior and Human Performance* 28: 78–95.

Green, R. 1983. The influence of divorce prediction variables on divorce adjustment: An expansion and test of Lewis' and Spanier's theory of marital quality and marital stability, *Journal of Divorce* 7: 67–81.

Green, R., and M. Sporakowski. 1983. The dynamics of divorce: Marital quality, alternative attractions and external pressures. *Journal of Divorce,* 7: 77–88.

Hatfield, E., and G. Walster. 1978. *A New Look at Love.* Reading, MA: Addison-Wesley.

Jones, W., J. Freemon, and R. Goswick. 1981. The persistence of loneliness: Self and other determinents. *Journal of Personality* 49: 27–48.

Jones, W., S. Hobbs, and D. Hockenbury. 1982. Loneliness and social skill deficits. *Journal of Personality and Social Psychology* 42: 682–89.

Jones, W., C. Sansone, and B. Helm. 1983. Loneliness and interpersonal judgments. *Personality and Social Psychology Bulletin* 9: 437–41.

Krain, M. 1977. Effects of love and liking in premarital dyads. *Sociological Focus* 10: 249–62.

Kupke, T., K. Calhoun, and S. Hobbs. 1979. Selection of heterosocial skills: II experimental validity. *Behavior Therapy* 10: 336–46.

Kupke, T., S. Hobbs, and T. Cheney. 1979. Selection of heterosocial skills: I criterion-related validity. *Behavior Therapy* 10: 327–35.

Lewis, R. 1973. Social reaction and the formation of dyads: An interactionist approach to mate selection. *Sociometry* 36: 409–18.

Mathes, E., and P. Wise. 1983. Romantic love and the ravages of time. *Psychological Reports* 53: 839–46.

Parks, M., C. Stan, and L. Eggert. 1983. Romantic involvement and social network involvement. *Social Psychology Quarterly* 46: 116–31.

Peplau, L., and D. Perlman. 1979. Toward a social psychological theory of loneliness. In M. Cook and G. Wilson, eds., *Love and Attraction.* New York: Pergamon Press.

Perlman, D., A. Gerson, and B. Spinner. 1978. Loneliness among senior citizens: An empirical report. *Essence* 2: 239–48.

Rusbult, C. 1980a. Commitment and satisfaction in romantic associations: A test of the investment model. *Journal of Experimental Social Psychology* 16: 172–86.

Rusbult, C. 1980b. Satisfaction and commitment in friendships. *Representative Research in Social Psychology* 11: 96–105.

Rusbult, C. 1983. A longitudinal test of the investment model: The development (and deterioration) of satisfaction and commitment in heterosexual involvements. *Journal of Personality and Social Psychology* 45: 101–117.

Rusbult, C., and D. Farrell. A longitudinal test of the investment model: The impact on job satisfaction, job commitment, and turnover of variations in rewards, costs, alternatives, and investments. *Journal of Applied Psychology,* in press.

Thibaut, J., and H. Kelley. 1959. *The Social Psychology of Groups.* New York: John Wiley & Sons.

Thompson, L., and G. Spanier. 1983. The end of marriage and acceptance of marital termination. *Journal of Marriage and the Family* 45: 103–13.

Weiss, R. 1973. *Loneliness: The Experience of Emotional and Social Isolation.* Cambridge, MA: MIT Press.

Zakahi, W., and R. Duran. 1985. Loneliness, communicative competence, and communication apprehension: Extension and replication. *Communication Quarterly* 33: 50–60.

Overview of Part Two

Anderson, S., C. Russell, and W. Schumm. 1983. Perceived marital quality and family life-cycle categories: A further analysis. *Journal of Marriage and the Family* 127–139.

Bailey, R., P. Finney, and B. Helm. 1975. Self-concept support and friendship duration. *Journal of Social Psychology* 96: 237–43.

Bandura, A. 1977. *Social Learning Theory.* Englewood Cliffs, NJ: Prentice Hall.

Bem, D. 1972. Self-perception theory. In L. Berkowitz, ed., *Advances in Experimental Social Psychology.* Vol. 6. New York: Academic Press.

Berscheid, E., and E. Walster. 1973. Physical Attractiveness. In L. Berkowitz, ed., *Advances in Experimental Social Psychology.* Vol. 7. New York: Academic Press.

Cahn, D. April, 1981. Feeling understood as a research concept. Unpublished paper, Central States Speech Association Annual Conference, Chicago.

Cahn, D. 1983. Relative importance of perceived understanding in initial interaction and development of interpersonal Relationships. *Pschological Reports* 53: 923–929.

Cahn, D. 1984. Relative importance of perceived understanding in students' evaluation of teachers. *Perceptual Motor Skills* 59: 610.

Cavior, N., and P. Boblett. 1972. Physical attractiveness of dating versus married couples. *Proceedings of the 80th Annual Convention of the American Psychological Association:* 175–76.

Crawford, M. 1977. What is a friend? *New Society* 42: 116–17.

Cushman, D., and D. Cahn. 1985. *Communication in Interpersonal Relationships.* New York: SUNY Press.

Cushman, D., B. Valentinsen, & D. Dietrich, 1982. A rules theory of interpersonal relationships. In F. Dance, ed., *Comparative theories of Human Communication:* 90–119. New York: Harper & Row.

Fromkin, H. 1970. The effects of experimentally aroused feelings of undistinctiveness upon valuation of scarce and novel experiences. *Journal of Personality and Social Psychology* 16: 521–9.

Fromkin, H. 1972. Feelings of interpersonal undistinctiveness: An unpleasant affective state. *Journal of Experimental Research in Personality* 6: 178–85.

Gibbs, S. 1977. A comparative analysis of friendship formation in six age groups of men and women. Ph.D. dissertation, Wayne State University.

Hill, C., Z. Rubin, and L. Peplau. 1976. Breakups before marriage: The end of 103 affairs. *Journal of Social Issues* 32: 147–68.

Homans, G. 1961. *Social behavior: Its elementary forms.* New York: Harcourt, Brace & World.

Jones, S. 1973. Self and interpersonal relations: Esteem theories versus consistency theories. *Psychological Bulletin* 79: 185–99.

Jones, W. 1981. Loneliness and social contact. *Journal of Social Psychology* 113: 295–96.

Kelvin, P. 1977. Predictability, power and vulnerability in interpersonal attraction. In S. Duck, ed., *Theory and Practice in Interpersonal Attraction.* London: Academic Press.

La Gaipa, J. 1977. Testing a multidimensional approach to friendship. In S. Duck, ed., *Theory and Practice in Interpersonal Attraction:* 249–70. New York: Academic Press.

McAdams, D., and C. Constantian. 1983. Intimacy and affiliation motives in daily living: An experience sampling analysis. *Journal of Personality and Social Psychology* 45: 851–61.

McCall, G., and F. Simmons. 1966. *Identities and Interactions.* New York: Free Press.

Murstein, B. 1972. Physical attractiveness and marital choice. *Journal of Personal and Social Psychology* 22: 8–12.

Pam, A., R. Plutchik, and H. Conte. 1973. Love: A psychometric approach. *Proceedings of the 81st Annual Convention of the American Psychological Association:* 159–60.

Peplau, L., and D. Perlman. 1979. Toward a social psychological theory of loneliness. In M. Cook and G. Wilson, eds., *Love and Attraction.* New York: Pergamon Press.

Perlman, D., A. Gerson, and B. Spinner. 1978. Loneliness among senior citizens: An empirical report. *Essence* 2: 239–48.

Prager, K. 1983. Development of intimacy in young adults, a multidimensional view. *Psychological Reports* 52: 751–56.

Shapiro, D. 1953. *Psychological Factors in Friendship Choice and Rejection.* Unpublished Dissertation. University of Michigan.

Swann, W., and C. Hill. 1982. When our identities are mistaken: Reaffirming our self-conceptions through social interaction. *Journal of Personality and Social Psychology* 43: 59–66.

Swann, W., and S. Read. 1981. Self-verification processes: How we sustain our self-conceptions. *Journal of Experimental Social Psychology* 17: 351–72.

Webster, M., and B. Kobieszek. 1974. *Sources of Self-Evaluation.* New York: John Wiley & Sons.

Wheeler, L., H. Reis, and J. Nezlek. 1983. Loneliness, social interaction, and sex roles. *Journal of Personality and Social Psychology* 45: 943–53.

Williams, J., and C. Solano. 1983. The social reality of feeling lonely: Friendship and reciprocation. *Personality and Social Psychology Bulletin* 9: 237–42.

Wise, L., and M. Lowenthal. 1975. Life-course perspectives on Friendship. In M. Lowenthal, M. Thurnher, D. Chiriboga, and Associates, eds., *Four Stages of Life: A Comparative Study of Women and Men Facing Transitions.* San Francisco, CA: Jossey-Bass.

Wright, P. 1977. Perspective on the psychology of self. *Psychological Reports* 40: 423–36.

Wright, P. 1978. Toward a threory of friendship based on a conception of self. *Human Communication Research* 4: 196–207.

Wright, P. 1984. Self-referent motivation and the intrinsic quality of friendship. *Journal of Social and Personnel Relationships* 1: 115–30.

Chapter Five

Argyle, M., and A. Furnham. 1983. Sources of satisfaction and conflict in long term relationships. *Journal of Marriage and the Family* 45: 481-93.

Argyle, M., and M. Henderson. 1984. The rules of friendship. *Journal of Social and Personal Relationships* 1: 211-37.

Argyle, M. and M. Henderson. *The Anatomy of Relationships* Heinemann: London, in press.

Barnlund, D. 1975. *Public and Private Self in Japan and the United States.* Tokyo: Simul.

Berger, C., and R. Calabrese. 1975. Some explorations in initial interaction and beyond. *Human Communication Research* 1: 99-112.

Berscheid, E., and E. Walster. 1973. Physical Attractiveness. In L. Berkowitz, ed., *Advances in Experimental Social Psychology.* Vol. 7. New York: Academic Press.

Booth, A. 1972. Sex and social participation. *American Sociological Review* 37: 183-92.

Cahn, D. 1983. Relative importance of perceived understanding in initial interaction and development of interpersonal Relationships. *Psychological Reports* 53: 923-929.

Cahn, D. 1984. Relative importance of perceived understanding in students' evaluation of teachers. *Perceptual Motor Skills* 59: 610.

Cavior, N., and P. Boblett. 1972. Physical attractiveness of dating versus married couples. *Proceedings of the 80th Annual Convention of the American Psychological Association* 175-76.

Crawford, M. 1977. What is a friend? *New Society* 42: 116-17.

Cushman, D., and D. Cahn. 1985. *Communication in Interpersonal Relationships.* New York: State University of New York Press.

Cushman, D., and E. Kunimoto. A rules theory of the mate formation process in two subcultures of the United States. In L. Kincaid, ed., *Communication from an Eastern and Western Perspective,* forthcoming.

Cushman, D., and T. Nishida. 1984. Mate selection in the United States and Japan. Unpublished manuscript, State University of New York at Albany.

Cushman, D., and Whiting, G. 1972. An approach to communication theory: Toward consensus on rules. *Journal of Communication* 22: 217-38.

Cushman, D., B. Valentinsen, and D. Brenner. 1981. An interpersonal communication theory of the friendship formation process. Unpublished paper, Annual Conference of the International Communication Association, Minneapolis, MN.

Cushman, D., B. Valentinsen, and D. Dietrich. 1982. A rules theory of interpersonal relationships. In F. Dance, ed., *Comparative theories of Human Communication:* 90–119. New York: Harper & Row.

Davis, K., and M. Todd. Friendship and love. In K. Davis and T. Michell, eds., *Advances in Descriptive Psychology* 2. Greenwich, CT: JAI Press, in press.

Duck, S. 1976. Interpersonal communication in developing acquaintances. In G. Miller, ed., *Explorations in Interpersonal Communication:* 127–145. Beverly Hills: Sage Publications.

Gibbs, S. 1977. A comparative analysis of friendship formation in six age groups of men and women. Ph.D. dissertation, Wayne State University.

Gudykunst, W., and T. Nishida. 1983. Social Penetration in Japanese and American Close friendships. Unpublished paper, annual Convention, International Communication Association, Dallas, TX.

Gudykunst, W., and T. Nishida. 1984. Individual and cultural influences on uncertainty reduction. *Communication Monographs* 51: 23–36.

Hacker, A. May 1979. Divorce a la mode. *New York Review of Books:* 23–30.

Harre, H., and P. Secord. 1972. *The Explanation of Social Behavior.* Totowa, NJ: Littlefield, Adams & Co..

Hill, C., Z. Rubin, and L. Peplau. 1976. Breakups before marriage: The end of 103 affairs. *Journal of Social Issues* 32: 147–68.

Johnson, C., and F. Johnson. 1975. Interaction rules and ethnicity: The Japanese and Caucasians in Honolulu. *Social Forces* 54: 452–66.

Kayser, E., T. Schwinger, and R. Cohen. 1984. Laypersons' conceptions of social relationships: A test of contract theory. *Journal of Social and Personal Relationships* 1: 433–58.

La Gaipa, J. 1977. Testing a multidimensional approach to friendship in S. Duck, ed., *Theory and Practice in Interpersonal Attraction:* 249–70. New York: Academic.

Mochizuki, T. 1981. Changing patterns of mate selection. *Journal of Comparative Family Studies* 12: 317–28.

Murstein, B. 1972. Physical attractiveness and marital choice. *Journal of Personal and Social Psychology* 22: 8–12.

Pam, A., R. Plutchik, and H. Conte. 1973. Love: A psychometric approach. *Proceedings of the 81st Annual Convention of the American Psychological Association:* 159-60.

Ross, R. and M. Ross. 1982. *Relating and Interacting* Englewood Cliffs, NJ: Prentice-Hall.

Takahara, N. 1974. Semantic concepts of marriage, work, friendship and foreigner in three cultures. In J. Condon and M. Saito, eds., *Intercultural Encounters with Japan.* Tokyo: Simul.

Wise, L., and M. Lowenthal. 1975. Life-course perspectives on Friendship. In M. Lowenthal, M. Thurnher, D. Chiriboga, and Associates, eds., *Four Stages of Life: A Comparative Study of Women and Men Facing Transitions.* San Francisco, CA: Jossey-Bass.

Chapter Six

Argyle, M., and A. Furnham. 1983. Sources of satisfaction and conflict in long term relationships. *Journal of Marriage and the Family* 45: 481-93.

Argyle, M., and M. Henderson. 1984. The rules of friendship. *Journal of Social and Personal Relationships* 1: 211-37.

Atsumi, R. 1980. Patterns of personal relationships: A key to understanding Japanese thought and behavior. *Social Analysis* 5/6: 63-78.

Bailey, R., R. Digiacomo, and O. Zinser. 1976. Length of male and female friendship and perceived intelligence in self and friend. *Journal of Personality Assessment* 40: 635-40.

Bailey, R., P. Finney, and B. Helm. 1975. Self-concept support and friendship duration. *Journal of Social Psychology* 96: 237-43.

Bell, R. 1981. Friendships of women and of men. *Psychology of Women Quarterly* 5: 402-17.

Caldwell, M., and L. Peplau. 1982. Sex differences in same-sex friendship. *Sex Roles* 8: 721-32.

Cissna, K., and E. Sieburg. 1979. Interactional foundations of interpersonal confirmation. Unpublished paper, International Communication Association, Speech Communication Association, and San Francisco State University Postdoctoral Conference in Honor of Gregory Bateson, Asilomar, CA.

Cook, M. 1977. The social skill model and interpersonal attraction. In S. Duck, ed., *Theory and Practice in Interpersonal Attraction.* New York: Acadamic Press.

Crawford, M. 1977. What is a friend? *New Society* 42: 116–17.

Cushman, D., and D. Cahn. 1985. *Communication in Interpersonal Relationships*. New York: State University of New York Press.

Cushman, D., B. Valentinsen, and D. Brenner. May 1981. An interpersonal communication theory of the friendship formation process. Unpublished paper, Annual Conference of the International Communication Association, Minneapolis, MN.

Cushman, D., B. Valentinsen, and D. Dietrich. 1982. A rules theory of interpersonal relationships. In F. Dance, ed., *Comparative theories of Human Communication:* 90–119. New York: Harper & Row, 1982.

Duck, S. 1973. Similarity and perceived similarity of personal constructs as influences on friendship choice. *British Journal of Social and Clinical Psychology* 12: 1–6.

Duck, S., ed., 1977. *Theory and Practice in Interpersonal Attraction.* New York: Academic Press.

Duck, S. 1981. A topography of relationship disengagement and dissolution. In S. Duck, ed., *Personal Relationships 4:* 1–31. New York: Academic.

Duck, S., and C. Spencer. 1972. Personal constructs and friendship formation. *Journal of Personality and Social Psychology* 23: 40–45.

Fisher, J., and L. Narus. 1981. Sex roles and intimacy in same sex and other sex relationships. *Psychology of Women Quarterly* 5: 444–55.

Friedman, P., K. Giffin, and B. Patton. 1978. The A-frame: Processes of authentic communication. Unpublished paper, Annual Convention of the Speech Communication Association, Minneapolis, MN.

Gibbs, S. 1977. A comparative analysis of friendship formation in six age groups of men and women. Ph.D. dissertation, Wayne State University.

Hays, R. 1984. The development and maintenance of friendship. *Journal of Social and Personal Relationships* 1: 75–98.

Hill, C., and D. Stull. 1981. Sex differences in effects of social and value similarity in same sex friendship. *Journal of Personality and Social Psychology* 41: 488–502.

Horowitz, L., and R. French. 1979. Interpersonal problems of people who describe themselves as lonely. *Journal of Consulting and Clinical Psychology* 47: 762–64.

Huston, T., and G. Levinger. 1978. Interpersonal attraction and relationships. *Annual Review of Psychology* 29: 115–56.

Kelley, H., and J. Thibaut. 1978. *Interpersonal Relations: A Theory of Interdependence.* New York: Wiley-Interscience.

Knapp, M. 1978. *Social Intercourse from Greeting to Goodbye.* Boston: Allyn & Bacon.

Krantzler, M. 1977. *Learning to Love Again.* New York: Thomas Y. Crowell.

La Gaipa, J. 1982. Rules and rituals in disengaging from relationships. In S. Duck, ed., *Personal Relationships 4: Dissolving Personal Relationships.* London: Acadamic Press.

Laumann, E. 1969. Friends of urban men: An assessment of accuracy in reporting their socio-economic attributes, mutual choice and attitude agreement. *Sociomentry* 32: 54–69.

Leefeldt, C., and E. Callenbach. 1979. *The Art of Friendship.* New York: Pantheon Books.

Lund, M. 1985. The development of investment and commitment scales for predicting continuity of personal relationships. *Journal of Personal and Social Relationships* 2:3–23.

Lundy, R. 1958. Self-perception regarding masculinity-femininity and descriptions of same and opposite sex sociometric choice. *Sociometry* 21: 238–46.

Nahemow, L., and M. Lawton. 1975. Similarity and propinguity in friendship formation. *Journal of Personality and Social Psychology* 32: 204–13.

Parks, M., C. Stan, and L. Eggert. 1983. Romantic involvement and social network involvement. *Social Psychology Quarterly* 46: 116–131.

Rusbult, C. 1980. Satisfaction and commitment in friendships. *Representative Research in Social Psychology* 11: 96–105.

Stokes, R., and J. Hewitt. 1976. Aligning actions. *American Sociological Review* 41: 838–49.

Sykes, R. 1983. Initial interaction between strangers and acquaintances. *Human Communication Research* 10: 27–53.

Thibaut, J., and H. Kelley. 1959. *The Social Psychology of Groups.* New York: John Wiley & Sons.

Thompson, W., and R. Nishimura. 1952. Some determinants of friendship. *Journal of Personality and Social Psychology* 20: 305–14.

Tognoli, J. 1980. Male friendship and intimacy across the lifespan. *Family Relations* 29: 273–79.

Trower, P. 1981. Social skill disorder. In S. Duck and R. Gilmour, eds., *Personal Relationships 3:* 97–108. New York: Academic Press.

Verbrugge, L. 1983. A research note on adult friendship contact: A dyadic perspective. *Social Forces* 62: 78–83.

Zakahi, W., and R. Duran. 1984. Attraction, communicative competence and communication satisfaction. *Communication Research Reports* 1: 54–57.

Chapter Seven

Bailey, R. C., and B. Helm. 1974. Matrimonial commitment and date/ideal-date perceptions. *Perceptual and Motor Skills* 39: 1245–46.

Bem, S. 1974. The measurement of psychological androgyny. *Journal of Consulting and Clinical Psychology* 42: 155–62.

Bentler, P., and M. Newcomb. 1978. Longitudinal study of marital success and failure. *Journal of Consulting and Clinical Psychology* 46: 1053–70.

Berscheid, E., and E. Walster. 1978. *Interpersonal Attraction* (2nd edition). Reading, MA: Addison-Wesley.

Berzins, J., M. Welling, and R. Wetter. 1976. Androgynous vs traditional sex roles and the interpersonal behavior circle. Paper, Annual Convention of the American Psychological Association, Washington, D.C.

Blood, R., and M. Blood. 1979. Amicable divorce: A new lifestyle. *Alternative Lifestyles* 2: 483–98.

Brown, J. 1980. Adolescent peer group communication, sex-role norms and decisions about occupations. In D. Nimmo, ed., *Communication Yearbook 4:* 659–78. New Brunswick, NJ: Transaction Books-International Communication Association.

Brunner, C., and L. Phelps. 1980. Interpersonal communication competence and androgyny. Unpublished paper, Annual Conference of the International Communication Association, Acapulco.

Butler, C. 1976. New data about female sexual response. *Journal of Sex and Marital Therapy* 2: 36–46.

Cavior, N., and P. Boblett. 1972. Physical attractiveness of dating versus married couples. *Proceedings of the 80th Annual Convention of the American Psychological Association:* 175–76.

Christensen, L., and L. Wallace. 1976. Perceptual accuracy as a variable in marital adjustment. *Journal of Sex and Marital Therapy* 2: 130–36.

Cissna, K., and E. Sieburg. 1979. Interactional foundations of interpersonal confirmation. Unpublished paper, International Communication Association, Speech Communication Association, and San Francisco State University Postdoctoral Conference in Honor of Gregory Bateson, Asilomar, CA.

Cushman, D., and D. Cahn. 1985. *Communication in Interpersonal Relationships.* New York: State University of New York Press.

Cushman, D., and E. Kunimoto. A rules theory of the mate formation process in two subcultures of the United States. In L. Kincaid, ed., *Communication from an Eastern and Western Perspective,* forthcoming.

Cushman, D., B. Valentinsen, and D. Brenner. May 1981. An interpersonal communication theory of the friendship formation process. Unpublished paper, Annual Conference of the International Communication Association, Minneapolis, MN.

Cushman, D., B. Valentinsen, and D. Dietrich. 1982. A rules theory of interpersonal relationships. In F. Dance, ed., *Comparative theories of Human Communication:* 90–119. New York: Harper & Row.

D'Augelli, J., and A. D'Augelli. 1977. Moral reasoning and premarital sexual behavior: Toward reasoning about relationships. *Journal of Social Issues* 33: 46–66.

Duck, S. 1981. A topography of relationship disengagement and dissolution. In S. Duck, ed., *Personal Relationships 4:* 1–31. New York: Academic Press.

Ellis, D., and L. McCallister. 1980. Relational control sequences in sex-typed and Androgynous groups. *Western Journal of Speech Communication* 44: 35–49.

Eman, V., K. Dierks-Stewart, and R. Tucker. May 1978. Implications of sexual identity and sexually identified situations on nonverbal touch. Unpublished paper, Annual Convention of the Speech Communication Association, Minneapolis, MN.

Erwin, P., and C. Arraham. 1983. Beauty: More than skin deep? *Journal of Social and Personal Relationships* 1: 359–361.

Friedman, P. Giffin, and B. Patton 1978. The A-frame: Processes of authentic communication. Unpublished Paper, Annual Convention of the Speech Communication Association, Minneapolis, MN.

Galvin, K., and B. Brommel. 1982. *Family Communication: Cohesion and Change.* Glenview, IL: Scott, Foresman & Co.

Greenblatt, L., J. Hasenauer and V. Freimuth. 1980. Psychological sex types and androgyny in the study of communication variables: Self-disclosure and communication apprehension. *Human Communication Research* 6: 117–29.

Hacker, A. May 1979. Divorce à la mode. *New York Review of Books:* 23–30.

Hill, C., Z. Rubin, and L. Peplau. 1976. Breakups before marriage: The end of 103 affairs. *Journal of Social Issues* 32: 147–68.

Hunt, R., and E. Rydman. 1976. *Creative Marriage*. Boston: Holbrook.

Huston, T., ed. 1974. *Foundations of Interpersonal Attraction*. New York: Academic Press.

Isenhart, M. 1980. An investigation of the relationship of sex and sex role to the ability to encode nonverbal cues. *Human Communication Research* 6: 309–18.

Karp, E., J. Jackson, and D. Lester. 1970. Ideal-self fulfillment in mate selection: A corollary to the complementary need theory of mate selection. *Journal of Marriage and the Family*. 32: 269–272.

Kelley, H. and J. Thibaut. 1978. *Interpersonal Relations: A Theory of Interdependence*. New York: Wiley-Interscience.

Knapp, M.L. 1978. *Special Intercourse from Greeting to Goodbye*. Boston: Allyn & Bacon.

Krain, M. 1977. Effects of love and liking in premarital dyads. *Sociological Focus* 10: 249–62.

Landis, J. 1946. Length of time required to achieve adjustment in marriage. *American Sociological Review* 11: 667–77.

Luckey, E. 1960. Marital satisfaction and congruent self-spouse concepts. *Social Forces* 39: 153–57.

Luckey, E. 1960a. Marital satisfaction and congruent self-spouse concepts. *Social Forces* 39: 153–57.

Luckey, E. 1960b. Marital satisfaction and its association with congruence of perception. *Marriage and Family Living* 22: 49–59.

Lund, M. 1985. The development of investment and commitment scales for predicting continuity of personal relationships. *Journal of Personal and Social Relationships* 2: 3–23.

MacCorquodale, P., and J. DeLamater. 1979. Self-image and premarital sexuality. *Journal of Marriage and the Family* 41: 327–39.

Margolin, G. 1978. A multilevel approach to the assessment of communication positiveness in distressed marital couples. *American Journal of Family Therapy* 6: 81–89.

McCauley, C., and C. Swann. 1978. Male-female differences in sexual fantasy. *Journal of Research in Personality* 2: 76–86.

Miller, S., E. Nunnally, and D. Wackman. 1975. *Alive and Aware: Improving Communication in Relationships*. Minneapolis: Interpersonal Communication Programs.

Montgomery, B. 1981. The form and function of quality communication in marriage. *Family Relations* 30: 21–30.

Montgomery, C., and M. Burgoon. 1977. An experimental study of the interactive effects of sex and adrogyny on attitude change. *Communication Monographs* 44: 130–35.

Murstein, B. 1971. Self ideal discrepancy and the choice of marital partners. *Journal of Consulting and Clinical Psychology* 37: 47–52.

Murstein, B. 1972a. Physical attractiveness and marital choice. *Journal of Personal and Social Psychology* 22: 8–12.

Murstein, B. 1972b. Person perception and courtship among premarital couples. *Journal of Marriage and the Family* 34: 621–27.

Murstein, B. 1976. *Who Will Marry Whom? Theories and Research in Marital Choice.* New York: Springer Publishing Co.

Navran, L. 1967. Communication and adjustment in marriage. *Family Process* 6: 173–84.

Newcomb, M., and P. Bentler. 1981. Marital breakdown. In S. Duck and R. Gilmour, eds., *Personal Relationships 3:* 57–94. New York: Academic Press.

Olson, D. October 1972. Marriage of the future: Revolutionary or evolutionary change? *The Family Coordinator* 21: 383–93.

O'Neill, N., and G. O'Neill. 1972. *Open Marriage.* New York: Avon Books.

Pam, A., R. Plutchik, and H. Conte. 1973. Love: A psychometric approach. *Proceedings of the 81st Annual Convention of the American Psychological Association:* 159–60.

Parks, M., C. Stan, and L. Eggert. 1983. Romantic involvement and social network involvement. *Social Psychology Quarterly* 46: 116–31.

Peplau, L., Z. Rubin, and C. Hill. 1977. Sexual intimacy and dating relationships. *Journal of Social Issues* 33: 86–109.

Putnum, L., and L. McCallister. 1980. Situational effects of task and gender on nonverbal display. In D. Nimmo, ed., *Communication Yearbook* 4: 679–97. New Brunswick, NJ: Transaction Books.

Rausch, H., W. Barry, R. Hertel, and M. Swain. 1974. *Communication Conflict and Marriage.* San Francisco: Jossey-Bass.

Rim, Y. 1979. Personality and means of influence in marriage. *Human Relations* 32: 871–75.

Rusbult, C. 1980. Commitment and satisfaction in romantic associations: A test of the investment model. *Journal of Experimental Social Psychology* 16: 172–86.

Rusbult, C. 1983. A longitudinal test of the investment model: The development (and deterioration) of satisfaction and commitment in heterosexual involvements. *Journal of Personality and Social Psychology* 45: 101–17.

Satir, V. 1964. *Conjoint Family Therapy.* Palo Alto, CA: Science and Behavior Books.

Scanzoni, J. 1972. *Sexual Bargaining.* Englewood Cliffs, N.J.: Prentice-Hall.

Shafer, R., R. Braito, and J. Bohlen. 1973. Self-concept and the reaction of significant others: A comparison of husbands and wives. *Sociological Inquiry* 46: 57–66.

Shantean, J., and G. Nagy. 1979. Probability of acceptance in dating choice. *Journal of Personality and Social Psychology* 37: 522–33.

Tamashiro, R. July 1978. Developmental stages in the conceptualization of marriage. *Family Coordinator:* 237–44.

Thibaut, J., and H. Kelley. 1959. *The Social Psychology of Groups.* New York: John Wiley & Sons.

Trower, P. Social skill disorder. 1981. In S. Duck and R. Gilmour, eds., *Personal Relationships* 3: 97–108. Academic Press.

Turner, T. 1970. *Family Interaction.* New York: John Wiley & Sons.

Westoff, L. 1977. *The Second Time Around: Remarriage in America.* New York: Viking Press.

Wheeless, V., and K. Dierks-Stewart. 1981. The psychometric properties of the Bem sex-role inventory. *Communication Quarterly* 29: 173–86.

Wheeless, V., and R. Duran. 1980. Sexual identity and flexibility as correlates of communication competence. Unpublished paper, Annual Conference of the International Communication Association, Acapulco.

Chapter Eight

Alpander, G. January 1974. Planning manpower training programs for organizational development. *Personnel Journal:* 15–25.

Baird, J., and J. Diebolt. 1976. Role congruence, communication, superior-subordinate relations and employee satisfaction in organizational hierarchies. *Western Speech Communication* 40: 260–67.

Barnlund, D. 1968. *Interpersonal Communication: Survey and Studies.* Boston: Houghton Mifflin.

Bass, B. M. 1981. *Stogdill's Handbook of Leadership.* New York: Free Press.

Cahn, D. 1976. The employment interview: A self-validation model. *Journal of Employment Counseling* 13: 150–55.

Cahn, D. 1979. Employee evaluation as a self-validation process. *Journal of Employment Counseling* 16: 31–37.

Cahn, D. 1985. Information technology and interpersonal behavior: Impact on supervisor-subordinate and teacher-student relationships. Unpublished paper, Annual Conference, Eastern Communication Association, Providence, RI.

Cahn, D. 1986. The role of perceived understanding in supervisor-subordinate communication and organizational effectiveness. *Central States Speech Journal* 37.

Cahn, D., and S. Tubbs. 1983. Management as communication: Performance evaluation and employee self-worth. *Communication* 12: 46–54.

Cissna, K. 1976. Interpersonal confirmation: A review of current theory and research. Unpublished paper, Annual Conference, Central States Speech Association, Chicago.

Cushman, D., and D. Cahn. 1985. *Communication in Interpersonal Relationships.* New York: State University of New York Press.

Cushman, D., B. Valentinsen, and D. Dietrich. 1982. A rules theory of interpersonal relationships. In F. Dance, ed., *Comparative theories of Human Communication:* 90–119. New York: Harper & Row.

Falcione, R., J. McCroskey, and J. Daly. 1977. Job satisfaction as a function of employees' communication apprehension, self-esteem, and perceptions of their immediate supervisors. In B. Ruben, ed., *Communication Yearbook 1:* 363–75. New Brunswick, NJ: Transaction Books-International Communication association.

Farrell, D., and C. Rusbult. 1981. Exchange variables as predictors of job satisfaction, job commitment, and turnover: The impact of rewards, costs, alternatives, and investments. *Organizational Behavior and Human Performance* 28: 78–95.

Friedman, P., Giffin, and B. Patton. 1978. The A-frame: Processes of authentic communication. Unpublished Paper, Annual Convention of the Speech Communication Association, Minneapolis, MN.

Gibb, J. 1961. Defensive communication. *Journal of Communication* 11: 141–48.

Gibb, J. June 1965. Defensive communication. *ETC: A Review of General Semantics:* 221–29.

Goldhaber, G. 1983. *Organizational Communication* (3rd edition). Dubuque, IA: Wm. C. Brown.

Hine, V. April–May 1977. The basic paradigm of a future socio-cultural system. *World Issues.*

Jablin, F. 1979. Superior-subordinate communication: The state of the art. *Psychological Bulletin* 86: 1201–22.

Katz, D., and R. Kahn. 1966. *The Social Psychology of Organizations.* New York: John Wiley & Sons.

Katz, D., N. Maccoby, and N. Morse. 1950. Productivity, supervision, and morale in an office situation. Ann Arbor, MI: University of Michigan, Institute for Social Research.

Kelley, H., and J. Thibaut. 1978. *Interpersonal Relations: A Theory of Interdependence.* New York: Wiley-Interscience.

Kindall, A., and J. Gatza. 1976. Positive program for performance appraisal. In J. Owen, P. Page, and G. Zimmerman, eds., *Communication in Organizations.* New York: West Publishing Co.

Knapp, M. 1978. *Social Intercourse from Greeting to Goodbye.* Boston: Allyn & Bacon.

Moskowitz, M. 1985. Lessons from the best companies to work for. *California Management Review* 27: 42–47.

Naisbitt, J. 1982. *Megatrends: Ten New Directions Transforming Our Lives.* New York: Warner Communications.

Pascale, R. 1985. The paradox of corporate culture: Reconciling ourselves to socialization. *California Management Review* 27: 26–41.

Redding, W. 1972. *Communication within the organization: An interpretive review of theory and research.* New York: Industrial Communication Council.

Reusch, J. 1961. *Therapeutic Communication.* New York: W.W. Norton & Co.

Sieburg, E. 1976. Confirming and disconfirming organizational communication. In J. Owen, P. Page, and G. Zimmerman, eds., *Communication in Organizations:* 129–49. New York: West Publishing Co.

Sieburg, E., and C. Larson. 1971. Dimensions of interpersonal response. Unpublished paper, Annual Conference of the International Communication Association, Phoenix.

Smith, P., L. Kendall, and C. Hulin. 1969. *The Measurement of Satisfaction in Work and Retirement.* Chicago: McNally.

Stogdill, R. 1974. *Handbook of Leadership.* New York: Free Press.

Thibaut, J., and H. Kelley. 1959. *The Social Psychology of Groups.* New York: John Wiley & Sons.

Tschirgi, H. December 1972. What do recruiters really look for in candidates? *Journal of College Placement:* 78.

Tubbs, S., and R. Widgery. 1978. When productivity lags, check at the top: Are key managers really communicating? *Management Review* 20: 20–25.

Watzlawick, P., J. Weakland, and R. Tisch. 1974. *Change: Principles of Problem Formation and Problem Resolution.* New York: W.W. Norton & Co.

Weissenberg, P., and M. Kavanagh. 1972. The independence of initiating structure and consideration: A review of the literature. *Personal Psychology* 25: 119–30.

Zunin, L., and N. Zunin. 1973. *Contact: The First Four Minutes.* New York: Ballantine Books.

Chapter Nine

Abrami, P., W. Perry, and L. Leventhal. 1980. Do teachers standards for assigning grades affect student evaluations of instructions? *Journal of Educational Psychology* 72: 107–18.

Andersen, J., R. Norton, and J. Nussbaum. 1979. Three investigations exploring relationships among perceived communicator style, perceived teacher intimacy, perceived teacher-student solidarity, teaching effectiveness and student learning. Unpublished paper, Annual Conference, American Education Research Association, San Francisco.

Andriate, G. 1982. Teacher communication and student learning: The effects of perceived solidarity with instructor and student anxiety proneness. In M. Burgoon (Ed.), *Communication Yearbook 6.* Beverly Hills: Sage Publications.

Armour, R. October 15, 1979. What do they expect of me? *The Chronicle of Higher Education:* 48.

Berenson, D. 1971. The effects of systematic human relations training upon classroom performance of elementary school teachers. *Journal of Research and Development in Education* 4: 70–85.

Bloom, B. 1976. *Human Characteristics and School Learning.* New York: McGraw-Hill.

Branan, J. 1972. Negative human interaction. *Journal of Counseling Psychology* 19: 81–82.

Brookover, W., S. Thomas, and A. Paterson. 1964. Self-concept of ability and school achievement. *Sociology of Education* 37: 271–78.

Cahn, D. 1982. The role of the feeling of being understood/misunderstood in student perceptions of teachers. Unpublished manuscript, State University of New York at Albany.

Cahn, D. 1984. Relative importance of perceived understanding in students' evaluation of teachers. *Perceptual Motor Skills* 59: 610.

Cahn, D. 1985. Information technology and interpersonal behavior: Impact on supervisor-subordinate and teacher-student relationships. Unpublished paper, Annual Conference, Eastern Communication Association, Providence, RI.

Cahn, D., and L. Frey. 1982. Interpersonal attraction and trust: The effects of feeling understood/Misunderstood on impression formation processes. Unpublished paper, Speech Communication Association Annual Conference, Louisville, KY.

Cahn, D., and G. Shulman. 1984. The perceived understanding instrument. *Communication Research Reports* 1: 122-25.

Carkhuff, R. 1971. *The Development of Human Resources: Education, Psychological, and Social Change.* New York: Holt, Rinehart, and Winston.

Coombs, A. 1959. *Individual Behavior.* New York: Harper & Row.

Cooper, P., L. Stewart, and W. Gudykunst. 1982. Relationship with instructor and other variables influencing student evaluations of instruction. *Communication Quarterly* 30: 308-15.

Crosswhite, F. 1972. Correlates of attitudes toward mathematics. In J. Wilson and E. Begle, eds., *National Longitudinal Study in Mathematics Achievement,* Report 5, #20. Palo Alto, CA: School Mathematics Study Group.

Cushman, D., and D. Cahn. 1985. *Communication in Interpersonal Relationships.* New York: State University of New York Press.

Cushman, D., B. Valentinsen, and D. Dietrich. 1982. A rules theory of interpersonal relationships. In F. Dance, ed., *Comparative theories of Human Communication:* 90-119. New York: Harper & Row.

Friedman, P., K. Giffin, and B. Patton. 1978. The A-frame: Processes of authentic communication. Unpublished paper, Annual Convention of the Speech Communication Association, Minneapolis, MN.

Giffin, K. 1968. An experimental evaluation of the trust differential. Research Monograph R/19. Communication Research Center, University of Kansas.

Guba, E., and J. Getzels. 1955. Personality and teacher effectiveness: A problem in theoretical research. *Journal of Educational Psychology* 46: 355.

Hogrebe, E. 1981. Digital technology: The potential for alternative communication. *Journal of Communication* 31: 170–76.

Kearney, P., and J. McCroskey. 1980. Relationships among teacher communication style, trait and state communication apprehension and teacher effectiveness. In D. Nimmo, ed., *Communication Yearbook 4:* 533–51. New Brunswick, NJ: Transaction Books-International Communication Association.

Knapp, M. 1978. *Social Intercourse from Greeting to Goodbye.* Boston: Allyn & Bacon.

Kryspin, W., and J. Feldhusen. 1974. Analyzing Verbal Classroom Interaction. Minneapolis, MN: Burgess.

Kulik, J., and W. McKeachie. 1975. The evaluation of teachers in higher education. In F. Kerlinger, ed., *Review of Research in Education 3.* Itasca, IL: Peacock.

Lunn, J. 1969. The development of scales to measure junior high school childrens' attitudes. *British Journal of Educational Psychology* 39: 64–71.

McGlone, E., and L. Anderson. 1973. The dimensions of teacher credibility. *Speech Teacher* 22: 196–200.

Meeth, J. 1976. The stateless art of teaching evaluation. *Change* 8: 3–5.

Rogers, C. 1951. *Client-Centered Therapy.* Cambridge, MA: Riverside Publishing Co.

Scott, M., and J. Nussbaum. 1981. Student perceptions of instructor communication behaviors and their relationship to student evaluation. *Communication Education* 30: 44–53.

Scott, M., and L. Wheeless. 1977. Instructional Communication: An overview of theory and research. In B. Ruben, ed., *Communication Yearbook 1:* 495–511. New Brunswick, NJ: Transaction Books-International Communication Association.

Shepps, F., and R. Shepps. 1971. Relationships of study habits and school attitudes in Mathematics and reading. *Journal of Educational Research* 65: 71–73.

Silberman, C. 1970. *Crisis in the classroom: The remaking of American Education.* New York: Random House.

Sorensen, G. 1981. The relationship between teachers' self-disclosive statements and student affect. Unpublished paper, Annual Conference of the International Communication Association, Minneapolis, MN.

Toffler, A. 1970. *Future Shock.* London: Pan Books.

Wittmer, J., and R. Myrick. 1974. *Facilitative Teaching: Theory and Practice.* Pacific Palisades, CA: Goodyear.

Chapter Ten

Note: Portions of Chapter Ten were previously published by Dudley D. Cahn and Jack T. Hanford, "Perspectives on Human Communication Research: Behaviorism, Phenomenology, and an Integrated View, *The Western Journal Of Speech Communication* 48 (Summer 1984): 277–292.

Aronson, E., and D. Linder. 1965. Gain and loss of esteem as determinants of interpersonal attractiveness. *Journal of Experimental Social Psychology* 1: 156–71.

Becker, H. 1960. Notes on the concept of commitment. *American Sociological Review* 66: 32–40.

Bergin, A. 1962. The effects of dissonant persuasive communications upon changes in a self-referring attitude. *Journal of Personality* 30: 423–38.

Blau, P. 1967. *Exchange and power in social life.* New York: John Wiley & Sons.

Buber, M. 1947. *Between Man and Man.* London: Routledge and Kegan Paul.

Byrne, D., and D. Nelson. 1965. Attraction as a linear function of proportion of positive reinforcements. *Journal of Personality and Social Psychology* 1: 659–63.

Cahn, D. 1976. Interpersonal communication and transactional relationships: Clarification and application. *Communication Quarterly* 24: 38–44.

Cahn, D. 1983. Relative importance of perceived understanding in initial interaction and development of interpersonal Relationships. *Psychological Reports* 53: 923–29.

Cahn, D. 1984. Teacher-student relationships: Perceived Understanding. *Communication Research Reports* 1: 65–67.

Cahn, D., and G. Shulman. 1984. The perceived understanding instrument. *Communication Research Reports* 1: 122–25.

Chisholm, R., ed. 1960. *Realism and the Background of Phenomenology:* 39–75. Glencoe, IL: Free Press.

Cushman, D., and D. Cahn. 1985. *Communication in Interpersonal Relationships.* New York: State University of New York Press.

Cushman, D., and R. Craig. 1976. Communication systems: Interpersonal implications. In G. Miller, ed., *Explorations in Interpersonal Communication, 5:* 37-58. Beverly Hills: Sage Publications.

Cushman, D., and G. Whiting. 1972. An approach to communication theory: Toward consensus on rules. *Journal of Communication* 22: 217-38.

Cushman, D., B. Valentinsen, and D. Dietrich. 1982. A rules theory of interpersonal relationships. In F. Dance, ed., *Comparative theories of human communication:* 90-119. New York: Harper & Row.

Delia, J. 1977. Constructivism and the study of human communication. *Quarterly Journal of Speech* 63: 66-83.

Farrell, D., and C. Rusbult. 1981. Exchange variables as predictors of job satisfaction, job commitment, and turnover: The impact of rewards, costs, alternatives, and investments. *Organizational Behavior and Human Performance* 28: 78-95.

Friedman, P., K. Giffin, and B. Patton. 1978. The A-frame: Processes of authentic communication. Unpublished paper, Speech Communication Association, Minneapolis, MN.

Gerard, H., and G. Mathewson. 1966. The effects of severity of initiation on liking for a group: A replication. *Journal of Experimental Social Psychology* 2: 278-87.

Gergen, K. 1969. *The psychology of behavior exchange.* Reading, MA: Addison-Wesley Publishing Co..

Goffman, E. 1959. *The presentation of self in everyday life.* New York: Doubleday.

Insko, C., and M. Wilson. 1977. Interpersonal attraction as a function of social interaction. *Journal of Personality and Social Psychology* 35: 903-11.

James, W. 1902. *The Varieties of Religious Experience* New York: Mentor Books.

Johannesen, R. 1971. The emerging concept of communication as dialogue. *Quarterly Journal of Speech,* 57: 373.

Katriel, T., and G. Philipsen. 1981. What we need is communication: Communication as a cultural category in some American speech. *Communication Monographs* 48: 301-18.

Kelley, H., and J. Thibaut. 1978. *Interpersonal relations: A theory of interdependence.* New York: Wiley-Interscience.

Knapp, M. 1978. *Social intercourse from greeting to goodbye.* Boston: Allyn & Bacon.

Laing, R., H. Phillipson, and A. Lee. 1966. *Interpersonal perception.* New York: Springer Publishing Co.

Lauer, R., H. and L. Boardman. 1971. Roll-taking: Theory, topology, and propositions. *Sociology and Social Research* 55: 137–48.

Maslow, A. 1967. Isomorphic interrelationships between knower and known. In F. Matson and A. Montague, eds., *The Human Dialogue:* 195. New York: Free Press.

Parks, M., C. Stan, and L. Eggert. 1983. Romantic involvement and social network involvement. *Social Psychology Quarterly* 46: 116–31.

Rubin, J. 1975. Conflict escalation and entrapment in international relations: A proposal. Research proposal.

Ruesch, J., and G. Bateson. 1961. *Communication: The Social Matrix of Psychiatry.* New York: W.W. Norton & Co.

Rusbult, C. 1980. Commitment and satisfaction in romantic associations: A test of the investment model. *Journal of Experimental Social Psychology* 16: 172–86.

Rusbult, C. 1983. A longitudinal test of the investment model: The development (and deterioration) of satisfaction and commitment in heterosexual involvements. *Journal of Personality and Social Psychology,* 45: 101–17.

Skinner, B. 1957. *Verbal Behavior.* New York: Appleton-Century-Crofts.

Stevens, S. 1950. A definition of communication. *Journal of the Acoustical Society of America* 22: 689.

Stewart, J. 1978. Foundations of dialogic communication. *Quarterly Journal of Speech* 64: 184.

Stokes, R., and J. Hewitt. 1976. Aligning actions. *American Sociological Review* 41: 838–49.

Thibaut, J. and H. Kelley. 1959. *The social psychology of groups.* New York: John Wiley & Sons.

Walster, E., V. Aronson, D. Abrahams, and L. Rottman. 1966. Importance of physical attractiveness in dating behavior. *Journal of Personality and Social Psychology* 4: 508–16.

Wylie, R.C. 1961, 1979. *The self-concept.* Lincoln: University of Nebraska.

Author Index

235

Subject Index